D0709727

WP 0800058 1

A Measure
of
Thatcherism

TITLES OF RELATED INTEREST

Classes in Modern Society
Second edition
Tom Bottomore

Gendered Jobs and Social Change
Rosemary Crompton and Kay Sanderson

Perspectives in Sociology
Third edition
E. C. Cuff, W. W. Sharrock and D. W. Francis.

The Problem of Sociology
David Lee and Howard Newby

Social Class in Modern Britain
Gordon Marshall, David Rose, Howard Newby and
Carolyn Vogler

In Praise of Sociology
Gordon Marshall

Global Capitalism and National Decline
The Thatcher Decade in Perspective
Henk Overbeek

Social Stratification and Economic Change
David Rose (editor)

A Nation of Home Owners
Peter Saunders

Industrial Societies
Crisis and Division in Western Capitalism and State Socialism
Richard Scase (editor)

A Measure of Thatcherism

A Sociology of Britain

STEPHEN EDGELL
&
VIC DUKE

HarperCollins*Academic*

An imprint of HarperCollins*Publishers*

Published by
HarperCollinsAcademic
77-85 Fulham Palace Road
Hammersmith
London W6 8JB
UK

First published in 1991

British Library Cataloguing in Publication Data

Edgell, Stephen, 1942–
  A measure of Thatcherism : a sociology of Britain in the 1980s.
  1. Great Britain – Sociological perspectives
  I. Title II. Duke, Vic
  301.0941
  ISBN 0-04-301247-7

Library of Congress Cataloging in Publication Data

Edgell, Stephen.
  A measure of Thatcherism : a sociology of Britain/Stephen Edgell
and Vic Duke.
    p.   cm.
  Includes bibliographical references and index.
  ISBN 0-04-301247-7 (HB) : $55.00. — ISBN 0-04-301248-5
(PB)
  1. Elections—Great Britain. 2. Voting—Great Britain. 3. Great
Britain—Politics and government—1979- 4. Public opinion—Great
Britain. I. Duke, Vic. II. Title.

JN956.E34 1991
320.941'09048—dc20
                                       90-22649
                                          CIP

Typeset in 10 on 11 point Bembo
by Mathematical Composition Setters Ltd, Salisbury, Wilts
and printed in Great Britain by Billings and Sons Ltd., Worcester.

CONTENTS

v

Contents

Contents

LIST OF TABLES

LIST OF FIGURES

ACKNOWLEDGEMENTS

Thanks to our research assistants Jackie Booth (SSRC), Frances Hayles (ESRC) and Sue Haslam (Nuffield) for their enthusiasm and persistent attention to detail. We would also like to take this opportunity of thanking all the interviewers who are listed in our SSRC and ESRC Reports. Over the years we have benefited from the support of our colleagues at the University of Salford, especially Chris Bryant and Rob Flynn in Sociology and Mike Goldsmith in Politics. Sue Smart and Sheila Walker have been towers of strength and good humour in the face of illegible writing and innumerable deadlines. Finally, our thanks to Phil Hodgkiss for suggesting the main title.

We thank all the following funding agencies for their financial support: SSRC, CAMPUS, ESRC and the Nuffield Foundation; plus the following journals for permission to draw upon previously published material: the *British Journal of Sociology* and the *International Journal of Urban and Regional Research*.

CHAPTER 1

Thatcherism: A Change in the Nature and Direction of British Society?

1 Introduction

The 1979, 1983 and 1987 British general elections were won by the Conservative Party led by Margaret Thatcher. The policies implemented during this period of political dominance have transformed British society to such an extent that the term 'Thatcherism' is now widely used to describe the distinctive set of policies adopted. The purpose of this book is to provide an overview of the political sociology of Britain in the 1980s. The genesis of our research and this book was the realization during the winter of 1979–80 that the nature and direction of British politics and society were about to undergo a period of profound change. In March 1980 we summarized this change in the following terms: 'The change in direction involves a reassertion of the "virtues" of competition, freedom of choice, self-reliance, incentives and non-intervention by the State in order that "initiative and enterprise" can be released and "commerce and industry" can prosper' (Edgell and Duke 1980: 1). We further argued that: 'such a change represents a victory for individualism and the market over collectivism and socio-economic needs' (Edgell and Duke 1980: 2). We concluded that the possible economic, political and above all the social implications of this 'major historical reversal of policy should not go unresearched' (Edgell and Duke 1980: 2). The end result was the Greater Manchester Study, which was carried out in two stages – 1980–1 (GMS1) and 1983–4 (GMS2) (for details of the GMS see Appendix 1).

In this introductory chapter, we need to locate our sociological analysis of this period in its historical context. It is necessary to assess the extent to which Conservative government policies since

1979 do in fact represent a major qualitative and quantitative break with the post-1945 social democratic political consensus regarding the management and character of the British version of a mixed industrial capitalist economy. The main policy issues that we will be reviewing, and which provide an essential historical backdrop to the subsequent analysis, include macro-economic perspectives, public spending, employment, trade unions, and, last but not least, privatization. We will then outline the main data sources that we will be drawing upon and the main theoretical issues of a substantive kind that we will be addressing in this book.

2 Historical Context

The severe international recession of the mid to late 1970s exacerbated Britain's long-term economic problems and created a sense of political crisis during this period of Labour government. Key statistics show that economic growth declined from an annual average rate of approximately 3 per cent between 1951 and 1973 to around 1 per cent between 1974 and 1979 (*Economic Trends*, Annual Supplement, 1984). In cross-cultural terms, these rates of economic growth compared unfavourably with most other industrial capitalist countries and led an official review of 'The British economy since 1945' to comment that this comparison 'probably more than anything else has produced a general feeling that the UK could, and should, do better' (*Economic Progress Report*, 1978: 5). The Labour governments of the late 1970s led by Wilson and then Callaghan also presided over extremely high levels of inflation. The annual average percentage increase in the retail price index between 1974 and 1979 was over 15 per cent, with a peak of 24.2 per cent in 1975 and a trough of 8.3 per cent in 1978 (Pliatzky 1984).

Meanwhile, unemployment more than doubled from just over half a million in 1974 to over 1.3 million in 1979 (*Employment Gazette*, 1980). This stagflationary situation was accompanied by a marked increase in the ratio of public expenditure (including debt interest) to gross domestic product (GDP) in the mid 1970s (41.5 per cent in 1973/4 compared with 46.5 per cent in 1974/5). Although the ratio declined to 41 per cent again in 1977/8 (HMSO 1980), it was rising steadily once more towards the late 1970s, as were both inflation and unemployment. Most significant of all politically perhaps was the massive rise in industrial conflict in 1979, which followed a period of relatively harmonious industrial relations. The latter was characterized by a policy of pay restraint

2

dating from August 1975 that was particularly hard on the public sector compared with the private sector and also on the low paid. From an annual average of over 2,000 strikes and about 7 million striker-days involving nearly 1 million workers between 1975 and 1978, in 1979 there was a steep increase in the number of striker-days (almost 30 million) and the number of workers involved (well over 4.5 million), although the number of strikes remained the same (*Employment Gazette*, 1980). Thus, in terms of economic trends, the crisis years were 1975/6 when inflation was at its peak and the symbolic 1 million unemployed milestone was passed. However, as far as social and political legitimacy are concerned, the crisis years were 1978–9, a period which hostile commentators dubbed the 'Winter of Discontent'.

This briefly is the historical context in which the Conservative election manifesto of 1979 promised a distinctive set of policies designed not merely to halt, but to reverse the long-term economic decline of Britain. According to the 1979 Conservative manifesto, Britain was 'faced with its most serious problems since the Second World War' and there were times when it 'seemed on the brink of disintegration'. Major responsibility for Britain's relative economic decline and current sense of 'helplessness' was placed at the door of the Labour Party, which had held power for most of the previous 15 years. More specifically, Labour was accused of practising the politics of class conflict and, in the process, altering the balance of power in favour of an enlarged state and 'militant' trade unions, 'at the expense of individual freedom' and 'enterprise'. Consequently, it was claimed that 'the very nature' of the Labour Party 'prevents them from governing successfully in a free society and mixed economy'. In marked contrast, the manifesto asserted that the Conservative Party was the only party fit to govern and capable of reversing the historical trend by rebuilding the economy and reuniting 'a divided and disillusioned people'.

3 Conservative Government Policies

A variety of labels have been attached to the policies adopted by the three Conservative governments since 1979, for example, 'new right', 'radical right' and 'political monetarism'. During this period, cabinet ministers have come and gone, but Margaret Thatcher has been the prime minister throughout, hence we prefer the term 'Thatcherism'. The policies implemented under Thatcher's leadership will be reviewed under five interrelated headings:

3

politico-economic policy; public spending and revenue policy; employment and unemployment; trade unions; and privatization.

Politico-economic policy

The phrase 'a new beginning' appeared at the end of the 1979 Conservative election manifesto and reappeared in the headline introducing the June 1979 budget in the *Economic Progress Report* (1979). It refers to the rejection of Keynesian demand management theory, which had informed postwar economic policies, in favour of an emphasis on the supply side of the economy. It was argued that economic growth could best be achieved by the control of inflation, and this in turn requires the control of the money supply, an increase in personal incentives, a reduced role for the state, and a general increase in competition and therefore efficiency. The adoption of this 'new strategy' made inflation the key policy objective, thereby replacing full employment. It also involved a preference for long-term rather than short-term solutions in an attempt to transcend the stop–go pattern of economic growth and overcome the long-standing problem of economic decline.

The much-vaunted postwar consensus dated from the 1945–51 Labour government, which considerably expanded the role of the state in the economy (state industries and state welfare) on the basis of Keynesian macroeconomic theory and with the general aim of achieving full employment in a mixed economy. For the next 30 years, the basic institutional structure of the British economy remained unchanged, notwithstanding many changes of government. However, the perceived ineffectiveness of policies inspired by Keynesian theory became a political issue in the mid 1970s under the impact of an international recession. The Labour government of that period, led by Wilson until March 1976, reacted to the economic crisis by introducing policies that directly contravened Keynesian orthodoxy – notably public spending cuts in general and cash limits on specific public spending programmes in particular. Further 'cuts' were announced in December 1976 by the Callaghan administration following the successful negotiation of a $3.9 billion loan from the International Monetary Fund (IMF). (Note that, throughout the book, billion is used to signify 1,000 million). Under the terms of the IMF loan, public expenditure was to be reduced by £1 billion in 1977/8 and £1.5 billion in 1978/9; most interestingly, the proposed terms also involved the sale of £500 million of government-owned shares in the British Petroleum Company (Holmes 1985). The relative success of these policies in controlling inflation inadvertently paved the way

4

for subsequent Conservative governments to adopt far more thoroughgoing anti-Keynesian policies. In other words, short-term expediency was replaced by a long-term commitment to the rejection of the Keynesian-based postwar consensus.

The 'new right' economic policies adopted by Conservative governments since 1979 place great emphasis on the market and a correspondingly much reduced emphasis on the state in the economy. The key ideas that inform this policy are summed up by the term 'economic liberalism' and as such derive from the contributions of Adam Smith (1723–90), de Tocqueville (1805–59), and more recently Hayek (1899) and Friedman (1912). Fundamental to classical and contemporary economic liberalism are two interrelated 'principles': (1) the maximum operation of free market forces in the production and distribution of goods and services, and (2) the minimal intervention of the state save for the provision of a legal framework to facilitate free economic exchange. Intrinsic to an economic system based on these twin principles is an unswerving belief in competitive individualism, both in the economic sense that public good flows inevitably from private self-interest, and in the political sense that economic freedom is the touchstone of political freedom.

In the context of the stagflationary situation of the mid to late 1970s in Britain, it is not difficult to see the appeal of monetarism, the modern version of classical economic liberalism. Monetarist macro-economic theory crucially focuses on the relationship between inflation and unemployment and argues that interfering with the 'natural' rate of unemployment, for example by increasing public spending, causes inflation (Friedman 1977). Consequently, the control of inflation is accorded primacy in economic policy and legitimizes a whole range of anti-Keynesian policies, foremost among which is the reduction of public spending.

Public spending and revenue policy

The claim that 'Public expenditure is at the heart of Britain's present economic difficulties' (HMSO 1979b: 1) has informed Conservative policy from the start of the first Thatcher administration in 1979. The strategy set out in the new government's first two White Papers on public expenditure was to 'stabilise public spending for the time being' (HMSO 1979b: 1) and then 'to reduce total public expenditure progressively in volume terms over the next four years, to a level in 1983–84 about 4 per cent lower than in 1979–80' (HMSO 1980: v). The stated main aims in both White Papers were the same: (i) 'to bring down the rate of inflation and

5

interest rates by curtailing the growth of the money supply and controlling Government borrowing'; (ii) 'to restore incentives'; and (iii) 'to plan for spending which is compatible both with the objectives for taxation and borrowing and with a realistic assessment of the prospects for economic growth' (HMSO 1980: 3). Thus, the Conservative government's first surveys of public expenditure represented a major change in direction compared with the plan to increase public expenditure by about 2 per cent a year in volume terms over the next four years outlined by the previous Labour government in its White Paper of January 1979 (HMSO 1979a). More precisely, the Labour government's intention to increase total public expenditure from £68,156 million in 1979/80 to £71,832 million in 1982/3 (£ million at 1978 survey prices) was altered to the Conservative government's intention to reduce total public expenditure from £74,551 million in 1980/1 to £71,400 million in 1983/4 (£ million at 1979 survey prices), which shows very clearly the scale of the change in direction.

In terms of their respective spending on individual programmes, the main differences concern the Conservative government's policy to give far greater priority to defence and law and order spending and yet at the same time reduce total public expenditure by cutting back on social expenditure, especially housing and education. The break with the post-1945 social democratic political consensus regarding the establishment of a welfare state was decisive: between 1978/9 and 1980/1, for the first time, the rise in social expenditure (defined as state spending on social security, health, education, housing and personal social services) was less than the overall increase in public expenditure (Walker 1982), whereas in the period to 1977 social expenditure had increased at a faster rate than the growth of gross domestic product (GDP) and 'also faster than public expenditure as a whole' (Gould and Roweth 1980: 357).

In line with their 'new right' economic theories regarding the 'need' to increase incentives and 'enlarge freedom', the first Conservative budget after the 1979 electoral victory initiated the process of rejecting progressive taxation policies in favour of markedly more regressive ones. The June 1979 budget cut the basic rate of income tax by 3 per cent to 30 per cent, cut the top rate on earned income by 23 per cent to 60 per cent and nearly doubled valued added tax by raising it from 8 per cent to 15 per cent. This new regressive taxation tradition has been maintained by a series of reductions in the basic rate of income tax (from 30 per cent to 29 per cent in 1986, to 27 per cent in 1987 and to 25 per cent in

1988) and the abolition of the four highest tax bands in 1988, leaving a top rate of 40 per cent in a two-tier system. Thus, in a relatively short historical period, the top rate of taxation has been reduced drastically to a point where it is now nearer the 1979 basic rate than is the current basic rate. Taken all together, these changes in income tax represent the most radical tax 'reforms' since the introduction of Pay As You Earn (PAYE) in 1944.

During the same period several other measures have reinforced this regressive trend, notably the attempt to limit the expansion of expenditure on social security in the face of growing numbers of unemployed and elderly people. In the first Thatcher administration, legislation was passed to end earnings-related unemployment benefit and to end the obligation to increase basic unemployment benefit in line with prices. Moreover, the obligation to increase state pensions and other long-term benefits in line with prices or earnings (whichever was higher) was replaced by a commitment to raise pensions in line with prices only. These policies had originally been introduced by Labour during the mid 1970s and the proposal to end them was announced as early as the 1979 Conservative budget. It has been estimated that the saving on state pensions alone between 1979 and 1988 amounted to a massive £4 billion (*Guardian*, 25 April 1988).

Last but not least, a poll tax (known as the community charge), the ultimate in regressive taxation, replaced domestic rates in Scotland in 1989 and in England and Wales in 1990. This major change in local taxation was inspired, like so many Thatcherist fiscal policies, by the desire to reduce public spending. In the words of the Green Paper, *Paying for Local Government*, one of the 'main strands' of Conservative local finance policy since 1979 has been to 'contain local government expenditure at affordable levels' (HMSO 1986a: 3). Moreover, the change from domestic rates to the community charge 'implied the end of local rates as a form of income redistribution ' (Butcher *et al.* 1990: 73).

The combined effect of the selective restructuring of public spending which disproportionately and adversely affects those dependent upon the state for wages/salaries, benefits, and/or services, and cuts in personal taxation which disproportionately and advantageously affect the wealthier members of society, has been to increase inequality (Walker and Walker 1987). For example, according to the Department of Employment's *New Earnings Survey* (1987), between April 1979 and April 1987 the highest-earning 10 per cent of full-time male workers received a 137 per cent rise in pay whereas the lowest-earning 10 per cent received a

7

93 per cent rise. This study focused on those in work and excluded the unemployed and others dependent upon the state for their income, and as a consequence tended to understate the extent of increasing economic polarization. A more representative study, which concentrated on household income rather than the earnings of employed individuals, and was also based on official statistics, has shown that the share of marketable wealth of the richest sections of the population has increased since 1979 (Stark 1987). More recent calculations that take into account the 1988 budget tax cuts for the rich have confirmed that the postwar trend towards greater equality has been reversed since 1979 (Riddell 1989). In other words, all previous postwar governments had been committed to reducing inequality via progressive fiscal policies in general and increased welfare spending in particular. The evidence provided by the Royal Commission on the Distribution of Income and Wealth, set up by Labour in August 1974 and abolished by the Conservatives in July 1979, showed that there had been some redistribution of income between 1949 and 1977, especially among the top half of income earners (HMSO 1979c). Since 1979 a new trend towards a more unequal society has been firmly established.

Lastly, a major anomaly in the official presentation of government income and expenditure has clear and important implications for economic inequality. As long ago as the late 1950s, Titmuss noted that direct cash payments from the government to individuals are treated as expenditure, whereas 'Allowances and reliefs from income tax, though providing similar benefits ... are not ... treated as social service expenditure' (1958: 44). This 'accounting convenience' conceals a massive state subsidy to the relatively well off. The best-known form of tax expenditure that does not appear in conventional appraisals of public spending is mortgage interest relief, which increased from less than £2 billion in 1978/9 to approximately £7 billion in 1989/90 (*Guardian*, 14 February 1990). Moreover, since there is no capital gains tax on house sales, the real cost in terms of income forgone by the exchequer in this respect is far greater. Government subsidies to council tenants, including housing benefit, on the other hand, appear in public expenditure accounts (Likierman 1988). In other words, public spending in the form of tax relief to 'middle-class' home-owners is not counted as public spending, whereas public spending in the form of state benefits to 'working-class' non-home-owners is counted as public spending. Under Thatcherism, this convention has become increasingly and acutely illogical and ideological. The perverse politics of public expenditure accounting is a little researched and debated issue of great class and sectoral significance (Hall 1983).

Employment and unemployment

The 1979 Conservative administration 'was the first government since the 1944 White Paper on Employment Policy not to make full employment one of its objectives' (Pliatzky 1984: 171). In May 1979 the number of people officially unemployed was 1.29 million; the trend was down, following a postwar peak reached during the winter of 1977–8. By mid 1979 this mini decline was arrested, and from the autumn onwards the official figures began a seemingly inexorable climb: the 2 million figure was passed in August 1980 and the 3 million in January 1982. The annual average level of unemployment remained at over 3 million until 1986, and, although it fell to just under 2 million in 1989, this is still higher than it was in 1979 (*Employment Gazette*, 1990).

These unemployment levels would have been even higher if it had not been for a major change in May 1982 in the way that the unemployment total is officially calculated, plus many other changes since. Before the Conservative election victory in 1979, in order to be counted as unemployed one needed to be officially registered as unemployed. In order to be counted as unemployed in 1982, one needed to be officially registered and in receipt of unemployment benefit. This key change in the basis of calculating the level of unemployment, combined with the expansion of government training schemes for adults and young people, had the effect of excluding large numbers of people seeking work (notably married women and young people) from the official estimate of unemployment. Drawing upon official data published by the Department of Employment and the General Household Survey, it was estimated at the time that these two sources alone reduced the total number of unemployed in mid 1982 by approximately 300,000 young people and 500,000 women (*Labour Research*, 1982). Clearly, Conservative government unemployment statistics are exceedingly conservative. Of 30 changes introduced by the Conservatives since 1979 in the manner in which unemployment is measured (*Guardian*, 4 December 1989), the vast majority have had the effect of reducing the total figure. This is an indication of the political sensitivity of these data, notwithstanding the consensus-breaking abandonment of 'full employment' as a policy objective.

The concomitant of cuts in public expenditure are cuts in public sector employment. Between 1961 and 1978 the private sector's share of employment fell by just over 1 million, whereas total public sector employment increased by approximately 1.5 million (Semple 1979). During the same period, social expenditure, that is expenditure on health, education and social services, actually doubled. To a new Conservative government committed to reducing 'the burden of financing the public sector, so as to leave room for commerce and industry to prosper' (*Economic Progress Report*, 1979: 1), reversing this particular historical trend was an urgent priority. In fact, this priority was made even more compelling by three other considerations: (a) the scale of public sector industrial conflict in the late 1970s (which was described in the Conservative manifesto of 1979 in crisis terms); (b) the rising cost of state spending on social security, owing partly to increasing unemployment and partly to demographic changes, notably Britain's ageing population; and (c) the expectation for 'economic activity to decline slightly over the next year or so', especially in manufacturing output (*Economic Progress Report*, 1979: 2).

In mid 1979 the public sector accounted for nearly 30 per cent of the total UK employed labour force of just over 25 million (Lomas 1980). By mid 1989 the public sector share of the UK labour force had declined to just over 23 per cent of the estimated 26 million workforce in employment (Fleming 1989). In terms of actual numbers, between 1979 and 1989 public sector employment fell by over 1 million and private sector employment increased by over 1 million. The marked decline in public sector employment can be illustrated by the achievement of the lowest number of civil servants since the Second World War in April 1984, a reduction of over 100,000 to 623,972 (or nearly 15 per cent between 1979 and 1984). At the time, this was a small but acclaimed contributory factor to the decline in public sector employment (*Economic Progress Report*, 1984).

The bulk of the change in the balance of private/public employment is due to the decline in the numbers employed in public corporations, that is, state trading organizations. In other words, this significant change in the postwar pattern of sectoral employment is related directly to the policy of 'privatization' that has developed apace since 1979. For example, the privatization of nine public corporations between February 1981 and February 1987 (British Aerospace, Cable and Wireless, National Freight Corporation, Britoil, Associated British Ports, British Telecom, Trust Ports (Great Britain), British Gas and British Airways) involved the reclassification of approximately 500,000 public sector employees

(Camley 1987). Moreover, changes in both unemployment and sectoral employment trends are not unrelated to the post-1979 Thatcherist aim of curbing the power of organized labour.

Trade unions
The postwar growth in the public sector in Britain was accompanied by the growth of public sector unionization and disputes. According to Price and Bain (1983), between 1948 and 1979 union density in the expanding public sector increased from 71 per cent to 82 per cent, union density in the contracting manufacturing sector increased from 51 per cent to 70 per cent and union density in the expanding private service sector increased from 15 per cent to 17 per cent.

In the 1970s, public sector disputes, often involving previously acquiescent occupational groups such as postal workers (1971) and firemen (1977), as well as traditionally less acquiescent groups like the coalminers (1972 and 1974), became increasingly prominent owing to their opposition to government economic policy and their perceived deleterious effect on the general public (Beaumont 1987). This trend culminated in the so-called 1978–9 'Winter of Discontent' during which over 1 million low-paid but essential public service and hospital workers were on strike for nearly three months (*Employment Gazette*, 1979). Following this high-profile dispute, the 1979 Conservative manifesto devoted more space to the reform of trade unions than to any other issue.

This manifesto advanced the view that the trade unions were the major cause of Britain's economic problems and claimed that the trade union movement was 'more distrusted and feared than ever before'. According to the Conservatives, the previous Labour government had 'enacted a "militants' charter" of trade union legislation', which had 'tilted the balance of power in bargaining throughout industry away from responsible management and towards unions'. In order to reduce industrial conflict and bring about economic recovery, the reform of trade unions was given a high priority in the first and second Thatcher administrations. Three major Acts of Parliament were passed to reduce the power of organized labour: Employment Act 1980, Employment Act 1982 and the Trade Union Act 1984. Taken together these three pieces of legislation have, among other things, reformed or constrained four key areas of trade union behaviour: picketing, secondary action, the closed shop and strike ballots. Lawful picketing is now defined as picketing which is peaceful, does not involve more than six strikers and is against the strikers' own employer or employer of a customer or supplier. Secondary action has been outlawed totally, closed shop agreements have been made more difficult to maintain, and strike ballots are compulsory. Moreover, legal immunities for what are now unlawful industrial actions, such as mass picketing, have been removed.

The implementation of a new (right) set of rules of the game was accompanied by a general exclusion of trade union leaders from the corridors of political power and a series of successful government encounters with public sector unions, notably the withdrawal of union membership rights at the Government Communications Headquarters (Cheltenham) early in 1984 and the defeat of the National Union of Mineworkers following a long and bitter dispute during 1984–5. Thus the close relationship that had developed in the postwar era of Keynesian consensus politics between governments and the trade union movement was decisively broken by the hostile union policies adopted by successive Conservative administrations. In other words, the tripartite management of the economy was rejected in 1979 and replaced by an essentially bipartite system involving the government and capital.

A labour market characterized by mass unemployment inevitably favours the buyers rather than the sellers of labour power. Since 1979, the relative weakness of labour vis-à-vis capital has been exacerbated by a sustained ideological and legal attack on trade union power and on the ability of trade unions effectively to organize workers and to defend and further their interests. This has resulted in a steep decline in both trade union membership and industrial conflict.

Between 1979 and 1987, 'aggregate trade union membership and density in Britain have declined significantly and continually for the first time since the period 1921–33' (Kelly and Bailey 1989: 54). Among unions affiliated to the Trades Union Congress (TUC), the drop in membership was a massive 25 per cent, from a peak of 12.2 million in 1979 to 9.1 million in 1987. Kelly and Bailey have suggested that: 'Together with changes in the scope and outcomes of collective bargaining, and the rise in unemployment, these trends suggest that union bargaining power has also declined in recent years' (1989: 54). Interestingly, the sharp decline in trade union membership over this period numerically parallels the rise in unemployment.

The number of industrial disputes has also declined, from an annual total in excess of 2,000 during the late 1970s to under 1,000 by the end of the 1980s, with a corresponding decline in the number of workers involved and worker-days lost in industrial disputes (*Social Trends*, 1990). Notwithstanding the unpropitious political, legal and economic climate of a Thatcherist Britain, rolling back the state in a highly selective pattern has, not surprisingly, meant that public sector disputes have tended to dominate industrial relations in the 1980s; for example, steel workers in 1980, civil servants in 1981, railway workers in 1982, health service workers in 1983, coalminers in 1984–5, teachers in 1985–6, university teachers in 1988–9, and ambulance workers in 1989–90 (*Employment Gazette*, 1979–90).

Thatcherism's concerted attempt to weaken the power of collective labour, to delegitimize trade unions and to de-unionize workers has been successful, despite widespread and, at times, prolonged resistance. Hyman (1984: 199) has called this process the 'coercive pacification' of trade unions. Central to this particular policy of reducing the power of trade unions in the market for labour and to the attempt to increase the role of market forces in all sectors of the economy, both of which fundamentally undermine Keynesian-based assumptions regarding the mixed economy, is the policy of privatization.

Privatization

The by now well-known term 'privatization' did not appear in the 1979 Conservative manifesto, although the policy of selling shares in state industries and the liberalization of licensing regulations were mentioned under the heading 'Nationalisation'. Yet, throughout the whole period of Conservative rule since 1979, privatization has developed into an increasingly important part of the overall policy of controlling the growth of public spending.

During the first Thatcher administration, the privatization policy gained in momentum and an 'official' definition was published by the Treasury in its *Economic Progress Report*: 'the return of industries, assets and activities to the private sector' (1982: 1). The reasoning behind this major reversal of the postwar trend towards increased state involvement in the economy was that market forces would increase competition and expand consumer choice. It was also argued that privatization would widen share ownership and help reduce the burden on the exchequer (*Economic Progress Report*, 1982: 1–2). By the time of the 1983 Conservative manifesto, privatization was mentioned explicitly in the context of transferring 'more state-owned businesses to independent ownership' (1983: 16–17). This manifesto also promised to extend the 'Right to Buy' housing scheme by including the right to buy houses on leasehold land and to buy on a shared ownership basis and by raising the maximum discount from 50 per cent to 60 per cent. The increasingly strong commitment of the post-1979 Conservative administrations to privatization is arguably the most distinctive feature of this period of new right politics by comparison with all previous postwar Labour and Conservative governments (Duke and Edgell 1984; Heald and Thomas 1986). The Conservative government's official statement on privatization refers to six ways of opening up the public sector to market forces (*Economic Progress Report*, 1982): (1) the public issue of shares on the Stock Exchange, e.g. British Telecom; (2) sale to consortia of employees and management, e.g. National Freight Company; (3) placement with institutional investors, e.g. minority shareholding in the British Sugar Corporation; (4) the sale of physical assets, e.g. British Rail hotels; (5) joint public/private ventures, e.g. the merger of British Rail's hovercraft service with Hoverlloyd; and (6) the contracting out of public services by central government and local authorities, e.g. office cleaning and refuse disposal.

This list emphasizes the withdrawal of industries from public sector production rather than the increased consumption of private services. At this point it is important to establish that the current debate on the Conservative privatization policy is concerned with economic privatization of both production and consumption. This process should not be confused with the social privatization of affluent workers identified by Goldthorpe *et al.* (1969), which involves an increase in individual family/home-centred ethos and life style. The two types of privatization are not unrelated, in the sense that the economic privatization of consumption, especially housing and transport, has extensive implications for social privatization. Unless otherwise indicated, hereafter all references to privatization are to economic privatization.

Discussions of privatization vary, depending on whether they adopt a broad or a narrow definition (see Chapter 7). Our own preference is to adopt a broad view on the grounds that it more accurately reflects the diversity and historical significance of the post-1979 Conservative privatization policy. In other words, privatization refers to altering the balance between the public and private sectors of the British economy in favour of the latter and as such is central to the key post-1979 Conservative policy objective of the restoration of market forces throughout the economy (Conservative manifestos of 1979 and 1983; *Economic Progress Report*, 1982). Following Heald's (1983) four components of the policy of privatization, but extending it to five, we consider that a broad definition of this policy should include: (1) increasing charges, that is, the privatization of the financing of a service produced by the public sector – this important component is noticeably absent from the official definition; (2) contracting out, that is, the privatization of the production of a service financed by the public sector; (3) denationalization (and loan shedding), that is, the transfer of activities from the public sector to the private sector; (4) liberalization, that is, the removal of formal obstacles that inhibit the private sector from competing against the public sector; and (5) the encouragement of private sector consumption, typically achieved by a combination of financial incentives to consume privately (for example, housing and health) and allowing the quantity and quality of public sector provision to deteriorate through selective cuts in spending, which intentionally or otherwise encourages privatization.

The pre-1979 British pattern of state intervention in the economy in general, and the nationalization of industries and services in particular, was one of increasing statism by both Labour and Conservative governments. Thus, after the boost to public ownership effected by the 1945 Labour government, the 1951 Conservative government did not reprivatize industries such as coal and the railways, or services like health. An exception was the denationalization of steel, which was then renationalized by Labour in 1967, and denationalized by the Conservatives yet again in 1988. Political party agreement regarding the maintenance of a mixed economy during the postwar era was further demonstrated by the Conservative nationalization of 'lame duck' industries such as Rolls-Royce Aero Engines in 1971.

From 1979 onwards this key part of the postwar social democratic political consensus was totally rejected, as the following statistical examples amply confirm. First, proceeds from central government privatization for the period 1979/80 to 1986/7 show that net receipts in cash terms rose steeply from under £0.5 billion per year during the first Thatcher administration to over £2 billion in 1984/5 and 1985/6, to over £4 billion in 1986/7 (HMSO 1986b, 1987, 1988). This component of the privatization policy has, as was shown above, made a major contribution to the policy of reversing the post-1945 growth in public sector employment. Second, proceeds from local government privatization, the most notable contribution to which is housing, exceeded £1 million each year between 1981/2 and 1986/7 (HMSO 1987, 1988). Third, largely as a result of the 'special sales of assets' (that is, privatization of public corporations), the number of shareholders increased from 7 per cent at the beginning of Thatcherism to 21 per cent by 1987

(*Social Trends*, 1990). Fourth, there was a growth between 1979 and 1989 in the private consumption of the following essential services: housing (owner occupation increased from 55 per cent to 63 per cent), transport (car ownership increased from 58 per cent to 64 per cent), health (private health insurance increased from 5 per cent to nearly 10 per cent), and education (private schooling increased from 6 per cent to 7 per cent) (*Social Trends*, 1990). Lastly, water was privatized in 1989 amidst claims of 'massive underpricing' and, at the time, public opposition (*Guardian*, 7 December 1989). In the light of the fact that privatization was not even mentioned as an objective in 1979, this is an impressive change in the direction of public policy.

4 The Historical Distinctiveness of Thatcherism: a Summary

The anti-Keynesian, consensus-breaking policies discussed above interrelate in many ways. In the sense that they tend to be mutually reinforcing in their effects, they represent a reasonably coherent package of social changes. For example, various forms of public spending cuts – notably increased charges and the reduction of state subsidies to nationalized industries – like the privatization policy, all strengthen market forces.

However, the package is not without its contradictions in theory or in practice (see Gough 1983; King 1987). For instance, the state has been rolled back, but very selectively, and reducing social expenditure in the short run may be a false economy in the long run, owing to the politics of increased poverty and the exacerbation of class and regional inequalities in the context of sustained economic growth since 1981 (*Economic Progress Report*, 1988). All of this may create new social and economic demands, as well as expand existing ones. At the beginning of the period of immense change that our study covers, public expenditure and, to a lesser extent, industrial relations were the central issues. During the mid-phase of the project, unemployment became the dominant issue. Over the ten years, privatization expanded inexorably in importance to become one of the key policies of Thatcherism.

The distinctiveness of the post-1979 Thatcher administrations is that their policies on public spending, public/private sector employment, public/private sector consumption and trade unions added up to a major qualitative and quantitative break with the post-1945 Keynesian-based political consensus regarding the character and management of the British economy. Rampant individualism replaced creeping collectivism. The growth in the public sector in terms of production and consumption was not just halted but reversed in many key respects. Privatization, broadly defined, increased in social, economic and political importance throughout the 1980s. The development of trade unionism in terms of membership and the unions' capacity to operate effectively was arrested in a period characterized by mass unemployment. The control of inflation took precedence over the achievement of full employment as a central, if not the central, policy objective. There had been hints of a change in direction by Labour on essentially pragmatic grounds during the economic crisis of the mid 1970s. In our view, however, the scale and depth of the changes in the political economy of Britain brought about by Conservative governments since 1979 under the leadership of Mrs Thatcher constitute the recrudescence of old values. Basically, these values include the virtues of competition, freedom of choice, self-reliance and incentives, and the creation of a new type of de-industrialized capitalist society.

5   Data Sources

The main data sources that will be drawn upon in this sociological study of Thatcher's Britain in the 1980s include the following:

- panel data from the Greater Manchester Study – see Chapters 2–8 below (the research design of the GMS is explained in Appendix 1);
- other survey data, notably 1987 data from the *British Social Attitudes* surveys (BSA) and the British Election Studies (BES) – see chapters 2, 3, 4, 7, 8 and Appendix 2;
- central and local government statistics with special reference to the period 1979–89 – see Chapters 5 and 6;
- local and regional press data collected as part of the GMS – see Chapter 5.

Appendix 3 outlines the base sample sizes in GMS, BSA and BES for the key sub-groups in this study, such as social classes and sectoral locations. Hence, sample sizes are not repeated in every single table.

In sum, this sociological measure of Thatcherism is based primarily on our panel survey covering the first two Thatcher administrations (GMS1 and GMS2), updated to 1987 on the basis of an analysis of BES and BSA survey data, and supplemented throughout with official central and local government statistics.

6 Plan of the Book

There are an increasing number of book-length accounts of 'Thatcherism', the vast majority of which have been concerned in a polemical way with its political and/or economic dimensions. For example, in chronological order: Hall and Jacques (1983); Riddell (1983 updated 1985); Keegan (1984); Holmes (1985); Krieger (1986); Kavanagh (1987); MacInnes (1987); Gamble (1988); Hall (1988); Jessop et al. (1988); Skidelsky (1988); and Brown and Sparks (1989). This veritable plethora of politico-economic analyses of Thatcherism is in marked contrast to the paucity of general sociological studies of Thatcherist Britain, although a number of studies have focused on some of the more obvious social consequences of Thatcherism – notably, social and economic inequality (see Field 1983; Marshall et al. 1988; Rose 1988), unemployment (see Harris 1987; Westergaard et al. 1989), regional divisions (see Walker and Walker 1987; Smith 1989), and privatization (see Hastings and Levie 1983; Ascher 1987). It is our contention that the nature, extent and social implications of the post-1979 'cuts' in public expenditure and associated policy changes in Britain, summarized by the term 'Thatcherism', should not be neglected by sociologists. Therefore the purpose of this book is to review a range of sociological and political theories about class, politics, and social welfare with reference to empirical data collected during the period of Thatcherist social change.

In Chapter 2 we are highly critical of what we call the traditional analytic class framework, which tends to concentrate on the occupational class position of the economically active. Following a comprehensive review of the research choices involved in operationalizing the concept class, we advocate and affirm the value of a social class and sectoral approach to the sociological analysis of contemporary Britain.

Chapter 3 considers the three election victories of the Conservative party led by Thatcher. The power to attempt to change society stems from continued success at the national polls, hence the social bases of British politics in 1979, 1983 and 1987 will be analysed with special reference to social class, plus production and consumption sectoral locations. Different theories of voting behaviour

18

will be reviewed, including conventional alignment theory based on a party identification model of voting, realignment theory based on the assumption of a decline in class voting, and alternative explanations based on a rejection of both alignment and realignment interpretations of voting behaviour.

In Chapter 4 the nature and extent of the mandate for Thatcher's policies will be examined, including public attitudes towards particular issues. Special attention will be given to the consistency of attitudes towards changes in the patterning of public spending over time. The interrelationship between values and political attitudes will also be considered.

Chapter 5 will focus on the problem of implementing central government policies at the local state level and the role of the local and regional press. More specifically, the extent to which local political control is a mediating factor at a time when the central government is trying to reduce and restructure public spending will be analysed on the basis of our case study of two different local authorities, one sympathetic to Thatcherism and the other antagonistic.

In Chapter 6, the nature and extent of knowledge and perception of the social impact of Thatcherism will be considered with reference to social class, sectoral location and stage in the family life cycle. This attempt to measure the perceived impact of Conservative policies will also involve the exploration of possible variations in social impact over time.

Of all the public expenditure 'cuts' strategies adopted by Conservative governments since 1979, privatization has developed into the most important in terms of political distinctiveness, economic value and social implications. Therefore in Chapter 7 the growth of the privatization programme over the past ten years and its future prospects will be examined with particular reference to welfare state privatization. This will include the attempt to clarify the conceptual confusion that surrounds this important issue and an analysis of the influences on attitudes to privatization.

In Chapter 8, the attempt by three successive Conservative governments to alter the balance of class forces in favour of capital and the balance of public and private sector production and consumption in favour of the market will be analysed with reference to theories about class, sector and social change. In other words, we considered that Britain under Thatcherism in the 1980s provided an ideal opportunity to test theories that seek to relate radicalization to the development of industrial capitalism. As part of this analysis, the persistence and patterning of dominant and radical value systems will also be examined on the basis of both attitudinal and behavioural data.

Lastly, Chapter 9 draws together the various measures of Thatcherism investigated in our study and includes an assessment of the sociological meaning of the claim that Britain has experienced a measure of Thatcherism. The GMS was designed specifically to measure Thatcherism empirically, hence our title.

CHAPTER 2

Class and Sector: Key Concepts in Understanding the Social and Political Effects of Thatcherism

1 Introduction

Between 1979 and 1989, the Conservative policy to restructure British society by enhancing the primacy of the market profoundly affected social and political divisions. The overall direction of this policy represented an attempt to alter the balance of class and sectoral forces in Thatcherist Britain, often by encouraging, both ideologically and practically, certain underlying economic trends (for example, by reinforcing the already relatively weak bargaining position of organized labour during a recession, and by providing added impetus to the historical growth of private transport and home ownership). The high priority given to reducing inflation compared with reducing unemployment, combined with legislation designed to restrict the effectiveness of trade unions, tipped the balance of class power in favour of employers and away from employees during the 1980s. Similarly, the centrality accorded to limiting public spending, plus the expanding privatization programme, modified the structure of public and private sector production and consumption in favour of private sector producers and consumers. Before we can analyse the changing pattern of class and sectoral forces in contemporary Britain, we need to consider the meaning and measurement of the key concepts – class and sector.

2 Class and Classes

Class is arguably the most widely used and abused concept in sociology. Nearly one hundred years have elapsed since Marx first

21

asked the question in the third volume of *Capital*: 'What constitutes a class?' ([1894] 1974: 886). His answer was that it depends upon one's relationship to the means of production and the stage reached in the development of the capitalist mode of production. Thus, according to Marx, the increasing concentration of the means of production was 'transforming labour into wage-labour and the means of production into capital' (1974: 885). This dichotomous model of the nineteenth-century British class structure and the revolutionary historical role that Marx assigned to the proletariat (Marx and Engels 1848) simultaneously popularized and controversialized the concept class.

The idea of class has remained at the centre of political and sociological attention ever since, although the Marxian conceptualization of class has not been the dominant one. Occupational class has become the conventional way to define class in British sociology. At the same time and somewhat ironically, Marxian theoretical issues have continued to be the main focus of class analysis. Thus, in Britain at least, the political role of the working class has remained high on the research agenda (see Chapter 8). Hence, the first issue that should be addressed in any study of the changing class structure is how to operationalize class.

3 Competing Definitions: Social and/or Occupational Class?

At the outset, it is important to note the confusing and annoying tendency for social scientific discussions of class to use the label 'social class' when the data being analysed involve occupational categories. This widespread propensity afflicts both official statistical analyses (namely, the Registrar-General's 'social classes') and mainstream sociological studies (see Reid 1989).

Throughout this study we use the term 'social class' to refer exclusively to the social relations of production and 'occupational class' to refer exclusively to the technical relations of production (Wright 1980). To illustrate the crucial theoretical differences between these two competing conceptualizations of class, take the case of an engineer. In a neo-Marxist social class scheme, such a person is defined in terms of their relationship to capital. Thus, if an engineer sells their labour power to a capitalist (i.e. employer), s/he would be classified as a worker (i.e. wage labourer); if s/he is in charge of workers, s/he would be classified as a controller (i.e. manager) of labour; if s/he was self-employed, s/he would be classified as petty bourgeois (i.e. small-scale capitalist); and, lastly, if s/he employed other people, s/he would be classified as a capitalist (i.e. employer). In contrast to these four theoretical possibilities within a social class scheme, in an occupational class scheme an engineer could be classified in one of two ways. If s/he is certificated to degree level and works in an office, s/he would be classified as higher managerial or professional 'middle class'. Alternatively, if s/he has undertaken an apprenticeship and works in a factory, s/he would be classified as skilled 'working class'. Crucially, if an engineer is self-employed or an employer of any size, s/he would still be classified as either a non-manual manager or a manual worker on the basis of their occupation.

Thus, the crux of the debate about social and occupational class concerns the theoretical primacy that is accorded either to one's social relations in an employment situation or to what one does at work. Consequently, social class and occupational class refer to distinct theoretical aspects of a capitalist social structure and this has important sociological implications (see Westergaard and Resler 1975).

First, the adoption of a social class scheme implies that the major societal division is between the owners and the non-owners of the means of production, whereas an occupational class scheme implies that the manual/non-manual cleavage is the main one in society. Second, a social class scheme is essentially a relational one which emphasizes conflict, whereas an occupational scheme is a hierarchical one which emphasizes shared values and therefore harmony.

These are sociologically significant considerations, yet there are occupational schemes that contain both social and occupational class categories. For example, in Britain over the past 20 years Goldthorpe has been associated with three 'impure' occupational class schemes: (1) the eight-category occupational classification that was used in the affluent worker research project was based on an earlier social grading of occupations (Goldthorpe *et al.* 1969; Hall and Jones 1950); (2) a new 36-category occupational scale that was constructed for the Oxford occupational mobility inquiry (Goldthorpe and Hope 1974) was based on procedures used in the British Census and is therefore compatible with official statistics; (3) the seven-category version of the already collapsed (36-category) occupational scale that was developed by Goldthorpe and Hope (Goldthorpe 1987). In all three versions, large proprietors and higher-grade professional and managerial workers are placed in the same top-ranking or dominant position. To paraphrase Murphy (1984), a class model that conflates social and occupational class is incapable of distinguishing between the wealth and power of Dr Edgell and Mr Maxwell.

Moreover, the 124-category Hope–Goldthorpe scale would seem to be infinitely flexible in that not only can it be collapsed by stages into seven categories, it can also be reduced to a basic three-class scheme and/or expanded slightly into an 11-class scheme (see Marshall *et al.* 1988: 22). However, whatever version of Goldthorpe is used, property relations and occupation are conflated at the apex of an essentially positional or hierarchical model of the class structure. Such a model tends to obfuscate the inherently antagonistic class relationship between labour and capital. This is regrettable since this form of class conflict is arguably the most significant in an industrial capitalist society – a point that is widely acknowledged by mainstream industrial sociologists (see Hill 1981).

4 Traditional Analytic Class Framework

A fundamental part of the Greater Manchester Study (GMS) of the social and political effects of the public expenditure cuts during the 1980s was a consideration of the relative advantages and disadvantages of the various ways of operationalizing class (Edgell and Duke 1981, 1985). We found that the vast majority of studies tend to define class in occupational terms, as well as assuming that the family is the basic unit of class analysis and that the class location of the family is determined by the occupation of the male 'head' of household. Furthermore, studies of class typically concentrate on people who are economically active on a full-time basis. We have called this approach the traditional analytic class framework, and it is instructive to consider some of the complex issues that are raised by its use, prior to outlining a critique and developing an alternative framework.

The first complexity encountered by a social scientist who wishes to conform to the traditional analytic class framework based on occupation is that there are many occupational class schemes to select from. In addition to essentially occupational schemes derived from one of the scales developed by Goldthorpe and his associates (discussed above), which are commonly used by sociologists, two other occupational class schemes are widely used in British social science. First, there is the historically important Registrar-General's occupationally based 'social classes' (Leete and Fox

1977). This is effectively an 'official' classification of occupations and consequently tends to dominate government and non-government statistics. Second, a social grading of occupations was developed in a study of political attitudes (Kahan *et al.* 1966). This scale closely followed the definitions of occupational grades developed by market researchers, and has tended to dominate political science in the 1970s and market research in Britain ever since (Butler and Stokes 1974; Monk 1985).

The Registrar-General developed an eight-fold classification of occupations into social groups in 1911, although occupational data had been collected from the very first Census in 1801 (Hakim 1980). The famous five 'social classes' date from 1921 (see Table 2.1), and were ranked according to social standing (Stevenson 1928). This semi-official occupational class scale remained in use until 1961, with only minor adjustments for changes in the standing of particular occupations. Examples of the changing fortunes of different occupations include: clerks, who started off in class I in 1911, were relegated to class II in 1921 and class III in 1931; and aircraft pilots, who were promoted from class III to class II in 1961 (Leete and Fox 1977; Hakim 1980).

In 1970 this scheme was modified by splitting class III into manual (IIIM) and non-manual (IIINM), thus creating a six-fold occupational scale that could be easily collapsed into a manual and non-manual dichotomy (Leete and Fox 1977). In 1980 the basis of the Registrar-General's social classes was changed without explanation from relative social standing to level of occupational skill, yet the class categories remained the same (Brewer 1986). Taken together, these two changes reaffirmed the by now widely adopted sociological practice of distinguishing between a non-manual middle class and a manual working class.

The same exercise can be and frequently is undertaken by users of the other two occupational class schemes, namely the social grade (SG) and the Hope–Goldthorpe (HG) scheme (see Table 2.1). Moreover, as in the case of the Hope–Goldthorpe occupational scale, the Registrar-General's social classes and the social grades also require information on both occupational unit group and employment situation. In each scheme the final class categories involve some merging of different employment situations into the same class category, notably in the case of the highest class, which invariably contains employers as well as managers and professionals. In this respect, RG and SG are almost as 'impure' as the HG scheme, but do not appear so from the labels used to describe the constituent class categories (see Table 2.1). Thus, the HG

25

Table 2.1 Occupational and social class coding schemes

Registrar–General (RG) (revised)		Social Grade (SG)		Hope–Goldthorpe (HG)		Wright Mark I		Wright Mark III	
I	Professional	A	Upper middle class	I	Higher professional, admin. and managerial plus large proprietors	1	Capitalists	1	Bourgeoisie
II	Intermediate	B	Middle class			2	Petty bourgeois	2	Small employers
III NM	Skilled non-manual	C1	Lower middle class	II	Lower professional, admin and managerial	3	Managers (con-trollers)	3	Petty bourgeoisie
								4/5	Expert managers & supervisors
III M	Skilled Manual	C2	Skilled working class	III	Routine non-manual	4	Workers	6/7	Semi-credentialled managers and supervisors
IV	Semi-skilled manual	D	Semi and unskilled working class	IV	Small proprietors and self-employed			8/9	Uncredentialled managers and supervisors
V	Unskilled manual	E	Residual: casual worker, state dependants	V	Lower-grade technicians			10	Expert non-managers
				VI	Skilled manual			11	Semi-credentialled workers
				VII	Semi-skilled manual			12	Proletarians

Source: OPCS 1980, Monk 1985; Goldthorpe 1987; Wright 1985.

26

scheme is distinctive in that large employers and small employers and the self-employed appear explicitly in classes I and IV respectively. In all other respects it is comparable with other occupational class schemes such as RG and SG, in the sense that it gives primacy to the manual/non-manual social division.

Many sociologists have argued that, in advanced industrial societies like Britain, the major 'line of cleavage falls between the manual and non-manual occupational categories' (Parkin 1971: 25; see also Roberts *et al.* 1977; King and Raynor 1981). Similarly, Kelley and McAllister (1985) have stated that the blue/white-collar occupational division is the dominant conception of class in political science. Certainly, as far as empirical sociological research in contemporary Britain is concerned, over 90 per cent uses a conventional occupational class scheme.

In addition to choosing to use an occupational class scheme, those who work within the traditional analytic class framework also tend to apply their occupational class categories to the household, using the occupation of the male 'head' as the indicator, and to economically active males rather than all the economically active population, or even all adult males.

The fullest statement defending the use of the male 'head' of the household approach to the operationalization of class was advanced by Goldthorpe in the context of the women and class debate (Goldthorpe 1983, 1984). He argued that:

> the family is the unit of stratification primarily because only certain family members, predominantly males, have, as a result of their labour market participation, what might be termed a directly determined position within the class structure. Other family members, including wives, do not typically have equal opportunity for such participation, and their class position is thus indirectly determined: that is to say, is 'derived' from the family 'head'. (Goldthorpe 1983: 468)

Consequently, 'lines of class division and potential conflict run between, but not through, families' (Goldthorpe 1983: 469). He summed up by noting that:

> what is essential to class analysis is the argument that family members share in the same class position, and that this position is determined by that of the family 'head' in the sense of the family member who has the greatest commitment to, and

continuity in, labour market participation. That this member is usually a male is then an independent empirical observation which is accounted for in terms of the dependence imposed on women by the conventional separation of sex roles within the family ... Thus, in the case where no male, or no economically active or employed male, is present, or where the family 'head' in the above sense is female, no difficulty arises in principle for class analysis in recognizing and accommodating these circumstances. A truly problematic situation would be created only if it could be shown that the extent and nature of female participation in the labour market is now such that in the more 'normal' conjugal family it is increasingly hard to say whether husband or wife could better be regarded as the family 'head' and that in many cases there are in effect two 'heads' with, quite often, different class positions. (Goldthorpe 1983: 470).

As will become apparent below, Goldthorpe's approach to the operationalization of class came under increasing attack from a variety of viewpoints. Goldthorpe responded to the scale and intensity of the criticisms by reiterating his case and by belatedly considering the class mobility of women (Goldthorpe 1984; Goldthorpe and Payne 1986; Erikson and Goldthorpe 1988). Goldthorpe referred to his approach as the 'conventional view' and it addressed only one part of the traditional analytic class framework to the extent that it did not question directly either the continued use of occupation as the most appropriate conceptual scheme, or the relative exclusion of the economically inactive from class analysis.

Another dimension of the traditional class analytic class framework is the concentration on the economically active in studies of the class structure, irrespective of the conceptual scheme(s) used (see Wright 1985; Marshall *et al.* 1988). This tendency assumes, first, that the distinction between the economically 'active' and 'inactive' is unproblematic and, second, that the 'inactive' are no longer part of the class structure. The first point ignores, among other things, the working unemployed (Henry 1982), the growth of part-time employment and the decline of full-time employment in the UK since the mid 1970s (Hurstfield 1987), and the indeterminate economic activity status of men who have taken early retirement (Casey and Laczko 1989). The second point implies that full-time labour force participation is a prerequisite for inclusion in class analysis. Taken together, these points suggest that it is increasingly indefensible to focus solely upon the economically

28

active if the object of the research is to develop generalizations about the whole class structure.

The problem of confining class analysis to the economically active, and thereby socially constructing a distorted view of the class structure, is compounded by the additional tendency to concentrate on economically active males (see Roberts *et al.* 1977). This is typically done for practical rather than theoretical reasons in order to 'hold the gender variable constant' (Roberts *et al.* 1977: 12). Interestingly, to our knowledge, no one has ever justified excluding men from class analysis on the grounds that they wished to 'hold the gender variable constant'. A male-dominated conception of work and employment that emphasizes full-time, uninterrupted economic activity outside the home seems to be present even in large-scale studies of the class structure. Yet, level of economic activity is related to both political attitudes and behaviour (Edgell and Duke 1983). Consequently, to concentrate on the economically active marginalizes women in class analysis, whereas to concentrate on economically active males excludes women altogether.

5 *Critique of the Traditional Analytic Class Framework*

The traditional analytic framework has tended to dominate empirical social research on class in postwar Britain. For example, three of the major sociological studies on the class structure were based upon samples of economically active male workers from a relatively narrow range of predominantly blue-collar occupations (Goldthorpe *et al.* 1969; Roberts *et al.* 1977; Gallie 1983). There have of course been other studies of class, but they have often been even more narrowly based. For example, there have been studies of male factory workers (Beynon 1975), male dockers (Hill 1976) and male agricultural workers (Newby 1977). We have calculated that studies of class that focus solely on economically active males exclude about 65 per cent of the adult population. The validity of generalizations that are based on such small and unrepresentative samples is questionable. Since 1979, the force of this point has been increased owing to the high level of unemployment and underemployment, plus the many public sector disputes involving large numbers of women – e.g. civil servants (1981), health service workers (1983), teachers (1985–86) – that have characterized this era.

Three lines of criticism of the traditional analytic class framework will be considered: (1) neo-Marxist; (2) feminist and (3) sectoral.

Neo-Marxist criticisms

Neo-Marxist criticisms of occupational class schemes have already been alluded to in section 3; the time has come to be more explicit.

First, there is what we would call the capitalist society critique. Occupational class schemes fail to recognize the capitalist nature of modern Britain in at least two related ways: (a) the capitalist class, the most economically powerful, disappears from the class structure; and (b) theories about the relationship between capitalists and workers cannot be adequately examined by class schemes that emphasize position in a class hierarchy, and anyway fail to identify the dominant class in the relationship.

Marshall *et al*. have countered this line of argument by pointing out that: 'Wright's operational definition of the bourgeoisie [i.e. owners with ten or more employees] is derived from a nineteenth century conception of family proprietorship which is wholly inadequate to the study of class processes in a late twentieth-century capitalist economy' (1988: 38 and 59). This criticism of Wright's preference for, and attempts to, operationalize social class along Marxian lines is reminiscent of Dahrendorf's (1959) thesis that the Marxist model of society was obsolete because of the 'decomposition' of both capital and labour. On the basis of Marshall *et al*'s, stated preference for a class scheme that conflates large proprietors and managers of large establishments (see section 3 above), it is implicitly managerialist. Yet, Marshall *et al*. did not address the claim that 'The managerial revolution, far from nearing completion, has not yet begun' (Scott 1985: 260), or the related claim that a propertied class 'can still be found at the head of the stratification systems of modern industrial capitalism' (Scott 1985: 255, see also Bottomore and Brym 1989). In our view, it is sociologically naive in a study of a capitalist society to adopt a class scheme that at worst renders the capitalist class invisible (e.g. the Registrar-General's scheme), or at best obscures its dominance (e.g. Goldthorpe's scheme).

The second strand of the neo-Marxist critique of the traditional analytic class framework concerns the vulnerability of occupationally based classifications to changes in the occupational structure. As a result of focusing on what a person does at work (i.e. technical relations of production), instead of on the relationships between classes (i.e. social relations of production), changes in the nature of work raise acute problems for occupationally based schemes. As was noted in section 4 above, social processes such as enskilling and deskilling mean that is is imperative continuously to review and if necessary revise the relative position of occupations. Thus, in addition to the examples given above, nurses were upgraded three times in British Censuses between 1861 and 1891 (Davies 1980).

Feminist criticisms

Feminist criticisms of the traditional analytic class framework have tended to dominate the debate about the operationalization of class in recent British sociology, largely, but not solely, in response to Goldthorpe's (1983) initial attempt to defend what he called the 'conventional view' (see section 4). In view of the extensive literature that has emerged on the issue of women and class analysis, what follows is a selective account, rather than an exhaustive one covering all the various contributions that have been published every year since Goldthorpe's original article (see Heath and Britten 1984; Stanworth 1984; Goldthorpe 1984; Dale *et al.* 1985; Crompton and Mann 1986; Abbott 1987; Abbott and Sapsford 1987; Erikson and Goldthorpe 1988; Leiulfsrud and Woodward 1988; Crompton 1989; Wright 1989a).

Briefly therefore, on this particular issue, we would concur with Marshall *et al.* who claimed that 'Class structures and the market processes behind them, are ... "gendered"' (1988: 84). Consequently, to allocate families to classes on the basis of the occupation of the 'head' of the household, who is usually male, produces a 'misleading picture of the class structure' (1988: 86). We have made this important point in the past in relation to both economically inactive adults in general *and* economically active females in particular (Duke and Edgell 1987: 453–4). Interestingly, Marshall *et al.* specifically excluded all those 'not in paid employment (including those who are married to employed spouses)' because 'it seems incongruous to investigate the current socio-political proclivities of respondents exclusively by reference to (perhaps) long-since changed work circumstances' (1988: 85–6). This is a point to which we will return later. For the moment it is relevant to note that the argument used to justify the exclusion of the unemployed from class analysis is predicated on an essentially occupational definition of class. Moreover, in an era when the official level of unemployment was at record levels in Britain (at the time of the Essex fieldwork in 1984 it was over 10 per cent of the working population), to exclude the economically inactive presents a potentially misleading picture of the class structure.

Sectoral criticisms

Sectoral criticisms of the traditional analytic framework concern the argument that sectoral cleavage theory (see section 3) fits better with social class categories than with occupational class (Duke and Edgell 1984). This is mainly because, in terms of the production sector, employers and the petty bourgeoisie are automatically classified as private sector. Therefore, the worker and the controller of labour classes can be divided neatly into public and private sectors. In view of the increased salience of sectoral cleavages during the 1980s (Dunleavy 1989), the ability to accommodate both class and sectoral effects in the same model is a marked advantage (Edgell and Duke 1983; Duke and Edgell 1984). Furthermore, the argument that the manual/non-manual distinction is a significant one in class analysis but is overlooked in social class schemes (see Marshall 1988) can be met by dividing the worker and controller classes into manual and non-manual groups if necessary, as Dunleavy and Husbands have demonstrated successfully (1985).

Considered together, the arguments in favour of a social class scheme that, in contrast to an occupational class scheme, can be neatly combined with sectoral analysis are strengthened by their political relevance since 1979. During the Thatcher era, the balance of class power between employers and workers has altered in favour of employers. Over the same period, the patterning of public and private sector production and consumption has altered in favour of the private sector. A class and sectoral model that captures these significant social changes in modern Britain would seem to have marked advantages over one that does not.

6   New Analytic Class Framework

As a result of our dissatisfaction with the traditional analytic class framework, we concluded that, in order systematically and comprehensively to translate the abstract idea of class into a measurable term, social researchers need to make three interrelated choices.

The first choice is which **conceptual scheme** to adopt: conventional occupational class, social class or a scheme that combines elements from both types? As was noted in section 3, this choice involves a theoretical preference for two quite different aspects of a capitalist class structure. The subsequent choices concern the application of the selected class categories, entailing two related but separate decisions: (a) should the **unit of analysis** be the individual respondent or the family/household group?; and (b) what is to be the **degree of coverage** of the population? In other words, should the classification be based solely upon the economically active individual respondent/group members or on all adult respondents/group members irrespective of whether or not they are currently economically active? Within this apparently clear and straightforward range of alternatives, the choices are in fact complex (see Table 2.2).

The choice of a *conceptual scheme* has been discussed extensively already. This decision involves a fundamental theoretical choice between diametrically opposed views regarding the nature of class in advanced capitalist societies. Occupational class schemes generally give primacy to the manual/non-manual boundary and then further subdivide according to varying skill levels within each category. By contrast, social class schemes emphasize the owner/non-owner division and then further subdivide on the basis of control over labour. Such schemes have the advantage of being compatible with sectoral categories, as indicated above in section 5.

One of the few advantages of occupational class compared with social class derives from its historical popularity among sociologists in Britain. By the selection of the class scheme that dominates empirical social research, comparability is enhanced (Bechhofer 1969). However, this argument is weakened by the greater vulnerability of occupational schemes to changes in the ranking of existing occupations and the inevitable introduction of new occupations. Comparisons across time are rendered highly problematic if the class scheme adopted is predicated on a changing occupational structure. Needless to say, social class schemes are far less susceptible to problems of this kind.

Furthermore, class schemes that are rooted in the occupational structure encourage class analysis to be concentrated on the employed population to the relative exclusion of large sections of the adult population – notably, the underemployed (such as part-time women workers and the intermittently employed, who are also often women), the unemployed and the non-employed (i.e. students and the retired). By the same token, in view of the extensive gender segregation that characterizes the labour market in Britain (see Gallie 1988), the occupational structure of women workers is different from that of men (Osborn and Morris 1979).

Consequently, occupational class categories are more contaminated by gender than social class categories. More specifically, it has been argued that the manual/non-manual divide has little relevance to women's work (Dale *et al.* 1985; Dex 1985; Heath and Britten 1984).

Table 2.2 The three choices in operationalizing class: conceptual and technical elements

Choice	Conceptual element	Technical element
1 Conceptual scheme	*What is the basis of class?* occupational class based on divisions within technical relations of production *versus* social class based on divisions within social relations of production	*Which particular operational scheme?* occupational class, e.g. Registrar General, Butler and Stokes, Goldthorpe *versus* social class, e.g. Erik Olin Wright Mark I, II and III
2 Unit of analysis	*What is the appropriate unit of class analysis?* the household or family *versus* the individual	*Which method of measuring household class?* single indicator, e.g. head of household, or combinations or dominance *versus* multiple indicators
3 Degree of coverage	*Who is included in class analysis?* economically active only *versus* include inactive as well	*Which definitions of economically active and inactive?* economically active: full/part-time boundary *versus* economically inactive: same or different rules for retired, housewives, unemployed, etc.

More generally, in a study of class attitudes and behaviour such as this, the appropriateness of the manual/non-manual occupational distinction is highly questionable, especially in relation to the small but distinctive employer and petty bourgeois social classes (see Chapter 8). Ironically, the Essex team have made a similar point, yet, on theoretical and empirical grounds (see section 2.5 and Table 2.2), they favoured Goldthorpe's class categories, which are primarily occupationally based and hence organized around the manual/non-manual divide (Marshall *et al.* 1988).

Whatever the presumed comparative advantage of occupational class schemes over social class ones, it has been increasingly lessened in the recent past following: (1) the attempts by Wright to operationalize class in terms of the social relations of production (see Wright 1976, 1979, 1985; Wright and Perrone 1977); and (2) the attempts by others to use his operational definitions (see Duke and Edgell 1984; Dunleavy and Husbands 1985; Marshall *et al.* 1988). However, the selection of a social class alternative to occupational class is complicated by the availability of three main versions of Wright's neo-Marxist model.

Wright's initial formulation comprised three basic social class locations – capitalists, petty bourgeois and workers – plus one 'contradictory class location within class relations' – managers (Wright 1985: 44–5). Subsequently Wright Mark II introduced further modifications, notably three levels of managerial control – top executives, managers and supervisors – plus two additional contradictory class locations, but this time between rather than within class relations – small employers and semi-autonomous employees (Wright 1985: 46–9). These elaborations resulted in his famous 'class map of capitalist society' (Wright 1985: 48). Wright introduced several more minor modifications prior to his extensive revisions on the basis of his own empirical research.

Wright Mark III retained the three class locations based on ownership of the means of production – bourgeoisie, small capitalists and petty bourgeoisie – but reclassified all non-owners in terms of their organization assets and skill/credential assets (1985: 87–8). This produced no fewer than nine types of non-owners: expert managers, supervisors and non-managers; semi-credentialled managers, supervisors and workers; and uncredentialled managers, supervisors and proletarians.

Wright's valiant conceptual efforts have been the subject of considerable criticism (see Carter 1985; Giddens 1985; Rose and Marshall 1986; Marshall 1988), not least from his own pen (Wright 1985, 1989b). The GMS pre-dates Wright Mark III and we found the semi-autonomous worker category of Wright Mark II unworkable. Thus our main focus was Wright Mark I combined with sector, which we were able to assess on the basis of the GMS. Briefly, we adopted the term 'controllers of labour' in preference to 'managers' (Dunleavy 1980c; Duke and Edgell 1984). Throughout the project we used Wright Mark I as the basic class scheme for advanced capitalism within which controllers and workers can be subdivided into public and private production sectors.

The second fundamental choice involved in operationalizing the concept class concerns the *unit of analysis*. It is part of the decision to whom to apply the occupational and/or social class categories: the respondent/individual or the family/household? This issue has also been broached earlier, notably in section 4.

The case for a respondent-based indicator is a relatively straight-forward one. It can be argued that respondent attitudes and behaviour should logically be analysed in terms of the direct experience of the respondent. Thus, in the context of the debate about women and class analysis, Stanworth (1984) suggested that the direct employment experience of married women is relevant to an understanding of their class fate and class action. Therefore wives' direct relationship to the class structure should not be denied on *a priori* grounds. This is a matter not just of theoretical inconsistency (Delphy 1981), it is also of considerable empirical concern (Acker 1973).

This is in contrast to the conventional view advocated by Parkin (1971), Giddens (1973) and Goldthorpe (1983, 1984), who claimed that the family/household is *the* unit of class analysis (see sections 4 and 5). The main argument in favour of a group measure is that the family/household acts as the basic unit of economic strategy in terms of both production (i.e. whether or not the spouse works) and consumption. It is in this sense that Goldthorpe asserted that lines of class division run between rather than through families.

Our essentially pragmatic solution is to suggest, following Erikson (1984), that both units are appropriate measures, but in different situations. More specifically, we suggest (a) that research into production-related behaviour and attitudes should include both men and women as individuals; and (b) that studies of consumption behaviour and attitudes should use a family/household measure. In other words, different units of class analysis are appropriate in different research contexts. Thus, we concur with Marshall *et al.* who noted that 'classes comprise neither families nor individuals but individuals in families' (1988: 85).

If the research situation requires a group measure of class, then the next question is how to measure class at the family/household level. Where there is only one adult in the household, the operational procedure is unproblematic, and in fact identical to a respondent-based indicator. However, where there are two or more adults in the household, and if these adults are not in the same class, the problem arises as to which should determine the household class measure. There are basically four possible solutions: male head of household; joint classification; the dominance principle; and multiple indicators.

We reject the male head of household approach on the grounds that it is empirically invalid and sexist (see Acker 1973; Dex 1985; Wright 1989a). In relation to joint classifications, such as the one advanced by Britten and Heath (1983), it has been argued that the 'utility' of this solution is undermined by the high instability that is found in the employment situations of married women (Goldthorpe 1984: 494). Also, it has been noted that, when joint classifications are applied to occupations, they are inherently problematic because 'work positions differ in several dimensions' (Erikson 1984: 503). The dominance principle – allocating household class on the basis of the 'highest' class member – overcomes the male 'head' of household problem (see Haug 1973; Erikson 1984). On the other hand, because it is applied upwards rather than downwards, it has the empirical effect of reducing the size of the working class. Also, the dominance method requires a hierarchical class scheme with a clear order of dominance. Although social class schemes are more 'relational' than 'hierarchical' compared with occupational class schemes, in a capitalist society it is appropriate for self-employment to take precedence. Consequently, we favour extending the use of this method to social class: the 'highest' is classified in descending order from employer, through petty bourgeois and controller, to worker. Lastly, where the technique of analysis permits it (e.g. multiple regression in Chapters 7 and 8), we include the social class location of both respondent and others in the household in the form of multiple indicators. This solution allows the influence of either or both to be displayed in the analysis.

The third choice in the operationalization of class relates to the *degree of coverage*, which in effect revolves around the issue of whether or not to include or exclude the economically 'inactive'. As noted already, this in turn involves the complicated question of the various sociological meanings that can be attached to the notion economic activity/inactivity. Typically, economic activity is divided into full- and part-time work, with a variable boundary line depending upon the purpose of the research. Similarly, economic inactivity can range from the permanently inactive (i.e. retired and disabled) to the temporarily inactive (i.e. unemployed, students and 'housewives'). Interestingly, the practice of excluding unpaid housework (and therefore women for the most part) from the official definition of economic activity dates from as recently as the 1881 Census in Britain (Hakim 1980).

A purely practical justification for opting for only the economically active rests on convenience and comparability: it obviates the necessity to decide what to do with the various inactive categories, and there is a preponderance of previous research based on this option. A general criticism of all studies that exclude the economically inactive, irrespective of whether they utilize a social class scheme (e.g. Wright 1985) or an essentially occupational class scheme (e.g. Marshall *et al.* 1988), is that this option invariably produces a restricted and therefore distorted view of the class structure (see section 4 above).

We support the view that all individuals/households are implicated in the class structure (Erikson 1984). The salience of this point is underlined by the high proportion of adults in contemporary Britain who fall into the economically inactive category by virtue of their status as housewife, student, retired, unemployed and/or part-time worker. Moreover, the potential political significance of such economically inactive groups should not be ruled out in advance.

The economically inactive can be included in class analysis by reference to their previous class location and/or their 'mediated class location', i.e. mediated via other members of one's family/household (Wright 1989a). Subject to the theoretical requirements of the project and the practical problems of gathering class data, we consider the case for classifying the economically inactive by their previous class location to be a strong one. This procedure is readily applicable to those who have had a direct relationship to the means of production in the past. However, for those who have never worked, it could be argued that 'location in the class structure is entirely constituted by mediated relations' (Wright 1989a: 41). Thus, this may be an appropriate way of including certain people in class analysis who would otherwise typically be excluded.

7   *Summary of the Interrelations between the Three Choices*

It is important to recognize the interrelations and implications of the operational choices reviewed. The various procedures have different consequences for the shape and hence character of the class structure. Table 2.3 illustrates some of these with special reference to the size of the working class and the unclassified population. Thus, the size of the working class is larger when using social class (SC) than it is with occupational class (OC), whatever the combination of unit of analysis and degree of coverage. Furthermore, 'respondent economically active' (REA) procedures provide a much narrower definition of what constitutes the class structure than do 'household all' (HALL) measures; for example REA measures result in the exclusion of 45 per cent.

In sum, different ways of operationalizing class produce different pictures of the class structure and much depends upon the sociological questions that are being addressed. Thus, if the focus is on production, REA should be the unit of classification combined with SC and/or OC, whereas HALL combined with SC and/or OC is the appropriate measure when consumption is the research object. Our theoretical and empirical preference for social class rather than occupational class was heavily conditioned by the basic aims of the GMS (see above and Chapters 1 and 8). Therefore, in the rest of the book we include the economically inactive in a household measure of social class (HALL/SC).

Table 2.3   The effect of alternative operationalizations of class on the size of the working class and the proportion of the sample unclassified

Unit of analysis	Degree of coverage	Conceptual scheme	% working class	% unclassified
Respondent	EA only	OC	24	45
Respondent	EA only	SC	39	45
Respondent	All	OC	45	5
Respondent	All	SC	71	5
Household	EA only	OC	24	34
Household	EA only	SC	39	34
Household	All	OC	35	3
Household	All	SC	60	3

$n = 3826$

Source: Adapted from British Election Study, 1987.

8 Sectoral Theory and the New Analytic Class Framework

In addition to our concern to assess the conceptual adequacy and empirical validity of class theory in the context of the economically and politically distinctive 1980s, we wished also to investigate sectoral theory. We considered that the attempt to increase the role of the market and reduce, albeit selectively, the role of the state in the economy, thus reversing the postwar historical trend, provided an opportune moment to research sectoral theory alongside the more familiar class theory. At the outset therefore, it was important to the project to be able to examine class and sectoral accounts of social change, as well as the possible relationship between them.

Sectoral theory refers to social divisions between those who are dependent upon the public sector for their employment (i.e. as producers) and/or for certain services (i.e. as consumers), and those who produce and/or consume in the private sector. In Britain, sectoral analysis has been championed by Dunleavy (1979, 1980a) and Saunders (1981), who have built upon the pioneering contributions of O'Connor (1973) and Castells (1977). Changes in Britain since 1945 in the structure of production and consumption owing to the growth of the state, especially the welfare state, were considered to be of political significance. The Conservative policy since 1979 has been to favour the private sector at the expense of the public sector, and this is thought to have heightened the political importance of sectoral cleavages. In other words, in a period of extensive state retrenchment and restructuring, the interests of public sector producers and consumers have been particularly threatened by the twin policies of public sector cuts and private sector growth. Consequently, it has become increasingly recognized that conflict and change in Britain in the 1980s cannot be fully understood without reference to the formation and politicization of production and consumption sectoral divisions (Edgell and Duke 1983; Duke and Edgell 1984; Dunleavy 1989; Hamnett 1989).

There are two aspects to sectoral location. First, production sectoral location refers to whether the respondent/household works in the public/state sector, the private/market sector, or in the self-employed sector. Second, consumption sectoral location refers to whether the household consumption of services is totally/mostly private or totally/mostly public (state).

Both aspects of sectoral location are linked to our conceptualization of social class outlined above. In the case of the production

40

sector, the self-employed are automatically employers or petty bourgeois; only the controller and worker classes are split into public and private sectors. On the relationship between class and consumption sector we side with Dunleavy and Husbands (1985) rather than Cawson and Saunders (1983) in arguing that consumption sectoral locations are cumulative and partially determined by household class position. Thus employers are more likely to be privatized on all services, whereas workers are more likely to be reliant on state provision for all services.

Much of the debate in sections 6 and 7 regarding the conceptualization of class is appropriate to production sectoral location. The same procedural decisions can be applied: (a) the sectoral locations of both the respondent and others in the household are taken into account; (b) the economically inactive are classified according to their previous sectoral location; and (c) for the household measure, public sector presence in the household is given primacy over private sector presence because of the research context of public spending cuts.

Our approach to consumption sectoral analysis and the question of the social and political effects of the public spending cuts during the 1980s can be located within Dunleavy's theoretical framework. Dunleavy suggested that consumption sectors may be said to exist wherever consumption processes involve competition between public/state and private/market forms of provision (Dunleavy 1979, 1980a). Dunleavy argued that: 'state intervention to provide collectively consumed services ... radically changes the level of politicisation and the nature of consumption cleavages' (1979: 419). The consequent polarization between the two modes of consumption arguably constitutes an important basis for the growth of social and political cleavages, for instance between the users of public and private transport. Different consumption locations lead to conflicting interests with regard to government spending, i.e. more/less state support for public/private provision of services such as transport, housing, and so on. More generally, the cuts in state spending on public provision represent an attack on those individuals/households who are dependent on collective consumption. In this sense the public spending cuts contribute to a potential for social and political polarization (Edgell and Duke 1982).

Consumption sectoral cleavages are therefore groupings of non-class interests, which may cross-cut (or overlap with) social class. In his original article, Dunleavy (1979) argued only for the partial independence of consumption sectors from social class. He demonstrated that class influenced access to housing and transport and

41

that sectoral locations nonetheless tended to cross-cut class lines. According to Dunleavy, the most salient cleavages develop where there is a high degree of fragmentation between state and market provision, as in the case of transport and housing. He also found that consumption locations in different consumption processes may overlap and thereby reinforce the process of fragmentation. Consequently, in contrast to Saunders (1981), it is involvement in wholly state or wholly market modes of consumption over several services that is particularly relevant to the polarization of consumption locations (Duke and Edgell 1984).

In our earlier work we pioneered the use of an index of overall household consumption location based on three services – housing, transport and health (Duke and Edgell 1984). Each of these three services may be dichotomized in terms of private/public consumption: housing into owner-occupiers and council tenants; transport into car owners and non-car owners who must rely on public transport; and health into those covered by private health insurance and those who are not and consequently have to rely exclusively on the NHS. Households are continuously involved in these three consumption processes. Education was not included in our measure because it is generally consumed intermittently by individuals at particular stages in the family life cycle.

Each household was classified according to the degree of private or public consumption of three services. Households may be totally private (all three services consumed privately), mostly private (two out of three services private), mostly public (two out of three services public), or totally public (all three services consumed publicly). The term 'mostly' private/public is used in order to avoid confusion with Dunleavy's distinction at the level of individual services between predominantly private and predominantly public (see below). Overall household consumption location will form the basis of our consumption sectoral analysis in later chapters.

Dunleavy (1979: 71) has argued that the ideological 'structuration' of sectoral consumption cleavages reflects the interests of the dominant social groups and that these ideological structures have been incorporated into the differentiation of the major political parties in contemporary Britain. Thus, debates over public spending cuts and privatization may be seen as crucial to consumption sectoral polarization within social classes. On the basis of occupational class categories, Dunleavy concluded that, because (manual) working-class consumption locations are more fragmented, the ideological and political structuration of these cleavages serves to weaken the link between the Labour Party and the working class. On the other hand, with respect to the overwhelmingly privatized (non-manual) middle class, the consumption effects tend to reinforce class effects and therefore strengthen the links between the middle class and the Conservative Party, which is associated more clearly with dominant class interests (Dunleavy 1979).

In his path-breaking discussion of sectoral consumption cleavages, Dunleavy usefully distinguished between predominantly private and predominantly public consumption processes (1980a). Housing and transport are examples of predominantly private consumption processes that have been favoured by Thatcherism. Since 1979 the private consumption of these services has increased to the extent that approximately two-thirds of all households have access to private transport and a similar proportion of dwellings are owner-occupied (*Social Trends*, 1990). Education and health services are examples of predominantly public consumption processes, the private consumption of which has also increased since 1979 as a result of being actively encouraged by successive Conservative governments.

Figure 2.1 shows the likely differential class impact of the two types of consumption processes. In the case of predominantly private consumption processes, since the majority of the 'middle class' are likely to be private consumers, fragmentation will be relatively more pronounced within the 'working class'. Conversely, in the case of predominantly public consumption processes, since the majority of the 'working class' are likely to be public consumers, fragmentation will be relatively more pronounced within the 'middle class'.

Table 2.4 indicates that consumption location for the four services did vary according to social class. Controllers emerged as

	Type of consumption process	
	Pred. private	Pred. public
'Working class'	Fragmented	Unfragmented
'Middle class'	Unfragmented	Fragmented

Figure 2.1 Differential impact of predominantly private and predominantly public consumption processes on the 'working class' and 'middle class'

Table 2.4 Predominantly private and predominantly public consumption locations by household social class

Consumption location	Employer	Petty bourgeois	Controller	Worker
		Household social class		
Housing: % own	84	78	84	63
Transport: % own car	92	87	85	65
Health: % private	19	16	27	12
Education: % private	17	13	13	5

Source: BES 1987

more privatized than workers on all services, and employers were predictably the most privatized on three of the four services. In the case of health, fully 27 per cent of controllers had private health insurance, in the case of 23 per cent paid for by their employers. The controllers had more perks than the bosses!

For the two predominantly private consumption processes (housing and transport), fragmentation was greatest among the working class. For instance, 28 per cent of workers lived in council housing and 35 per cent did not have a car. On the other hand, class fragmentation for health and education (predominantly public) was relatively more pronounced among controllers than workers. The former had 15 per cent more private health insurance

Table 2.5 Household consumption location by household social class: GMS 1983–4 and BES 1987

Consumption location	Employer	Petty bourgeois	Controller	Worker
		Household social class		
GMS 1983–4:				
% totally private	21	10	11	5
% mostly private	75	71	61	52
% mostly public	0	11	18	24
% totally public	0	3	3	10
BES 1987:				
% totally private	17	15	25	9
% mostly private	62	58	53	43
% mostly public	9	12	11	23
% totally public	1	3	5	16

and 8 per cent more private education. The degree of 'middle-class' fragmentation on education and health can be expected to increase if the current policy of privatization continues.

Larger social class differences are evident when overall house-hold consumption location is examined. Table 2.5 indicates that the working class was most fragmented with respect to overall con-sumption location for both GMS and BES: 39 per cent of BES workers and 34 per cent of GMS workers consumed at least two of the three services in the state mode. By contrast, 78 per cent of BES controllers and 72 per cent of GMS controllers were mostly/totally private.

In conclusion, this chapter has argued in favour of using social class rather than occupational class, and of measuring social class at the level of the household rather than the respondent. The econ-omically inactive are also to be incorporated into class analysis. Furthermore, sectoral analysis, in terms of both production and consumption, has been shown to be of growing importance. A combination of social class and sectoral analysis is therefore the most appropriate framework – theoretically and empirically – for measuring the effects of Thatcherism in the 1980s.

CHAPTER 3

The Social Bases of British Politics: the 1979, 1983 and 1987 General Elections

1 Introduction

In the national competition for votes between 1979 and 1987, the Conservative Party led by Thatcher won three consecutive contests – May 1979, June 1983 and June 1987. As a result of this electoral success, Conservative governments have been able to implement a distinctive set of policies for over a decade and, taken together, they have become known as 'Thatcherism'. In modern British politics at least, it is unique for a leader to lend their name to a political philosophy or programme. How did this virtual 'elected dictatorship' come about? What are the social bases of Thatcherism? How did the Conservatives manage to retain power in Britain for over a decade?

The purpose of this chapter is to review the political success of the Conservative Party in three consecutive general elections. The strategy will be to outline the origins of Thatcherism, present the basic political facts of the 1979, 1983 and 1987 elections, and review critically the political sociological theories that are available to explain them.

2 The Origins of Thatcherism

The 1970s in Britain were a time of economic crisis and political turbulence. Economic crisis took the form of continued economic decline accompanied by growing unemployment and intermittent social disorder. The attempted political solutions to what appeared to be increasingly intractable problems provide a neat and simple division of the 1970s into two periods: (i) Conservative 1970–4; and (ii) Labour 1974–9. What these two ostensibly contrasting political periods have in common is that they both 'failed'. First, their economic policies seemed to exacerbate rather than alleviate, let alone remedy, persistent economic decline. Second, their economic failure resulted in political failure in the sense that the respective Conservative and Labour governments of the period were perceived to be out of control of the economy (indeed, some would say, the country) and consequently were rejected decisively at the polls. In 1974 the Conservative Party won 277 parliamentary seats out of a total 635 (43.6 per cent) and in 1979 the Labour Party won 269 seats (42.4 per cent). Moreover, the 1970–4 Conservative government and the 1974–9 Labour government both failed after their respective attempts to implement broadly national state interventionist policies associated with social democratic consensus politics. That is to say, they operated within what is often referred to as the postwar Keynesian model of a mixed corporatist economy in which the owners of capital (represented institutionally by the Confederation of British Industry, CBI) and the sellers of labour power (represented institutionally by the Trades Union Congress, TUC) cooperate with the government of the day to achieve economic progress. Ironically, the Conservative interventionist policies of the early 1970s were marked by the intervention of the National Union of Mineworkers (NUM), and the Labour interventionist policies of the late 1970s were marked by the intervention of the International Monetary Fund (IMF). The failure of the Conservatives led to the election of Thatcher as leader of the Conservative Party in 1975, whereas the failure of Labour led to the election of Thatcher as leader of the country in 1979.

In response to these 'failures', Thatcher and her political allies, notably Joseph, rejected the whole basis of the postwar social democratic consensus. This involved abandoning central government planning, on the ethical grounds that it infringes individual liberty and on the practical grounds that it is less efficient than the free market. It also involved abandoning the associated corporatist approach to policy-making on similar grounds – namely, that it was undemocratic and therefore unethical to the extent that it bypassed parliament, and that it was ineffective and therefore impractical to the extent that it produced conflict rather than cooperation.

The public sector industrial conflicts that preceded the downfall of the Conservative government in 1974 and of the Labour government in 1979 illustrate the limitations of the twin policies of interventionism and corporatism. More specifically, the successful miners' strike of 1974 is thought to have led directly to the demise not only of the Heath government in 1974 but also of the interventionist and corporatist policies with which it was associated. Similarly, the so-called 'Winter of Discontent' of 1978–9 is held by many to have been the major factor in the defeat of the Callaghan government in 1979, and along with it the bipartite form of corporatism championed by the Labour government between 1974 and 1979 (MacInnes 1987).

Thatcher, in contrast, offered a distinctive political alternative to Keynesian macroeconomic policies that emphasized an enhanced role for the market and a reduced role for the state with a view of reversing Britain's long-term economic decline. Thus, the initial appeal of Thatcherism was based as much on the political opprobrium that attached to the failed policies of her predecessors, both Conservative and Labour, as on the attractiveness of an alternative that promised an end to conflict and stagflation. This culminated in the set of policies discussed in Chapter 1 under the headings: public spending/revenue; employment/unemployment; trade unions; and privatization.

3   Key Electoral Political Facts: 1979, 1983 and 1987

Table 3.1 shows the performance of the main political parties in the parliamentary elections of 3 May 1979, 9 June 1983 and 11 June 1987. It shows that the Conservative Party had a clear majority over all the other political parties at each general election, despite a decline in its percentage share of the total votes cast at each elec-

Table 3.1   Party results in the 1979, 1983 and 1987 elections

Party	1979 % of total votes	1979 % of total seats	1983 % of total votes	1983 % of total seats	1987 % of total votes	1987 % of total seats
Conservative	43.9	53.4	42.4	60.1	42.3	57.8
Labour	37.0	42.4	27.6	32.2	30.8	35.2
Centre parties	13.8	1.7	25.4	3.5	22.6	3.4
Others	5.3	2.5	4.6	3.2	4.3	3.5
Totals	100%	635	100%	650	100%	650

Source: Adapted from Butler and Kavanagh 1988, p. 283

tion. Its overall majorities were 43 in 1979, 144 in 1983 and 102 in 1987. These figures understate the extent of its parliamentary dominance during this period because the Northern Ireland independent Unionist MPs invariably support the Conservatives and the other non-Conservative parties cannot be relied upon to vote with Labour on every issue. In terms of its share of the total number of parliamentary seats, the Conservative Party dominated the House of Commons after each of the three elections: 53.4 per cent in 1979, 61.0 per cent in 1983 and 57.8 per cent in 1987. Yet Thatcher has never received the electoral support of more than a large minority of voters. In 1987 the Conservative government was elected on a smaller percentage of the vote than any of the ruling parties among the 17 liberal democracies in Western Europe (*Guardian*, 10 August 1987). Clearly, in an electoral system not based on proportional representation, the percentage share of the total vote is not a good guide to a party's percentage share of the total number of parliamentary seats. In other words, the first past the post electoral system tends to result in governments that represent only a minority of the electorate.

Table 3.1 also reveals that, between 1979 and 1983, the combined electoral support for the two major political parties declined from over 80 per cent of the vote to exactly 70 per cent of the vote, although it recovered to 73 per cent in the 1987 general election. This noticeable trend reflects the rise and fall of centre parties in Britain during this period. The Social Democratic Party was formed in 1981 by ex-Labour Party members, and fought the next two general elections with the Liberal Party as the Alliance. However, the marked change in the pattern of electoral support for the major political parties between 1979 and 1987 was not reflected in the distribution of parliamentary seats. Despite the sharp decline in their support, the two major parties together consistently won over 600 seats (608 in 1979, 606 in 1983 and 605 in 1987). As recently as 1970, the combined electoral support for the two major parties was almost 90 per cent, which was typical of the postwar trend of support.

The relative stability of the Conservative vote and the party's parliamentary dominance between 1979 and 1987 have led to the comment that, in an era of emergent Conservative hegemony, the Labour Party may be 'destined to permanent minority status' (Harrop 1988: 34). Throughout the 1980s, in the aftermath of three crushing electoral defeats, it was suggested that the changes in the class structure, combined with internal divisions within the Labour Party, represented a weakening of the class basis of politics in general and of manual working-class support for the Labour Party in particular, and a threat to the political credibility of the Labour Party in the longer term (see Sarlvik and Crewe 1983; Butler and Kavanagh 1984, 1988; Robertson 1984).

Reference to the decline of the manual labour force and the corresponding expansion of the non-manual labour force, as well as to the increased importance of 'immediate economic interest – rather than class membership in the old sense' (Sarlvik and Crewe 1983: 88 and 332), is reminiscent of the political sociological debates in Britain under equivalent circumstances a generation ago. In 1959, the reaction to Labour's third successive electoral defeat also raised questions about changes in the class structure, Labour Party disunity and its political future. For example, Labour's defeat in 1959 was initially attributed to divisions within the Labour Party, and, more importantly, it was assumed that 'The ethos of class solidarity is beginning to crumble in the face of the new fluidity of our society, the new opportunities for advancement through individual effort' (Abrams *et al.* 1960: 119). Subsequent empirical research showed conclusively that this theory was simplistic and ultimately wrong; working-class solidarity and its relationship to Labour Party support was not necessarily or automatically undermined by changes in the occupational class structure (Goldthorpe *et al.* 1968a,b, 1969).

The historical parallel between the debates about class and the future of the Labour Party in these two periods of electoral failure has also been noted by Heath *et al.* (1985) in the context of the wider debate about the decline of class voting, a topic to which we now turn.

4   Age of Alignment: Voting in Britain in the 1950s and 1960s

In the postwar period to 1970, parliamentary politics in Britain was dominated by the Conservative and Labour parties, which together consistently won over 90 per cent of votes at elections. The reliable and stable voting support enjoyed by the two major parties during this period was widely thought to be due to two related factors: class and partisan alignment. Consequently, this period in British politics can usefully be called the age of alignment.

Class alignment refers to the tendency in this period for the majority (about two-thirds) of the manual working class to vote for the Labour Party, and the majority (about four-fifths) of the non-manual middle class to vote for the Conservative Party. (Technically, this clear postwar pattern of class voting should be referred to as occupational class alignment since this is how the concept class is usually operationalized in voting studies, as in British sociology in general – see Chapter 2.)

Partisan alignment refers to the tendency for the majority (about four-fifths) of voters to identify with one of the main political parties, Conservative or Labour. In the 1960s over half of all major party identifiers typically expressed a 'very strong' commitment (Sarlvik and Crewe 1983: 334). The source of partisanship is thought to be political socialization in one's family of origin which ensures that political identification is passed on from parents to children (Butler and Stokes 1974).

Taken together, the extent and strength of voter loyalty to the Conservative and Labour parties between 1950 and 1970 in terms of class and party alignment were thought to be responsible for the marked stability in electoral behaviour that sustained the two-party system in Britain during this period. Unsurprisingly, the clear and consistent association between occupational class and political party loyalty on the one hand, and the tendency for the vast majority of voters to express support for one of the major political parties on the other, became a political science orthodoxy that is often referred to as the political identification model of voting behaviour (Dunleavy and Husbands 1985). According to Butler and Stokes (1974), two of the most renowned proponents of this model, class was the key variable that influenced voting behaviour in the 1950s and 1960s. In fact they noted that 'partisanship has followed class lines more strongly in Britain than anywhere else in the English-speaking world' (Butler and Stokes 1974: 67).

5   Decade of Dealignment: Voting in Britain in the 1970s

The key assumption behind the class-based two-party political stability of postwar Britain was that it was 'natural' for the working class (defined as manual occupational groups) to vote for the Labour Party and for the middle class (defined as non-manual occupational groups) to vote for the Conservative Party. Voting along these class lines in Britain has long been regarded as logical in terms of the historical class origins and current class interests of the two major political parties – in other words, the capital and 'middle'-class character of the Conservative Party and the labour and 'working'-class character of the Labour Party.

People who did not vote along these 'normal' class lines were regarded as 'deviant'. However, a disproportionate amount of effort was directed at explaining the failure of manual workers to vote for the Labour Party (e.g. Runciman 1966; Parkin 1967; McKenzie and Silver 1968; Crewe 1973), compared with the problem of explaining why certain non-manual workers did not vote for the Conservative Party (Parkin 1968; Rallings 1975; Jary 1978). Working-class conservatives were thought to be more likely to think of themselves as 'middle-class' and/or deferential than traditional working-class Labour Party supporters. Conversely, middle-class support for the Labour Party was usually explained with reference to the marginality and/or the altruism of middle-class radicals.

According to Butler and Stokes, during the 1960s 'the declining strength of the association between class and party is one of the most important aspects of political change of this decade' (1974: 203). They examined the relationship between partisan alignment and both occupational grade (class) and class self-image (subjective class) for 1963 and 1970. This showed that there was a strong relationship between occupational grade and partisan allegiance in 1963 but a weaker one in 1970. A similar yet even more pronounced trend was observable in their data on class self-image and partisan allegiance. In Table 3.2, occupational grades I–IV include the non-manual middle classes and occupational grades V–VI include the manual working classes. The decline in working-class support for the Labour Party and the corresponding increase in

Table 3.2 Partisan allegiance by occupational grade and class self-image, 1963 and 1970

Party	1963				1970			
	Occupational grade		Class Self-image		Occupational grade		Class Self-image	
	I–IV	V–VI	M/C	W/C	I–IV	V–VI	M/C	W/C
	%	%	%	%	%	%	%	%
Conservative	75	28	79	28	70	36	68	37
Labour	25	72	21	72	30	64	32	63
	100	100	100	100	100	100	100	100

Source: Adapted from Butler and Stokes 1974, p. 203

working-class support for the Conservative Party between 1963 and 1970 is readily apparent from this table, as is the marked decline in middle-class support for the Conservative Party. Butler and Stokes concluded on the basis of this and other evidence that the 'weakening of the dominant class alignments' (1974: 206), especially during the late 1960s, was related to the historic fall in voting turnout between 1950 and 1970 (from 84 per cent to 72 per cent), and to the increasing volatility of party support.

The theory that by the 1970s British electors had become less inclined to vote according to the logic of their class found support in a number of separate studies, often on the basis of different measures of class dealignment. Analysis of the class pattern of voting between 1959 and 1979 by Sarlvik and Crewe (1983) showed that class voting over this period had declined, albeit slowly and unevenly. All three of their measures of class voting pointed in the same direction:

> The class index of Labour voting stood at forty in 1959, fell to thirty-three at the next Conservative win in 1970, and again by a similar amount to twenty-seven in 1979. The Somer's d correlation followed an exactly parallel path. The proportion of manual Labour + non-manual Conservative votes dropped from 65 per cent in 1959 to 55 per cent in 1974 and 1979. (Sarlvik and Crewe 1983: 86)

In order to facilitate comparisons with other studies of British voting behaviour, Sarlvik and Crewe adopted Butler and Stokes' 'social grades of occupation' (1983: 75). In other words, they operationalized class in the familiar manual/non-manual occupational dichotomy to represent the working and middle classes respectively. They also classified everyone by their own current or former occupation, except married women, who were classified according to their husband's occupation, 'even if in paid employment' (Sarlvik and Crewe 1983: 75).

Three further book-length studies of voting behaviour confirmed, in their different ways, the increasingly popular class dealignment thesis: McAllister and Rose (1984); Himmelweit *et al.* (1985) and Franklin (1985).

In their study of the 1983 general election, McAllister and Rose noted that: 'Since the 1960s the importance of class differences in party politics has tended to decline' (1984: 15). By class they really meant occupational class. They portrayed the Conservative Party as a success in terms of its ability to 'draw about half their vote from working-class electors' (1984: 14). In contrast, they suggested that the Labour Party was 'becoming a failed ghetto party' as a result of its inability to win the support of the majority of manual workers (1984: 15–16). They concluded: 'In the past quarter-century the influence of class-related differences upon party preferences has declined by more than a half' (1984: 15).

Himmelweit *et al.* prefaced their conclusions regarding the class dealignment trend in Britain in the recent past with the important point that 'class-based voting has never been very strong in post-war Britain. If it had, given that the electorate contains more working than middle class voters, Labour would have been continuously in office' (1985: 88). More specifically, they noted that in 1959 approximately 65 per cent of the electorate voted according to the logic of their occupational class, yet 'by 1983 only half did so' (1985: 88). They also noted that this decline in class voting was more marked among the working than the middle class. For example, in 1979 the vote for the Conservative Party increased by 15 per cent among the skilled and 12 per cent among the semi-skilled and unskilled working-class.

In the most complex statistical analysis of the debate thus far, Franklin (1985) weighed in with strong support for the class dealignment thesis. On the basis of his causal models of electoral behaviour, Franklin claimed to have been able to 'pin-point both the nature and occasion of the mainspring in the decline of class voting in Britain' (1985: 104) and concluded:

(1) About half of the decline in support for the Labour Party that occurred between 1966 and 1979 can be attributed to changes in the social structure which had the effect of reducing the size of class groups that had provided the bulk of Labour votes in 1974.

(2) The rest of the decline that took place up to 1979 ... is attributable to the reduced appeal of Labour to the groups that had traditionally supported it. A similar decline in Conservative support among traditionally Tory social groups made this a quite general phenomenon of declining class voting. (Franklin 1985: 176)

These contributions to the debate about class dealignment that is thought to have occurred in Britain during the late 1960s and 1970s are representative of the burgeoning theoretical consensus concerning the historical relationship between occupational class and voting behaviour. Furthermore, these studies encompass the main explanations of class dealignment – notably, changes in the occupational class structure and party political changes. It is suggested that British society is becoming more middle class in the sense that the proportion of manual workers is decreasing while the proportion of non-manual workers is increasing. This has had the effect of reducing support for the Labour Party as instrumentalism replaces traditional solidarism. Meanwhile, it is also suggested that the appeal of the Labour Party among working-class electors and the appeal of the Conservative Party among middle-class electors have both declined as each party has sought to broaden its class appeal.

An alternative explanation of class dealignment was advanced by Dunleavy and Husbands (1985), who argued that production and consumption sectoral cleavages have replaced occupational class cleavages as the main determinants of voting behaviour in Britain. In other words, social location is still the key factor influencing party choice, but (a) private sector workers and consumers have replaced non-manual workers as the 'natural' Conservative Party supporters; and (b) public sector workers and consumers have replaced manual workers as the 'natural' Labour Party supporters. According to this theory, the decline in working-class support for the Labour Party is explained by such factors as the increase in private sector housing among manual workers. At the same time, the decline in middle-class support for the Conservative party is explained by such factors as the increase in public sector employment among non-manual workers.

The emergent consensus regarding the decline in class voting in Britain, notwithstanding the existence of different explanations for this recent historical trend, was shattered by the claim that 'Contemporary accounts of the decline of class are no more plausible than those of the 1950s' (Heath *et al.* 1985: 29). It is at this point that the debate about class dealignment becomes somewhat complex and acrimonious. The Heath *et al.* rejection of dealignment theory involved a redefinition of class, a new measure of class voting, and the production of data on the basis of these methodological changes that show that class differences in party support 'have remained at much the same level throughout the post-war period' (1985: 39). They concluded that Britain remains a class-divided society, that Labour's social base is shrinking, that it had become a less successful party between 1964 and 1983, and that the 'trendless fluctuation' in voting behaviour has 'as much to do with political as with social sources of change' (1985: 39).

Reaction to this attempted refutation of class dealignment theory was swift and strong, and a lively debate ensued. First Crewe (1986), a leading class dealignment theorist, responded at length and in great detail to Heath *et al.*'s challenge to the political orthodoxy. Briefly, Crewe defended the traditional way of measuring dealignment, namely in terms of absolute class voting ('the working class Labour plus middle class Conservative vote as a proportion of the total vote'), against what he argued were misplaced criticisms by Heath *et al.*, and attacked their alternative measure, namely relative class voting ('the relative probability of the two classes voting against rather than for their respective "natural" parties' – 1986: 622). Crewe concluded: 'in elections, unlike election books, it is absolute numbers, not relative probabilities, that count' (1986: 638).

Heath *et al.* (1987) replied to Crewe's critique in an even longer but equally detailed article in which they restated the case for their alternative measure of class voting. Like Crewe, they claimed that the criticisms were misplaced. Heath *et al.* concluded: 'There is not, and never has been, any disagreement about the fact of declining absolute class voting' (1987: 276). Consequently, the debate 'centres around the alleged decline in relative class voting, since the measurement of relative class voting better enables us to disentangle a long-term loosening of the classes from the transitory political fortunes of the parties' (1987: 276–7).

The crux of this dispute concerns the respective measures adopted by the main protagonists. Crewe is part of what had become the conventional wisdom in electoral studies and thus favours the manual/non-manual occupational class scheme and an absolute class voting measure. Conversely, Heath *et al.* favour new measures of both class and class voting – the former involving a distinction between the proletariat and the salariat, and the latter involving the calculation of relative class voting. These two approaches produce quite different patterns of class voting over time in Britain. Crewe's measures show con¬lusively that the relationship between class and voting has weake: d: between 1945 and 1983 'the overall level of class voting ... fel rom 62 per cent to 47 per cent' (1986: 620). Heath *et al.*'s meas :es, on the other hand, show equally conclusively that between tl same dates there was no clear pattern of class voting, only 'trei less fluctuations' (1987: 259). The key question is, which of tl two approaches is the most appropriate way of testing the theory of class dealignment?

In an attempt to answer this question it is first of all necessary to consider the two models of class that are being used. The inadequacies of the occupational class scheme adopted by Crewe are well known and extensive (see Chapter 2), but this scheme is widely used and therefore facilitates comparability. The Heath *et al.* alternative class scheme produces a big reduction in the size of the working class between 1964 and 1983, from 47 per cent to 34 per cent of the electorate, and a corresponding increase in the size of the salariat, from 18 per cent to 27 per cent (1985: 36). We are sympathetic to the arguments advanced by Heath *et al.* for rejecting occupational class in favour of their scheme, which emphasizes economic interests rather than income levels, but we are not convinced about the superiority of the new class model. This is because to operationalize class in terms of economic interests and then exclude the capitalist class (apart from the petty bourgeoisie) undermines their own case for rejecting occupational class. Moreover, Heath *et al.* operate a restrictive definition of the 'working class' that excludes routine white-collar workers and blue-collar foremen and technicians. Lastly, it has also been noted that coding errors cannot be ruled out in a major recoding exercise of the kind Heath *et al.* had to undertake (Denver 1986; Dunleavy 1987).

The other part of this dispute concerns the adequacy of the two competing measures of class voting. Absolute class voting, namely 'the proportion of the electorate voting for its natural class party' (Heath *et al.* 1987: 259), has the virtue of being simple to calculate and has long been regarded by most researchers as an appropriate measure of class dealignment. Relative class voting refers to 'the relative strength of the parties in different social classes' (Heath *et al.* 1987: 259), and as such is a more complex measure. However, it has been criticized for being very sensitive to small changes in class voting (Dunleavy 1987). Although Heath *et al.*'s methods and conclusions are not without support (Marshall *et al.* 1988), their approach to class voting has yet to be accepted as the most appropriate way of assessing class dealignment.

If class and class voting are considered together, Heath *et al.*'s exclusion of routine non-manual workers plus foremen and technicians from their analysis of class dealignment is regrettable. Arguably, these are strategic classes in a test of the class dealignment thesis, since their very marginality would lead one to expect that they are the classes most likely to change their vote.

In sum, regarding the two frameworks within which the debate about class dealignment has been conducted, absolute class voting measures tend to support the theory of class dealignment whereas relative class voting measures do not. Moreover, there are competing explanations of class and electoral trends in post-1950s Britain, and these will be considered in section 7 below. Lastly, as far as partisan dealignment is concerned, this is widely thought to have occurred throughout the 1970s (Crewe *et al.* 1977; Crewe 1984).

6 Era of Realignment? Voting in Britain in the 1980s

So far we have considered voting behaviour in postwar Britain in terms of class and partisanship. We have noted that in the 1950s and 1960s it was thought that voting patterns could be explained largely by reference to an elector's occupational class and party identification. In the 1970s there was considerable evidence of both class and partisan dealignment. In other words, voting behaviour became less class based and less a matter of party loyalty, although it should be remembered that there is more consensus regarding partisan dealignment than class dealignment. Following the decline of class voting and partisanship, some commentators have discussed the 1980s in terms of the rise of issue voting.

According to Butler and Stokes (1974), there are four stages in issue voting:

1 knowledge of an issue;
2 attitude about an issue;
3 perception of party differences on an issue;
4 issue voting.

This model of issue voting implies that, for an issue to affect an elector's voting behaviour, the elector needs to be well informed about political issues, to develop a distinct attitude towards an issue and to be cognizant of party differences regarding various issues. It also implies that the major political parties have contrasting policies on the key issues in a general election.

Issue voting theory is 'based on the idea of the "rationality" of the voter' who 'wishes to maximize his or her expected utilities, that is, the advantages that might accrue from the opportunity of having competing choices' (Himmelweit *et al.* 1985: 114). This consumer model of voting behaviour emphasizes a voter's choice of party at an election, not their social background (i.e. class) or past voting history (i.e. partisanship). Strictly speaking, therefore,

'This is a consumer model not of voting but of parties: voting for a party "purchases" the party' (Himmelweit *et al.* 1985: 117).

Franklin has measured the rise of issue voting between 1964 and 1983 at the level of the individual and the electorate as a whole and concluded that issue voting 'increased in step with the decline of class voting' (1985: 152). It is argued that voters have become more 'rational' and 'the British electorate has moved to a more sophisticated basis for voting choice', to the extent that issue-based party preferences now structure partisanship (Franklin 1985: 152).

In support of this thesis, Crewe has claimed that, in 1979, 'It was issues, not organization or personalities, that won the election for the Conservatives' (1981: 282). Moreover, Crewe has argued that it is not 'sufficient for an issue to be important and for that party to be preferred on it. The issue must also be regarded as soluble and the party's proposals as credible', and this was the key to electoral victory in 1979 (1981: 284–5).

Crewe advanced a similar argument to explain the result of the 1983 election, when unemployment was regarded by voters as the most salient issue (1985). According to Crewe, Labour was the preferred party to solve this problem but its credibility on this issue was weak. This was also the post-Falklands' war election and, although the 'government's popularity soared' at the time (Butler and Kavanagh 1984: 72), it is not thought to have been a factor that influenced the outcome of the election one year later (Dunleavy and Husbands 1985).

Issue voting theory has been applied somewhat less successfully to the 1987 election. In order to explain the fact that Labour lost, despite its clear lead over the Conservative Party on three of the four most salient issues (unemployment again, the National Health Service and education), Crewe (1987) suggested that in this election voters were particularly concerned with maintaining their personal prosperity. Although this is still an issue argument, it is a 'valence' issue rather than a 'position' issue. That is to say, it is not an issue 'on which the parties may appeal to rival bodies of opinion', but an issue 'on which there is essentially one body of opinion on values or goals' (Butler and Stokes 1974: 292).

More generally, there are innumerable and complex problems associated with issue voting theory. For example, Himmelweit *et al.* (1985) listed no fewer than 21 issues that voters may take into account, and this was before they began to grapple with the problems of salience and party credibility. Following from this point, a more fundamental criticism of issue voting theory is that it treats voters as atomized individuals who behave electorally in a highly rational way on the basis of considerable knowledge of political issues and political parties. It may well be that some voters are very knowledgeable politically and make up their minds about whom to vote for during the course of an election campaign, and that the proportion of such voters has increased in Britain recently. However, this model of voting behaviour is asking a lot of an elector. It also ignores the fact that voters are social beings who are located in a class structure with all that implies in terms of economic interests, and that voters have a history in terms of their own, or their family of origin's party preferences.

Thus, although issue voting was proposed by many researchers to fill the theoretical 'vacuum left by a decline in the class-structuring of voting choice' (Franklin 1985: 150), it has been the object of sustained and, in our view, quite damaging criticism. Others, notably Dunleavy and Husbands (1985), are not only highly critical of issue voting, but have discussed voting patterns in Britain in the 1980s in terms of a realignment by class and sector.

On the basis of a detailed study of the 1983 general election, Dunleavy and Husbands questioned the key assumptions behind the rational issue voter. They presented data to show that political attitudes towards electoral issues are neither stable over time nor logically consistent. Consequently, they 'reject the emphasis placed by issue-oriented approaches upon issue attitudes as determinants of voting decision' (Dunleavy and Husbands 1985: 181).

As a 'radical' alternative to the presumed increase of issue voting in Britain in the 1980s, they suggested that a voter's social situation continues to structure their electoral behaviour. They concentrated on five factors that they claimed are the main influences on voting behaviour in contemporary Britain: (a) social class; (b) gender and household situation; (c) production location, including trade union membership; (d) consumption location; and (e) state dependency. The Dunleavy and Husbands' model of voting is 'radical' in several senses. First, the conventional occupational class scheme was replaced by a social class scheme that is considered to be less arbitrary and correspondingly more theoretically informed, namely, the neo-Marxist theory of economic interests. Second, the convention of using a husband's class to categorize his wife's class was replaced by a non-sexist classification of all married women on the basis of their current or last job. Third, they analysed production and consumption sectoral locations, and the extent to which a person is dependent upon the state to supplement their pension or other income.

Dunleavy and Husbands found that analysing voting behaviour in relation to social as opposed to occupational class revealed a clear relationship between class and party in the expected direction for Labour and Conservative, but not for the Alliance Party (1985: 124). They also found evidence that gender, production sector and consumption sector all affected voting in distinctive ways in the 1983 election. For example, unsurprisingly, owner-occupiers were more inclined to vote Conservative and, conversely, council tenants were more likely to vote Labour. Degree of state dependence proved difficult to operationalize and Dunleavy and Husbands' findings concerning this variable were less conclusive. Overall, however, their alternative approach to voting behaviour was generally vindicated by their data. In the 1983 election, there was considerable evidence for realignment in terms of class and sector in relation to the major political parties, Conservative and Labour. Support for the Alliance Party, on the other hand, was mixed in terms of class, sector and gender. This suggests that the extent of class dealignment during the 1970s may have been overstated; class alignment was never total and certainly did not disappear altogether. As far as the 1980s are concerned, class dealignment theory would seem to apply best to the rise of centre party voting, but this trend has since declined, and with it the validity of class dealignment explanations in this respect.

7   *Class and Politics in Britain: Social or Political Forces?*

Thus far we have concentrated on the alleged trends, or lack of them, in the patterning of party support along class lines in postwar Britain. In the process we have highlighted the importance of the different ways of measuring the key variables, class and class voting. At the same time, we have made only passing reference to the various theories that have been advanced to explain the changing relationship between class and politics during the recent past in Britain. Hence, it is now necessary to focus on the forces that are thought to have shaped class politics, and ultimately the political success and failure of the major parties at general elections in Britain.

Proponents of the class dealignment thesis tend to be united on two points: first, that social forces have affected classes in ways which have reduced their influence on party support; and, second, that issue politics has replaced class politics in contemporary

Britain. Conversely, critics of class dealignment tend to emphasize political forces in addition to social forces, but otherwise occupy a less unified theoretical position. Somewhat paradoxically, political scientists have been at the forefront of social explanations of changes in electoral behaviour, whereas sociologists have on the whole favoured political explanations.

More specifically, explanations of the decline in the class basis of British politics emphasize the 'loosening' of the class structure in general, including the numerical decline and fragmentation of the working class in particular. One of the fullest social explanations of class dealignment was advanced by Butler and Kavanagh (1984: 8):

> As social structure became 'looser', so Britain became less two-party and two class. Between 1964 and 1979 manual workers declined from 65% to 56% as a proportion of the work force: by 1983 the figure had fallen to 50%. Class consciousness was also low: the Essex election study of 1979 indicated that less than half of British voters gave themselves a class identity and only 39% of manual workers called themselves 'manual workers'. The working class became more fragmented, socially and politically. The spread of home ownership, including council house sales, meant that by 1983 60% of households were privately owned. The working class was evenly divided between those who owned their own homes and those who were council tenants. The spread of other symbols of affluence besides housing – for example, cars and telephones – also weakened working-class attachment to the Labour party. Research in 1979 showed that wage-earners who possessed any of these were more likely to vote Conservative than Labour. The leakage of working class support from the Labour party was marked in 1979 ... But there were also some middle-class defections from the Conservatives; little more than half of British voters actually voted for the party of their 'natural' class in 1979.

The argument that the working class has shrunk and that, among those who are left, there is an increased willingness to vote Conservative, owing to a change in their economic situation and class consciousness, was echoed by Crewe (1986). Commenting on Heath *et al.*'s analysis of the decline in popularity of nationalization and the corresponding increase in popularity of privatization between 1964 and 1983 among the whole electorate, including the working class, Crewe claimed that this indicates 'a precipitous decline in the ideological consciousness and solidarity of the working class' (1986: 633).

Proponents of class dealignment have suggested two further social, as opposed to political, explanations of this change in the basis of party support in Britain. First, the majority response has been to champion instrumental issue voting (see Butler and Stokes 1974; Crewe 1981; Himmelweit *et al.* 1985; Franklin 1985). This explanation focuses on the voter as a rational consumer who supports a party on the basis of its policies on particular issues. In many ways, the so-called rise of issue voting is the logical development of the decline of traditional working-class solidarity that is thought to have been behind class dealignment.

Second, the minority response has been to develop the social explanation of class dealignment by suggesting that production and consumption sectoral divisions have increased in political importance in modern Britain (Dunleavy 1980a; Duke and Edgell 1984; Dunleavy and Husbands 1985). The sectoral explanation is predicated on the growth of sectoral divisions and on the analysis of voters in terms of their sectoral location and of parties in terms of their sectoral policies. Thus, it is argued that public sector producers and consumers tend to support Labour, whereas private sector producers and consumers tend to support the Conservative Party. A sectoral explanation of recent British politics has been advanced as an alternative to class explanations (Duke and Edgell 1984; Dunleavy 1989).

According to the opponents of class dealignment theory, recent electoral patterns in Britain can be explained partly by reference to changes in the occupational class structure, and partly by reference to the political credibility of the main parties (for example, Heath *et al.* 1985; Marshall *et al.* 1988). The clearest statement in favour of a mixture of social and political factors to explain trendless electoral behaviour in Britain between 1964 and 1983 has been made by the primary critics of class dealignment:

> On the sociological side we show that there have been major long-term changes in the shape of the class structure, the working class, for example, shrinking from 47 per cent to 34 per cent of the electorate. This contraction of the working class could explain nearly half of Labour's electoral decline over the period as a whole, but not the precipitate decline between 1979 and 1983 ... We suggest that political factors are largely responsible for the other half. These factors include the economic failures of the 1966 Labour government and of the 1970 Con-

servative government ... Since then, there has been a perceived movement of the Labour and Conservative parties away from the centre, leaving vacant territory for the Alliance parties. (Heath *et al.* 1987: 257)

Heath *et al.* rejected class dealignment on the grounds that class continues to shape political attitudes and behaviour in an age when party support seems to be increasingly sensitive to the policies and credibility of political parties.

The evidence and arguments for and against class dealignment, with the notable exception of sectoral theorists, converge on one key point – the decline in the size of the working class by around 25 per cent, despite their different measures of class. The Butler and Kavanagh definition of the working class refers to manual workers as a proportion of the work force. The Heath *et al.* definition of the working class also refers to manual workers, but in this case as a proportion of the electorate sampled in their study. As noted above, their definition also excludes the 'marginal' working class, namely foremen and technicians. Their measure is therefore a stricter operational definition of the working class, hence its smaller size over the period in question (see Chapter 2). Both measures uncritically exclude the problematic routine white-collar labour force, and also appear to exclude the unemployed. This is to be regretted since over this period unemployment increased markedly from under 0.5 million to nearly 3 million, despite many restrictive changes in the official definition of the unemployed (see Chapter 1). Since virtually all adults in Britain are entitled to vote, and typically 75 per cent do so at general elections, theories of voting behaviour are arguably best tested using samples of the whole population rather than a proportion of it.

8 *The Social Bases of Thatcherism: 1979, 1983 and 1987*

As we saw in Chapter 2, different operationalizations of class have contrasting effects on the character of the class structure (see especially section 7). In order to overcome the problems associated with either an occupational class scheme or ones that conflate occupation and employment, and thereby examine more effectively the class and electoral behaviour debate, we favour a social class scheme that is compatible with sectoral analysis, both of which can be operationalized according to the principles outlined above.

The pattern of party support (as measured by vote) in the 1979, 1983 and 1987 general elections in terms of social class, production sector and consumption sector is shown in Table 3.3. It is important to note that the postwar electoral domination of the major parties was reduced during the 1980s following the breakaway of dissenting Labour Party supporters who formed the Social Democratic Party (SDP) in 1981. The SDP and the Liberal Party fought the 1983 and 1987 elections together as the Alliance and increased the third party share of the vote to over 25 per cent in 1983 and nearly 23 per cent in 1987, largely at the expense of the Labour Party (Butler and Kavanagh 1988). In view of the electoral impact of the Alliance during this period, we have included a non-Conservative, or anti-Thatcher, vote column in the table.

Tables 3.3 and 3.4 indicate distinct and consistent patterns of political party support. First, the overall social class pattern is clear and in the expected direction of declining support for the Con-

Table 3.3   Vote in the 1979 and 1983 general elections by social class, household production sector and household consumption sector

Sub-group	% vote 1979				% vote 1983			
	Con.	Lab.	Lib.	Non-con.	Con.	Lab.	All.	Non-con.
Social class:								
Employer	67	16	0	16	64	14	7	21
Petty bourgeois	62	26	3	29	53	21	16	37
Controller	48	36	7	43	37	29	22	51
Worker	34	46	5	51	27	39	21	60
Household production sector:								
Controller private	45	35	8	43	37	28	19	47
Controller public	51	37	6	43	37	29	25	54
Worker private	32	47	5	52	26	41	20	61
Worker public	36	45	5	50	28	36	24	60
Household consumption sector:								
Totally private	61	19	11	30	53	22	14	36
Mostly private	45	39	ʹ6	45	36	28	23	51
Mostly public	37	43	5	48	27	41	18	59
Totally public	23	50	25	75	17	54	15	69

Sources: 1979 and 1983 data based on GMS1 and GMS2.

Table 3.4 Vote in the 1987 general election by social class, household production sector and household consumption sector

| | % vote 1987 | | | |
Sub-group	Con.	Lab.	All.	Non-con.
Social class:				
Employer	60	12	15	27
Petty bourgeois	42	19	20	39
Controller	49	18	21	39
Worker	31	33	21	54
Household production sector:				
Controller private	52	15	20	35
Controller public	45	21	21	42
Worker private	32	32	19	51
Worker public	30	33	24	57
Household consumption sector:				
Totally private	59	10	18	28
Mostly private	42	21	23	44
Mostly public	27	40	18	58
Totally public	16	50	14	64

Source: Based on BES 1987.

servative Party and increasing non-Conservativism as one descends the social class structure. Thus, the majority of employers (consistently over 60 per cent) voted for the Conservative Party in the three elections and a majority of workers voted for non-Conservative opposition parties (consistently over 50 per cent). Furthermore, in each of the elections only a minority of workers voted for the Conservative Party, typically one-third or less. There are two minor exceptions to this trend, both in the 1987 election when support for the Conservative Party declined markedly to 42 per cent among the petty bourgeoisie and recovered to nearly 50 per cent among controllers.

Second, when the two employee classes (controllers and workers) are subdivided by production sector, the production sector effect on voting became more marked between 1979 and 1987. The difference between public sector controllers compared with private sector controllers in non-Conservative voting was zero in 1979 but widened to 7 per cent in the next two elections.

Non-Conservative voting among workers in general increased between 1979 and 1983, and was evenly divided between public and private sector workers. By the time of the 1987 election, however, the public sector vote was 6 per cent greater than the private sector vote. This suggests that Parkin's 'middle class radicals' reside mostly in the public sector and have been 'radicalized' rather than 'deradicalized' by Thatcherism (see Parkin 1968 and Chapter 8). Once again, the historical context of the data, notably the attack on public spending in general and public sector employment in particular, is crucial here.

Third, the pattern of voting in relation to consumption sectoral location is the most distinct and consistent of all. In each of the elections, the Conservative and non-Conservative vote varied systematically with consumption sectoral location: the greater the public consumption of services, the lower the level of the Conservative Party vote, and vice versa.

The tables also show that the social bases of Thatcherism are relatively narrow, in that majority support was present in very few sub-groups. Thus, in 1979 the only Conservative majorities were found to be among the employer (67 per cent) and petty bourgeois (62 per cent) classes, public sector controllers (51 per cent) and totally private consumption sector households (61 per cent). In 1983, the two capitalist classes again supported the Conservatives (64 per cent and 53 per cent respectively), along with a majority of totally private consumption sector households (53 per cent). In the 1987 national sample, employers (60 per cent), private sector controllers (52 per cent) and totally private consumption sector households (59 per cent) were the only groups to contain a majority of support for the Conservatives.

The social bases of the anti-Thatcher or non-Conservative vote, on the other hand, are spread over more sub-groups. In 1979, workers (51 per cent), private (52 per cent) and public (50 per cent) sector, plus totally public consumption households (75 per cent) displayed non-Conservative majorities. In 1983, workers (60 per cent), private (61 per cent) and public (60 per cent) sector, and totally public consumption sector households (69 per cent) again contained non-Conservative majorities and were joined by public sector controllers (54 per cent), plus mostly public (59 per cent) and mostly private consumption sector households (51 per cent). Lastly, in 1987, workers (54 per cent), private (51 per cent) and public (57 per cent) sector, plus mostly public (58 per cent) and totally public consumption sector households (64 per cent) all contained non-Conservative majorities.

In sum, between 1979 and 1987,. the highest and most consistent level of support for the Conservative Party was among employers and totally private consumption sector households, and the highest and most consistent non-Thatcher voters were workers and totally public consumption households. Thus, British politics remains markedly (social) class based, but it has also become increasingly sectoral in terms of both production and consumption sectoral locations. We would anticipate that if the policy to privatize the production and consumption of goods and services is maintained the sectoral dimension of politics in Britain in the 1990s is likely to be of increasing significance.

9   Conclusions

The debate about class alignment and dealignment in Britain is conventionally discussed in terms of occupational class, with approximately three-fifths of the non-manual middle class voting Conservative and two-thirds of the manual working class voting Labour (see sections 4 and 5). It is more instructive to examine this psephological debate in relation to the data presented in Tables 3.3 and 3.4. This is because the comparative distinctiveness of the voting pattern of the employer and petty bourgeois classes is concealed by occupational class but revealed very clearly by social class. Overall, the data support class alignment theory in the sense that Conservative voting increased systematically with each step up the social class structure, in contrast to non-Conservative voting, which increased with each step down the social class structure.

Moreover, the combination of social class and production sectoral analysis also reveals politically important voting trends that are hidden by a conventional occupational class approach to class alignment theory. In a period of declining 'working-class' support for the Labour Party, plus the emergence of a third party (Alliance), non-Conservative voting actually increased among certain sectors of the 'working class', namely public sector employees.

Thus, our support for class alignment theory is qualified by reference to social class rather than occupational class voting trends between 1979 and 1987, plus consideration of the production sectoral location of controllers and workers. Furthermore, examination of the consumption sectoral evidence presented in Tables 3.3 and 3.4 suggests that class alignment theory needs to be qualified in one other way. The greatest non-Conservative vote occurred among households that were totally dependent upon the public provision of services. These variations in consumption and production sector effects between 1979 and 1987 are due to the differential impact of the public spending cuts on consumers and producers, and are discussed in detail in Chapter 6.

The expanding privatization programme (see Chapter 7) is of enormous political significance in terms of both production and consumption sector effects. This is because the policy of increasing the role of the market at the expense of the role of the state in effect changes the economic interests and therefore the political orientations of producers and consumers in ways that favour the Conservative Party. Thus, the growth of private sector employment and private sector consumption tends to increase the Conservative vote. It is these sectoral changes in the structure of British society, and not class dealignment, that helped the Conservative Party led by Thatcher to win three successive general elections between 1979 and 1987.

In addition to our own research, the recent work of Saunders (1990) in three English towns demonstrates that the division between home-owners and council tenants is the most significant consumption factor associated with voting behaviour. Furthermore, his index of overall consumption location has an important impact on vote, especially within the (manual) working class.

Interestingly, our conclusions regarding the social bases of contemporary British politics have been confirmed by the Essex study on class but not on sector (Marshall *et al.* 1988). In other words, we agree that class dealignment is a myth, but our data also suggest that sectoral factors are an important influence on the variation in voting behaviour from one election to another, depending on particular historical circumstances.

Lastly, we have shown that the social bases of Thatcherism are relatively narrow compared with the non-Conservative vote. This suggests that the electoral success of Thatcherism between 1979 and 1987 had more to do with a divided opposition in a system without proportional representation than with the popularity of Conservative policies. In the next chapter, the nature and extent of Thatcher's mandate for change will be considered in more detail with reference to the support for specific Conservative policies among both Conservative and non-Conservative voters.

CHAPTER 4

A Mandate for Thatcherism? Attitudes and Values in the 1980s

1 Introduction

Politicians are disposed to interpret electoral success as a mandate to carry out all the policies in their manifestos. The three Thatcher governments have been no exception to this tendency, despite the fact that each victory was based on a minority of the national vote. This chapter will examine the survey evidence on the extent of the mandate for Thatcherism.

Thatcherism has been viewed by some theorists (most notably Stuart Hall) as a deliberate attempt radically to alter the terms of political debate and restructure political values in Britain (Hall 1980, 1983, 1985). In Hall's own terms, Thatcherism is a hegemonic project, whose aim is to destroy the previous postwar social democratic consensus and replace it with a pro-market, anti-collectivist set of values.

To examine the full range of attitudes and values in the 1980s is beyond the brief of this chapter. A comprehensive monitoring service of attitudes and values is provided by the *British Social Attitudes* series (Jowell and Airey 1984; Jowell and Witherspoon 1985; Jowell *et al.* 1986, 1987, 1988). We will concentrate on the core topics covered by the Greater Manchester Study (GMS), namely, attitudes to public spending (particularly on the welfare state) and related issues such as unemployment, local government autonomy and trade unions. Attitudes to privatization are considered separately in Chapter 7 and the overall notion of attitudinal radicalization is dealt with in Chapter 8.

GMS data will be supplemented and updated with reference to the *British Social Attitudes* (BSA) series and the 1987 British Election Study (BES). Prior to examining specific policy issues, the next two sections will briefly review the literature on the level of support for

Thatcherism among Conservatives and the influences on attitudes to public spending and welfare state issues.

2   *The Level of Support for Thatcherism among Conservatives*

An important article on ideological change in the Conservative Party by Crewe and Searing (1988) argued that the brand of radical Conservatism associated with Thatcherism sits uneasily with traditional one-nation Conservatism. The question arises as to the extent of Thatcherism among Conservative politicians and Conservative voters.

Crewe and Searing defined Thatcherism in terms of three principal political ideals: (a) discipline – emphasizing law and order; (b) free enterprise, i.e. rolling back the state; and (c) statecraft, i.e. strong central government. They showed that on the eve of Thatcherism only one-quarter of Conservative MPs endorsed free enterprise and strong government. Moreover, those approving of all three ideals amounted to a mere 10 per cent.

Later estimates of the level of Thatcherite support among MPs ranged from 10 per cent (King 1983) to 25 per cent (Riddell 1985). There is no suggestion here that the majority of Conservative MPs are adherents of Thatcherism. On the other hand, in a more specific study of MPs' attitudes to welfare, Taylor-Gooby and Bochel (1988) confirmed that the majority of Conservatives favoured a minimalist state.

At the level of Conservative voters, there was even less enthusiasm for the three political ideals on the eve of Thatcherism. Only 17 per cent of Conservative identifiers endorsed both free enterprise and strong government (Crewe and Searing 1988). Furthermore, in the period 1974–83 public opinion shifted to the right on only one out of ten key issues (the exception being denationalization/privatization of industry). This hardly constitutes evidence of a seachange in political values or a new consensus in favour of radical Conservatism.

3   *Influences on Attitudes to Public Spending and the Welfare State*

Most attitudinal studies on the welfare state in the 1980s centred on either the level of public expenditure on services or the public–

private balance in service provision (see Chapter 7 on the latter). There is overwhelming evidence of a large consensus for maintained or increased spending on the main services such as health and education (Edgell and Duke 1982; Lewis and Jackson 1985; Hyde and Deacon 1986; Taylor-Gooby 1988).

Bosanquet (1986) argued that a broad collectivism characterizes British attitudes to the welfare state. Indeed, he showed that between 1983 and 1985 attitudes moved consistently in a collectivist direction and away from non-interventionist policies. This phenomenon of a high level of mass support for welfare state spending is not confined to Britain. In a study of Western Europe, North America and Japan, Alber (1988) found no sign of a general welfare backlash or a legitimation crisis.

A consistent finding in previous research was the joint influence of self-interest and ideology on attitudes to public spending and the welfare state. In their work on public expenditure preferences in Britain, Lewis and Jackson (1985) presented systematic patterns associated with occupational class and party identification. Similarly, both Mouritzen (1987) on public spending attitudes in Denmark and Hawthorne and Jackson (1987) on tax policy in the USA singled out the importance of self-interest and ideology. In our own work, social class and sectoral locations constitute indicators of self-interest, whilst partisanship is an indicator of ideological position.

The strong and enduring support for the welfare state should not be allowed to obscure the existence of negative experiences of state welfare, especially at a time of expenditure restraint (Hyde and Deacon 1986; Taylor-Gooby 1988).

General attitudes to public spending

The commitment of the first Thatcher government to reduce public expenditure meant that the GMS began during a period of great debate over spending cuts, actual or proposed (see Chapter 1). We asked respondents whether they approved or disapproved of the spending cuts in general. First-stage results (in 1980–1) indicated 34 per cent approval of the spending cuts (only 5 per cent strong approval) and 53 per cent disapproval (23 per cent strong disapproval). By the second stage of the GMS (1983–4), disapproval had risen by 10 per cent to 63 per cent (25 per cent strong disapproval), whilst approval had fallen to 27 per cent.

As can be seen from Table 4.1, there are distinct and consistent patterns in relation to social class, consumption sector and par-

Table 4.1 General attitude to the spending cuts by household social class, household consumption sector, partisanship and household production sector

Sub group	GMS1		GMS2	
	% approve	% disapprove	% approve	% disapprove
	spending cuts in general		spending cuts in general	
Household social class:				
Employer	68	27	41	48
Petty bourgeois	54	41	42	52
Controller	42	48	31	61
Worker	23	66	19	73
Household consumption sector:				
Totally private	54	36	40	53
Predominantly private	37	52	28	63
Predominantly public	31	61	23	71
Totally public	22	67	10	85
Partisanship:				
Conservative	74	14	53	35
Labour	7	87	9	88
Liberal/SDP/Alliance	35	55	21	72
Household production sector:				
Controller private	40	50	39	58
Controller public	44	45	24	64
Worker private	25	65	20	72
Worker public	22	68	19	75

Source: GMS1 and GMS2

tisanship at both stages. The production sectoral cleavage is more apparent at the second stage than the first. All sub-groups moved in the direction of greater disapproval. At GMS1 there was majority approval of the spending cuts among employer households, petty bourgeois households, totally private consumers and Conservative identifiers. By GMS2 only the last retained majority approval (53 per cent).

A persistent refrain of the first Thatcher administration was that 'there is no alternative' (TINA) to government economic policy in general and public expenditure restraint in particular. Thus we investigated whether or not respondents considered the spending cuts inevitable. At the first survey (GMS1), a majority (53 per cent) thought the cuts inevitable and 37 per cent regarded the cuts as not inevitable. By GMS2 there was a 10 per cent increase in those disputing the inevitability of the cuts to 47 per cent, resulting in an even split with the inevitables (48 per cent).

Once again, attitudes to the inevitability of the spending cuts exhibited systematic differences in relation to social class, consumption sector and partisanship. An interesting shift in opinion occurred among those employed in the public sector. At GMS1 both public sector controller households (57 per cent) and public sector worker households (52 per cent) thought the cuts inevitable. By GMS2 a majority of the controllers (54 per cent) regarded the cuts as not inevitable, whereas the workers continued to accept inevitability (55 per cent). Clearly, more public sector controllers have begun to question whether there is no alternative. The public sector controller group will emerge again as distinctive in Chapter 8.

The GMS revealed no mandate of approval for the spending cuts, nor by the second stage was there a majority accepting their inevitability. The direction of change identified was of increased opposition to government policy. This trend can be confirmed in a national sample by looking at BES data.

The BES has regularly asked a question regarding the relative balance of taxation and spending on government services such as health, education and welfare. The three options offered are: to cut taxes (and therefore services); to leave as they are; and to extend services (and therefore increase taxes). The proportion of service increasers rose dramatically from 37 per cent in 1979 to 52 per cent in 1983 and 64 per cent in 1987. Correspondingly, tax cutters dwindled from 37 per cent in 1979 to 24 per cent in 1983 and 13 per cent in 1987. The national data clearly corroborate the direction of change indicated in the GMS.

Specific attitudes to public spending

Specific attitudes towards public spending were investigated in more detail during the first GMS survey by asking respondents whether or not they would like to see more or less spent on six major types of publicly funded services: defence, education, health, police, social services and transport. There were majorities for more spending on health (78 per cent), education (72 per cent), social services (58 per cent) and the police (51 per cent). Sizeable minorities wanted more spending on transport (42 per cent) and defence (35 per cent). When respondents were questioned about particular areas of social provision, there was vast support for increased public expenditure, especially on the main welfare state services.

At GMS2 two further areas of public spending (housing and welfare benefits) were added to the six investigated at the first interview. There were clear majorities for more spending rather than less on five of the eight services, namely health (83 per cent), education (74 per cent), personal social services (64 per cent) and housing (64 per cent) and welfare benefits (61 per cent). For two other services more spending was the modal answer, i.e. transport (44 per cent) and police (43 per cent). Only in the case of defence spending was there a majority (just 50 per cent) for less spending, with a mere 20 per cent favouring more spending.

The most significant change among the panel was a clear drop in support for more defence spending (– 15 per cent) and a surge in support for less defence spending (+ 17 per cent). In fact, of those favouring more defence spending at the first interview, only 37 per cent continued to do so at the second. By contrast, there was a steady increase in support for more spending on the welfare state services: health (+ 5 per cent), education (+ 2 per cent) and social services (+ 6 per cent).

The 1987 BSA survey confirmed the continuation of these preferences with a national sample. Asked to name the two most important priorities for spending, there was overwhelming agreement among all sub-groups on health (79 per cent) and education (56 per cent). Furthermore, the same survey exhibited majorities for less defence spending and more spending on welfare benefits. Earlier in the 1980s our pattern of spending preferences was corroborated by Lewis and Jackson (1985).

Further analysis of the relationship between general attitudes of approval/disapproval towards the cuts and support for more or less public expenditure on specific services proved highly instructive. Table 4.2 indicates that, among those at GMS1 who strongly approved of the public expenditure cuts, a clear majority nonetheless supported greater public spending on the police and defence. This is in contrast to other types of public expenditure, which they either endorsed less strongly (for example, health) or positively disapproved of (for example, transport, social services and education). Moreover, the same table clearly shows that, among those who strongly disapproved of the cuts, the majority favoured more public spending on all the services investigated except the police and defence. In other words, there would seem to be a marked ideological patterning of public spending preferences. Strong approval of the cuts in fact meant approval of certain cuts only, and

Table 4.2 Attitude to spending on specific services by general attitude to the spending cuts

General attitude to cuts	Police	Defence	% wanting more spending on:[a] Health	Education	Transport	Social services
Strongly approve (*n* = 48)	69 (1)	67 (2)	40 (3)	25 (4)	25 (4)	21 (6)
Approve on the whole (*n* = 275)	61 (2)	46 (4)	63 (1)	55 (3)	33 (6)	39 (5)
Disapprove on the whole (*n* = 284)	48 (4)	30 (6)	90 (1)	86 (2)	45 (5)	69 (3)
Strongly disapprove (*n* = 212)	44 (5)	26 (6)	93 (1)	91 (2)	57 (4)	80 (3)

Note: [a]The rank order of spending priorities for each level of general attitude is given in brackets.
Source: GMS1

indeed meant more spending on defence and the police. Conversely, strong disapproval of the cuts did not mean disapproval of all cuts, but also involved a low priority for spending on the same two law and order areas of provision.

At GMS2 approval/disapproval of the cuts remained highly selective. The 'strong approvers' had no majorities for more spending on any of the six services, but their two most preferred services continued to be the police and defence. 'Strong disapprovers' on the other hand had majorities for more spending on all services except the police and defence.

Lewis (1982) has pointed out the dangers of asking questions on public expenditure where it is not made clear to respondents that increases in expenditure require increases in taxation (or charges). Thus at the second interview we asked respondents whether they would be prepared to pay more in taxes/rates so as to avoid cuts in the service (those not paying taxes/rates were asked if they would like to see taxes increased so as to avoid cuts in the service).

The responses in Table 4.3 reveal a strong correlation between the two forms of question. Our panel sample were prepared to put their money where their preferences lay. Majorities were willing to pay more so as to avoid cuts in five out of eight service areas, the exceptions being housing (41 per cent), transport (36 per cent) and defence (28 per cent). The fact that housing and transport are now predominantly privately consumed is important in understanding the greater reluctance to pay more for these services.

Table 4.3   Responses to (a) wanting more or less spending on eight services and (b) willingness to pay more in taxes/rates so as to avoid cuts in the eight services

(a) % wanting more spent		(b) % prepared to pay more taxes/rates	
Health	83	NHS	82
Education	74	Schools	75
Personal social services	64	Personal social services	69
Housing	64	Housing	41
Welfare benefits	61	Unemployment benefit	54
Public transport	44	Local buses	36
Police	43	Police	51
Defence	20	Defence	28

Source: GMS2 (n = 685)

There was a marked party political patterning of specific attitudes towards public spending. Conservative partisans were more favourable to increased public spending than Labour and Liberal/SDP Alliance supporters on two of the eight services, namely defence and the police (i.e. law and order spending). On the other hand, they were less favourable to increased spending on the other six services (i.e. welfare state spending). Interestingly, Liberal/SDP Alliance partisans were closer in spending preference to Labour than to Conservative identifiers on seven out of the eight services (the exception was police spending, where they were roughly equidistant). This set of relationships between party identification and expenditure preferences was confirmed by Lewis and Jackson (1985) with a national sample.

Household social class location was clearly related to attitudes on welfare spending, with (predictably) the lower the class the more spending wanted. However, there were no systematic class-related differences in relation to defence and police spending. Similarly, household consumption sectoral location was a good predictor of attitudes to spending on welfare state services but not to law and order spending. This is to be expected in that there is no public–private sector cleavage in relation to law and order spending – yet!

4   Unemployment and Jobs

If public spending cuts dominated debate at the time of the first GMS survey, by the second stage the key issue had been unemployment for some time and was about to become privatization (see Chapter 1). The increased salience of unemployment to our panel is clearly evident in Chapter 6 on the impact of government policy.

The first Thatcher government had broken the postwar consensus in abandoning the commitment to full employment. Control of inflation thus became a higher priority than maintaining full employment. To what extent was this view endorsed by the electorate?

At GMS2 we used a question from the *British Social Attitudes* survey relating to the policy choice between inflation and unemployment: if the government had to choose between keeping down inflation or keeping down unemployment, to which should it give the highest priority? A clear majority (62 per cent) chose unemployment and only 29 per cent selected inflation. The detailed responses, broken down by social class, sector and partisanship, are

Table 4.4 Choice of inflation or unemployment as the priority by household social class, household consumption sector, partisanship and household production sector

Sub-group	% choosing inflation as priority	% choosing unemployment as priority
Household social class:		
Employer	37	56
Petty bourgeois	32	59
Controller	31	62
Worker	27	66
Household consumption sector:		
Totally private	41	58
Predominantly private	30	62
Predominantly public	22	70
Totally public	24	73
Partisanship:		
Conservative	49	43
Labour	14	82
Liberal/SDP/Alliance	26	67
Household production sector:		
Controller private	30	64
Controller public	31	60
Worker private	28	67
Worker public	27	66

Source: GMS2

presented in Table 4.4. All sub-groups had majorities selecting unemployment as the priority, except Conservative partisans. Even among Conservatives only 49 per cent echoed Thatcherite policy by prioritizing inflation. Clear differences emerged according to household consumption sector, but there was no systematic patterning in relation to production sector.

The 1983 *British Social Attitudes* survey confirmed our findings with national data. The mandate for inflation as *the* priority was even less in the national sample, at 27 per cent, whereas fully 69 per cent selected unemployment as the priority. By the 1987 *British Social Attitudes* survey, opposition to the declared government priority had become even greater, with only 23 per cent for inflation and 73 per cent for unemployment. Even 58 per cent of Conservative partisans chose unemployment in 1987.

Interestingly, the unemployment/inflation choice is strongly related to general attitude to the spending cuts. 'Strong approvers' of the cuts were overwhelmingly in favour of inflation as the priority (77 per cent), whereas 83 per cent of 'strong disapprovers' chose unemployment. Our respondents had manifestly made the connection between different aspects of government policy.

※ The Thatcherite view on unemployment breaks with the postwar social democratic consensus by insisting that it is not the state's responsibility to provide jobs for everyone; it is up to the individual to 'get on his/her bike' (to quote Norman Tebbitt, the former Employment Secretary) and find work. Accordingly, at GMS1 we asked respondents two questions which tapped into these two related themes.

First, contrary to Thatcherite dogma, 68 per cent of our sample thought that it is up to the government to ensure that everybody has a job and an adequate standard of living; even 52 per cent of Conservative partisans agreed with this view. More recently, the 1987 *British Social Attitudes* survey asked a similar question and 57 per cent agreed that the government should provide a job for everyone who wants one. Only Conservative partisans (38 per cent), employers (48 per cent) and totally private consumers (39 per cent) failed to exhibit majorities in agreement.

On the second question, only 32 per cent of our GMS1 sample endorsed the Thatcherite view that it is up to workers to move to another part of the country to find work. Fully 57 per cent disagreed. The only sub-group with a majority in favour was employer households (60 per cent) and 49 per cent of Conservative partisans agreed with the proposition. A related question was asked in the 1987 *British Social Attitudes* survey: 41 per cent of the national sample agreed that most of the unemployed could find a job if they wanted one, whereas 42 per cent disagreed. The sub-groups endorsing the Thatcherite line were, once again, Conservative partisans (57 per cent), employer households (56 per cent) and totally private consumers (52 per cent).

5   Local Government Autonomy

As part of their overall concern to reduce public expenditure and also ensure that policies such as privatization of services are carried out everywhere, the Thatcher governments have strengthened central control of local government (see Chapter 5 for details). This feature of radical Conservatism is at odds with the strong element

of local autonomy in traditional Conservatism (Butcher *et al.*
1990).

There was little support among the electorate for this centraliz-
ation of control and associated reduction of local autonomy. At
GMS2 we asked respondents whether central government should
tell local authorities what to spend their money on or whether local
government should be independent. An overwhelming 79 per cent
favoured local independence and only 11 per cent wanted central
control. The breakdown of responses into sub-groups is displayed
in Table 4.5. All sub-groups endorsed local independence,
including 70 per cent of Conservative partisans and 89 per cent of
Labour partisans. Support for local autonomy was also systematically related to household social class, with 83 per cent of workers

Table 4.5 Central control or local independence by household social
class, household consumption sector, partisanship and household
production sector

Sub-group	% central control	% local independence
Household social class:		
Employer	11	64
Petty bourgeois	16	74
Controller	11	80
Worker	9	83
Household consumption sector:		
Totally private	12	73
Predominantly private	11	79
Predominantly public	8	85
Totally public	10	90
Partisanship:		
Conservative	20	70
Labour	6	89
Liberal/SDP/Alliance	6	84
Household production sector:		
Controller private	14	79
Controller public	9	81
Worker private	10	81
Worker public	7	87

Source: GMS2

in favour, and also to household consumption sector, with 90 per cent of totally public consumers in favour.

The 1983 *British Social Attitudes* survey asked a similar question and 13 per cent wanted more central government control of local authorities, a figure very close to our own 11 per cent. By the 1987 survey this same question elicited 19 per cent support for more central control, most notably among Conservative partisans (30 per cent) and employers (35 per cent). There was thus a 6 per cent increase between 1983 and 1987 in the level of agreement with the Thatcherite position, but this remains far short of a mandate.

A further related question was employed in the 1987 *British Social Attitudes* survey. Fully 60 per cent of the sample thought that the level of rates should be up to the local council rather than

Table 4.6 Government should introduce stricter trade union laws by household social class, household consumption sector, partisanship and household production sector

Sub-group	GMS2 % should	BES 1987 % should
Household social class:		
Employer	74	72
Petty bourgeois	67	64
Controller	51	59
Worker	49	48
Household consumption sector:		
Totally private	60	62
Predominantly private	52	54
Predominantly public	45	49
Totally public	67	47
Partisanship:		
Conservative	79	76
Labour	30	28
Liberal/SDP/Alliance	50	48
Household production sector:		
Controller private	54	60
Controller public	49	58
Worker private	51	50
Worker public	46	45

Sources: GMS2 and BES 1987

central government. Even 63 per cent of Conservative partisans shared this view, which confirms the presence of localism in traditional Conservatism.

6 *Trade Union Autonomy*

A major plank in the hegemonic project of Thatcherism has been to alter the balance of class forces in favour of capital and to the disadvantage of labour. Hence the Thatcherite concern to restrict the power of trade unions in general and public sector trade unions in particular.

Since 1979 the British Election Study has included a question on whether the government should or should not introduce stricter laws to regulate the activities of trade unions. There was strong support for stricter laws in 1979 (following the 'Winter of Discontent'), with 70 per cent wanting the government to introduce them. By the 1983 BES, the proportion in favour had dropped to 56 per cent, and by the 1987 BES still further to 50 per cent. Although the direction of attitudinal change is against further restrictions on trade unions, it is important to bear in mind that in between these elections stricter trade union laws were introduced.

GMS2 asked exactly the same question as the BES. The result was a fairly even split, with 50 per cent in favour and 43 per cent against stricter laws. Detailed responses by class, sector and party are documented in Table 4.6 for both GMS2 and BES 1987. Consistent systematic patterns emerged in relation to social class, partisanship and production sector, but totally public consumers in the GMS constituted an anomaly.

Compared with other aspects of Thatcherite policy, trade union reforms are fairly popular. However, it is important to realize that trade unions are still regarded as necessary. At GMS1, 70 per cent of the sample agreed that it is still sometimes necessary for people to go on strike to make a decent living and by GMS2 this proportion had risen to 73 per cent.

7 *Conclusions*

The mandate for Thatcherism is distinctly lacking in relation to the core issues discussed in this chapter. Only in the case of trade union reform have we witnessed popular support for the Thatcherite agenda. There is opposition to most of the policy shifts away from the postwar consensus. Nor is there overwhelming backing from Conservative partisans on several of the issues.

We must therefore agree with Jessop *et al.* (1985) and Gamble (1988) that there is little evidence of a new Thatcherite consensus. What Thatcherism has achieved is a shift in the terms of political debate. Whereas in the 1970s debate centred on more or less nationalization, in the 1980s discussion centred on more or less privatization (see Chapter 7). The national media have played a crucial role in facilitating the shift in political debate onto Thatcherite terrain (Dunleavy and Husbands 1985).

Given that Thatcherism in its broader sense remains a minority viewpoint, it is clear that Mrs Thatcher's three election victories were attained despite, rather than because of, Thatcherism. In both 1983 and 1987 the anti-Conservative vote was split, so that a minority share of the popular vote was translated into a parliamentary landslide. It is the workings of the British electoral system in relation to the regional variations in support which has perpetuated the electoral success of the Conservative Party.

The influence of both self-interest and ideology on attitudes and values is evident from the data presented in this chapter. Thatcherism's key sub-groups are employers, the petty bourgeoisie, totally private consumers and Conservative partisans.

Overall we would wish to stress the transparent yet highly selective class and party political nature of reactions to the cuts in public expenditure. It is not simply that those at the top of the class structure and Conservative partisans tend to support the public spending cuts, whilst those lower down the class structure and Labour voters tend not to do so, but that there are sharply contrasting value systems in public spending priorities. Those who expressed the more extreme attitudes illustrate this point very clearly; the strong approvers of the cuts in general had majorities in favour of more spending on only two services – the police and defence; whereas the strong disapprovers had majorities on all services except the police and defence. In other words, the first two spending preferences of the strong approvers were the last two preferences of the strong disapprovers.

Within the context of the particularly distinct party political patterning of attitudinal reactions to the spending cuts, the predilections of the Liberal/SDP Alliance partisans were most interesting. In terms of attitudes they were closer to the Labour partisans than to the Conservative partisans, for example in their support for more welfare state spending. The contrasting value systems of the 'strong approvers' and 'strong disapprovers' noted

above can also be interpreted in the context of ideological polarization. The Liberal/SDP Alliance bid for the centre ground of
British politics is in itself indicative of perceived polarization of the
two main parties. This polarization of policy alternatives is equally
evident at the local authority level, as we shall see in the next chapter.

CHAPTER 5

Central–Local Government Relations: A Case Study

1 Introduction

The first decade of Thatcherism witnessed a significant transformation in the relationship between central and local government. According to Duncan and Goodwin (1988), local authorities are in the front line for three reasons: first, as big spenders they are central to the aim of reducing public expenditure; second, as a major provider of collective services – such as cheap public transport and subsidized council housing – they are a prime target for Thatcher's attack on collectivism; third, they constitute a site where alternative socialist policies and values may be established, a veritable anathema to Thatcherism. The attack on local government is apparent in the unleashing of over 60 Acts of Parliament since 1979 which pertain to local government (*Local Government Trends*, 1989).

However, it is important to remember that the latest era of public spending cuts was initiated by the Labour administration between 1975 and 1979. This policy has been continued somewhat differently but more thoroughly and enthusiastically by the Conservatives since 1979. Arguably the current phase differs from all previous versions of this policy in the sense that it represents an explicit attempt to reverse the historical trend of public expenditure growth and in the process to restructure the welfare state. In this view, the spending cuts involve a reassertion of market forces and individualism as opposed to the welfare state and collectivism. This 'rolling back of the state' can be seen as the end of the postwar Butskellite consensus on the welfare state. The nature of the restructuring exercise is indicated by the scale and selective scope of the current policy, which is based on a package of interrelated public expenditure and revenue strategies (see Duke and Edgell 1984).

The most significant congruence in the expenditure patterns of

Table 5.1   Trends in central and local government spending, 1976–1983

	Average annual rates of change (in real terms)	
	1976–9 Labour %	1979–83 Conservative %
Total central government spending	+ 1.9	+ 1.6
Total local government spending	– 2.4	– 1.0
Local government capital spending	– 11.5	– 9.0
Local government current spending	+ 0.2	+ 0.5

Source: Local Government Trends, 1989

both governments is over the discrepancy between central and local state expenditure. Table 5.1 highlights trends in central and local spending during the Labour and Conservative periods of spending cuts. In both periods central government spending increased whereas local government spending decreased. It was local capital spending which took the brunt of the cuts – not surprisingly, given its lower political visibility. The cancellation of proposed new buildings is politically safer than the closure of existing buildings. The proportion of GDP accounted for by local government expenditure declined consistently from 12.2 per cent in 1976/7, to 10.7 per cent in 1978/9, to 10.1 per cent in 1982/3, to 9.7 per cent in 1986/7.

Local authority employment data confirm the decline of local government during the first Thatcher government, with a small decrease from 2.368 million in 1979 to 2.301 million in 1983 (Fleming 1988). However, there were slight increases in the local authority workforce during both the second Thatcher regime and the Labour administration of 1974–9.

In addition to the cuts in spending, the Thatcher governments have markedly increased the central government's control over local authorities. During the first regime, the Local Government Planning and Land Act 1980 introduced a new block grant system which set spending targets for individual authorities and imposed grant penalties for overspending authorities. Any marginal expenditure beyond a fixed threshold fell more heavily on local rates.

Local authorities were required to publish information on costs and performance in order to facilitate identification of overspenders. A second piece of legislation, the Local Government Finance Act 1982, banned the raising of a supplementary rate by local authorities and introduced the possibility of retrospective rate support grant penalties for alleged overspending. If a local authority spent excessively in one year, they received proportionately less grant the following year.

The second Thatcher administration intensified the control over individual local authorities. The Rates Act 1984 gave central government the power to set the level of rates for specific local authorities. This led to the ratecapping of several predominantly Labour authorities (Newton and Karran 1985). By the mid 1980s the system of targets and penalties became so complex that only local and central government accountants could fully understand it. The Local Government Act 1985 paved the way for the abolition of the Greater London Council and the metropolitan authorities in 1986, all of which were big-spending Labour authorities.

Further legislation ensued early in the third Thatcher government. The Education Reform Act 1988 gave schools the right to opt out of local authority control and adopt a semi-independent grant-aided status. This policy change strikes at the core local service of education, which accounts for around half of all local spending. Another local government change involved the imposition of competitive tendering for six areas of local government service. Most significantly of all, the Local Government Finance Act 1988 set up the introduction of a community charge (or poll tax) for Scotland in 1989 and England/Wales in 1990 to replace the local rates.

The new community charge is a flat-rate per capita tax on all adults, which is highly regressive in its incidence. Local taxpayers pay the full marginal cost of extra spending in each local authority, through either a higher community charge or increased fees/charges for services (Gibson 1987). As a result of this, local authorities are likely to rely increasingly on central grants rather than local taxation. Preliminary research by Bramley *et al.* (1989) in Cheshire has shown that the incidence of poll tax deviates systematically from the pattern of service usage and is therefore not a good benefit tax. Bramley argues that local accountability is liable to be extremely limited.

Thatcherism's obsession with reducing public spending embraces several other strategies that affect local provision of collective services. These are the imposition of cash limits, decreased subsidies to public services, increases in charges for services and privatization. The last is considered in detail in Chapter 7.

The strategy of imposing **cash limits** below the rate of inflation was first introduced by Labour in 1976 and then more widely adopted by the Conservatives after 1979 (Pliatzky 1984). Cash limits operate most effectively in relation to public sector pay restraint (Bevan *et al.* 1981; Elliott 1986). A prolonged period of spending restraint and cash limits has led to the end of incrementalism in local social service budgets (Kelly 1989). Other latent consequences of cash limits are (a) underspending as departments aim low in an attempt to keep within the limit set (Else and Marshall 1981), and (b) 'quickspend' towards the end of the financial year (Midwinter 1980). A further related development is that the 1982 White Paper presented the expenditure plans solely in cash terms for the first time, a procedure which provoked severe criticism from the Treasury and Civil Service Committee (Fifth Report 1981–2) and resulted in the rapid return of spending analyses in real terms (i.e. allowing for inflation) as well as in cash terms (see section 3 in Chapter 6).

Subsidies to local public services, especially housing and public transport, have been systematically reduced since 1979 in line with the ideological shift towards market forces. The Transport Act 1982 curbed local authorities' discretion to subsidize fares, while central government subsidies to local authority housing decreased by 50 per cent between 1978/9 and 1982/3. At the same time, the subsidization of mortgaged house-owners and company car users remained undisturbed, although company cars are now taxed (*Guardian*, 12 February 1990). It has been argued that such tax expenditures should be included in the overall analysis of public expenditure (Titmuss 1958; Pond 1982; Hogwood 1989). Tax allowances and reliefs are still not 'counted' in the politics of public expenditure accounting, unlike direct subsidies and benefits.

Increased charges for services are another strategy to reduce the level of public spending. The burden of payment is shifted towards the users of the service rather than the state and as such it may be regarded as a form of privatization (see Chapter 7). For example, both council house rents and public transport fares increased substantially during the first Thatcher government. Additionally, a survey showed that 22 out of 63 authorities increased home help charges between 1979 and 1981 (Ferlie and Judge 1981).

Other effects of the policy shift in relation to local government include:

- the erosion of local government functions – e.g. the increased role of the Manpower Services Commission (now the Training Commission) in relation to further education, and the removal of housing benefit administration from local authorities in 1982;
- the growth of single-purpose non-elected bodies – e.g. the joint boards introduced in the wake of abolition of the metropolitan authorities, and the Urban Development Corporations;
- the fostering of a contracting-out ethos in local government (Stallworthy 1989), which owes much to the influence of multinational auditing companies and their espousal of value-for-money accounting (Kaser 1988);
- professional norms and expectations in local government being under challenge (Young 1988);
- increased use of creative accounting measures to overcome spending restrictions, such as the movement of spending from one year to another and from current expenditure to capital expenditure, and the signing of lease-back arrangements.

However, not all the government's legislative changes are in the direction of greater central control. The contradictory nature of government policy is indicated by several instances of increased local autonomy. The Education Act 1980 restored the power of local authorities to pay pupils' fees at independent schools and removed the restrictions on school meals charges. The Housing Act 1980 enabled local authorities to sell council houses at an increased discount on the market price (on the other hand, it also gave the Secretary of State the power to enforce sales where the local authority is opposed to privatization). The underlying rationale of government policy seems to involve increased central control over total local authority expenditure and spending on subsidies (especially housing and transport), whilst increasing local autonomy over privatization and higher charges for services.

The attempt to reorganize central–local relations in the context of prolonged and selective retrenchment has led to increased conflict between local authorities and central government, irrespective almost of the political party character of the protagonists. Traditional Conservative municipalism has always valued local political autonomy and the notion of service to the community. Nonetheless, Labour authorities have been at the forefront of any conflict. Central–local relations deteriorated to such a degree that the 1980s witnessed a series of unprecedented legal cases over local authority spending/privatization (Stoker 1988).

This chapter is a case study in two senses. First, central–local relations in general provide an excellent insight into the workings of Thatcherist government. Second, the main part of this chapter will examine a case study of two contrasting local authority districts in Greater Manchester and how they have reacted to the various shifts in government policy. The behaviour of these districts will be contrasted for both the Labour central government's spending cuts in 1976–9 and the Conservative era 1979–83. Prior to that, we lay down a theoretical framework for the case studies.

2   Social Consumption and the Local State

We have found a number of theoretical analyses helpful in comprehending the recent pattern of public expenditure cuts in Britain and the associated increase in conflict at the local authority level. It is our intention here to draw upon relevant conceptual distinctions and resultant hypotheses in order to establish a framework to which our empirical data can be related.

The seminal work of O'Connor (1973) on the fiscal crisis of the state is clearly pertinent to the study of public expenditure cuts. O'Connor discerned a long-term trend in advanced capitalist societies to the socialization of costs as the state increasingly provides necessary services which individual capitalists find it unprofitable to supply. At the same time, the private appropriation of profits continues to be accentuated. The end result of these two related processes is an ever-widening gap between state expenditure and state revenue, which O'Connor called the fiscal crisis of the state.

O'Connor viewed the state as performing two contradictory functions: first, facilitating accumulation in the interests of monopoly capital and, second, legitimating the system in order to pacify the working class. State expenditure plays a key role with regard to these functions. The first function is achieved through a combination of social investment, to increase productivity and profits, and social consumption to provide social and material support for the non-capitalist classes. The second function is served by social expenses, which include both law and order maintenance and welfare benefits.

Although no individual item of state expenditure may be unambiguously assigned to local investment, to social consumption or to social expenses, most may be allocated according to their primary function. Thus the current Conservative government's spending cuts can be seen to be increasing social expenses (notably law and order, and unemployment) whilst decreasing social consumption (notably housing and education). O'Connor's schema thus retains considerable heuristic value even if his wider theory is flawed by an overly restrictive and instrumental view of the state (Saunders 1981).

The application of O'Connor's conceptual framework to the British context was pioneered admirably by Gough (1979). He discussed the problems raised by the very scale of state expenditure, the rising relative costs of the welfare state and the long-term decline in the profitability of British Capitalism. Gough differed from O'Connor in emphasizing the relative autonomy of the state from monopoly capital. He adopted Poulantzas' notion that the state responds to the balance of class forces at any one time (Poulantzas 1973). This position recognizes the role of class conflict in the development of the welfare state, as well as the conventional explanation couched in terms of the functional needs of monopoly capital. For Gough, the requirements of capital thus set parameters within which class conflict may determine social policy.

In Gough's view, the current crisis highlights the inherently contradictory relationship between, on the one hand, the need for economic restructuring in order to reassert the long-term profitability of capital and, on the other hand, the need for a social wage to maintain the legitimacy of the system (see Habermas 1976). A good example of this contradiction is provided by the present government's monetarist policies resulting in new demands (both parliamentary and extra-parliamentary) for increased expenditure on youth unemployment.

The only long-term solution for capital, according to Gough, is for the state to weaken the power of the organized working class, that is, to alter the balance of class forces. It is in this context that the Conservative government's twin policies of selective public spending cuts and trade union regulation should be located. The importance of attempts selectively to restrict public sector pay increases through cash limits is that they serve both aims.

Gough concluded (in 1979, prior to the Conservative government) that the spending cuts were intended as a restructuring rather than a dismantling of the welfare state. A clear indication of restructuring in favour of capital is evidenced by the Conservative policy of privatizing the more profitable sections of the public sector, which can be clearly linked to the function of capital accumulation. The selection of social consumption policies to bear the brunt of the spending cuts is further evidence of the restructuring process.

In addition to the class struggle, political conflict in response to selective cuts in public spending takes two main forms: (a) there is a marked deterioration in local–central government relations as the latter brings pressure to bear on the former to carry out proposed cuts in spending; and (b) the sectoral cleavage between public and private modes of consumption intensifies as the public mode suffers (and is seen to suffer) relative to the private. The second of the two conflicts was considered in Chapter 2. The first identifies the main question addressed in this chapter, that is, to what extent is local political control a mediating factor in relation to the nature and severity of the cuts?

Building upon the work of O'Connor and others, Saunders (1981, 1984, 1986) developed an ideal-type analytical framework for studying central–local relations. First, he suggested that, whereas central/regional government is concerned primarily with social investment, local government's main economic function is social consumption. Second, whilst social consumption policies are resolved largely in competitive political struggles, social investment has been insulated by means of a corporatist mode of interest mediation (see also Jessop 1978). The latter suggests that the functional economic interests of capital (e.g. the CBI) and organized labour (e.g. the TUC) have been incorporated into policy-making. Third, the dominant ideology in British capitalist society exhibits a tension between the two contradictory principles of profit and social need (see Abercrombie *et al.* 1980).

Drawing together these three strands (see Figure 5.1), Saunders argued that central and regional government are typically concerned with social investment, corporatist policies and private sector profitability. Local government, on the other hand, is concerned mainly with social consumption, competitive politics and social need. According to Saunders, the tensions between these contrasting functions, modes of political mediation and ideologies are to some extent insulated by being located at different levels of government. Moreover, the dominance of central over local government can best be understood with reference to the dominance of investment over consumption, corporatism over democracy, and profit over need.

Thus, although local government is constrained by central government powers and priorities, Saunders hypothesized that there will be local variations, even to the extent of non-capitalist

	Central/ regional	Local	Tension (central control vs. local autonomy)
Economic function	social investment	social consumption	economic vs. social policy priorities
Mode of interest mediation	corporate bias	competitive struggles	rational direction vs. democratic accountability
Ideological principle	private property	citizenship right	profit vs. need

Source: Saunders 1982

Figure 5.1   The specificity of the local state

interests prevailing at this level. It is in this context that the attempt by the Conservative central government throughout the 1980s to reassert market values in the face of considerable opposition at the level of local government needs to be seen. The consequent deterioration in central–local relations is particularly acute for, but far from limited to, Labour local authorities which are politically and ideologically opposed to the current government's cuts policy. A radical workers' party may capture power at the local level and thereby have some influence on social consumption, but its power does not directly threaten key social investment policies (Boddy and Fudge 1984).

Acceptance of the Saunders' model has significant implications for two longstanding debates in political science. First, the model assumes that the local state is not merely an agent of the central government, in that non-capitalist interests may succeed at the local level in influencing social consumption policies. Second, the existence of competitive political struggles over social consumption at the local level highlights the importance of local political control and the party political effect on expenditure patterns.

The traditional view of local government stressed its prescribed and restricted role as solely managing a bundle of separate independent services (Redcliffe-Maud 1967). Proponents of both orthodox political science and Marxist political economy came to accept the idea that local government was the agent of central government (Broadbent 1977; Cockburn 1977). Considerable emphasis was placed on an increasing financial dependence on the centre.

On the other hand, Ashford's study of the effect of central finance on the British local government system concluded that the common view of central dominance and local subjection was 'exaggerated if not totally incorrect' (Ashford 1974: 320). Simi-

larly, Rhodes (1979) argued that local authorities possess substantial political, financial and legal resources, and two literature
reviews both concluded that local government has considerable
autonomy (Dearlove 1979; Elcock 1982). The public choice
theorists' view of local bureaucrats as budget or staff maximizers
also implied that the local state has a degree of autonomy (e.g.
Niskanen 1973).

Duncan and Goodwin (1988) explained the existence of local
government and how local politics became differentiated in terms
of the uneven development of capitalist society; hence Thatcherism's concern to undermine any resultant resistance from
peripheral authorities. Cockburn (1977) also integrated local
politics into the wider view of the capitalist state, but combined
this with a restricted view of the state's role.

Saunders' model has been most frequently criticized on the
grounds that it tends to exaggerate the differences between the
central and local levels of the state. For example, Clegg (1982) has
argued that transport is part social investment and part social consumption. Also, Flynn (1983) has documented the importance of
social investment in local structure planning and found that both
modes of interest mediation operated at the local level. On the
same theme, Martlew (1982) has emphasized the interdependence
between central and local government and has suggested that
Saunders' dualistic approach overlooks the links between them.
His conclusion was that the vertical divisions within central and
local government are greater in extent than the horizontal divisions
between them. For example, production sectoral cleavages apply
equally to both local authority and central government workers
(Dunleavy 1980b). More generally, the Saunders model was based
on an *a priori* allocation of functions to the local and national levels,
and assumed pluralist politics at the local level (Goodwin 1989).

3   Party effects on local policies?

In a review of international research, Fried (1976) concluded that
political variables were not as important as socioeconomic variables in explaining local expenditure patterns, but nonetheless con-
ceded that the party effect was most noticeable in British studies.
There is in fact a considerable body of literature on the relationship
between political party control and local expenditure patterns in
Britain. Alt's study of 44 county boroughs from 1958/9 revealed
a correlation between greater Labour representation on councils

and higher spending on housing, education and health, but lower spending on the police service (Alt 1971). Boaden (1971) concluded that party political control affects priorities both between and within services after analysing the spending patterns of 81 county boroughs in 1965/6. For example, in education, Labour authorities were associated with higher per capita spending and a lower proportion of secondary pupils in selective grammar schools; in housing, Labour control was correlated with a higher level of rate subsidy of council house rents and a lower proportion of new houses built by the private sector. In a study of children's services, Davies *et al.* (1972) concluded that Labour was the spending party.

In contrast, Oliver and Stanyer (1969) and Nicholson and Topham (1972) concluded that there was no evidence of a significant political effect on expenditure patterns. In both cases, however, the findings are somewhat limited in that Nicholson and Topham considered only capital expenditure and Oliver and Stanyer were concerned solely with total revenue expenditure. Newton and Sharpe (1977) stressed the importance of disaggregating total expenditure into individual services and even to the level of specific items within services.

The historical debate on the earlier period continues without agreement. Sharpe and Newton (1984) concluded that local discretion resulted in significant service variations in the period 1957–73. Hoggart (1987) contradicted Sharp and Newton's conclusion on party effects for a similar period (1947–74).

The research discussed above relates only to the period of growth in local authority expenditure. For the Labour-prompted spending cuts from 1975/6 to 1978/9, Greenwood (1981) concluded that in England and Wales there was no evidence that the political complexion of a council *per se* affected an authority's response to fiscal pressure. Although there was resistance from some Labour councils, overall the differences were negligible. Indeed, there is some evidence that in Scotland from 1976/7 to 1977/8 Labour authorities were more likely to respond to the call from a Labour central government to reduce the rate of local authority expenditure growth (Page 1978).

According to Cooper and Stewart (1982), the more recent era of Conservative-induced spending cuts reveals a growing level of disparity between Conservative and Labour authorities. For the years 1979/80, 1980/1 and 1981/2, on average Labour-controlled authorities increased total expenditure by about 2 per cent more than their Conservative counterparts. However, this overall pattern conceals considerable overlap: 66 per cent of Labour authorities were reducing current expenditure in real terms compared with 69 per cent of Conservative authorities. The larger Labour authorities have been most prone to increase expenditure and thereby enhance the political visibility of Labour–Conservative differences.

Bassett (1982) suggested that initially most Labour councils chose either to carry through the cuts and blame the Conservative central government, or to protect key services by rate increases. A study of social services cuts in 63 authorities confirmed that many Labour authorities regarded central guidelines as legitimate (Ferlie and Judge 1981). Elcock (1986) concluded that most local authorities eventually responded to demands for spending cuts, but without major service reductions or compulsory redundancies. Duncan and Goodwin (1988) found significant variations in local service delivery, especially over the subsidization of council housing. Some London boroughs were found to be making a profit on council house renting.

4 Local Authority Mediation in Greater Manchester

A major part of the overall Greater Manchester Study project involved a case study of two local authority districts during the first Thatcher government. (Full details of the research design are provided in Appendix 1.) One of these districts was represented by a Conservative MP and controlled at the local government level by the Conservative Party (Torytown). The other was represented by a Labour MP and controlled locally by the Labour Party (Labourville). The research design thus possessed a built-in contrast of local political control in order to assess the extent of local authority mediation.

Chartered Institute of Public Finance and Accountancy (CIPFA) indicators of local authority service provision and data supplied by the treasury departments of Torytown and Labourville provided a basis for assessing the extent to which Labourville and Torytown reacted differently to the spending cuts policies of the two central governments, Labour 1976–9 and Conservative 1979–83. Before presenting empirical data of actual expenditure on services in the two districts, and an analysis of local press data it is pertinent to consider the conceptual and practical difficulties involved with the system in operation at that time.

Problems with CIPFA and local treasury data

Expenditure on local authority services can be measured in numerous ways, as can be seen in Figure 5.2. There are two (at least) definitions of net expenditure, which differ in their inclusion or exclusion of specific government grants. These grants are earmarked for specific purposes and are therefore distinct from the general rate support grant (RSG) to each authority. CIPFA tends to present comparative spending data inclusive of specific grants, that is, in terms of net local rate/grant-borne expenditure. The addition of income from fees and charges produces the gross expenditure figure.

The importance of these conceptual distinctions is that local authorities have considerable discretion to influence two of the four sources of finance. First, they can attempt to maintain total net expenditure by increasing rates to compensate for central government reductions in rate support grant. Second, they can attempt to maintain gross expenditure on particular services by increasing fees and charges. Thus, whereas a reduction in gross expenditure represents a decreased level of service provision by the authority, a reduction in net rate/grant-borne expenditure may indicate simply a higher proportion of expenditure met through fees and charges.

Both the expenditure accounts released by Labourville and Torytown districts and the series of actual statistics (as opposed to the estimates series) published by CIPFA presented expenditure data in cash terms. In order to assess whether there had been real

Source of finance		Measure of expenditure
1. Rates		—
+		net local expenditure borne by rates/rate
2. Rate support grant	=	support grant
+		
3. Specific government grants	=	total net local rate/ grant-borne expenditure
+		
4. Fees and charges	=	gross expenditure

Figure 5.2 Alternative measures of local authority expenditure

cuts in spending from one year to another it was necessary to convert these cash figures into constant prices which allow for the rate of inflation. In the tables below the analysis is conducted at 1978/9 prices for the Labour period and 1982/3 prices for the Conservative period.

A number of practical and technical difficulties are involved in comparisons of expenditure data between districts. Tables 5.2 and 5.3 below are based on accounts published by Labourville and Torytown. First, the expenditure categories used by the authorities may vary. For instance, some items classified as housing expenditure by Labourville were located under environmental health spending by Torytown. Every attempt must be made to ensure that genuine comparisons are being made.

Second, the volume and nature of the data collected by local authority accountancy departments at any given point in time are governed largely by the returns which authorities are legally obliged to submit to central government. Thus a change in the returns form results in a change in the data collected, which hinders comparability over time. Furthermore, authorities often do not systematically collate and retain additional data which, although not legally required, may be of interest to the researcher.

A related set of problems existed in analysing data from the various CIPFA publications. A drawback was the changing nature of many indicators over time. Most of the changes involved the welcome provision of greater detail in more recent years, but it was therefore not possible to derive a continuous series since local government reorganization in 1974. Lastly, although no blame can be attached to CIPFA, there were frequent instances of missing data for particular authorities. Torytown was notable for the above-average occurrence of missing data, particularly involving personal social services. It did thus not prove possible to obtain in full, and for the whole period, data as categorized in Figure 5.2. The changing definition of specific grants over time was the most serious problem encountered.

Overall responses to Labour central government's cuts, 1975/6–1978/9

Changes in total expenditure by Labourville and Torytown districts for the period of Labour spending cuts are summarized in Table 5.2. During the Labour central government's spending cuts between 1975/6 and 1978/9, total net expenditure (excluding specific grants) declined in real terms in both districts. By 1978/9, net expenditure was lower by 4.3 per cent in Labourville and 7.5

Table 5.2 Changes in total local authority expenditure and spending on major programmes during the Labour period of cuts, 1975/6–1978/9 in cost terms (1975/6 = 100: 1978/9 prices)

Expenditure	Labourville				Torytown			
	1975/6	1976/7	1977/8	1978/9	1975/6	1976/7	1977/8	1978/9
Total expenditure:								
net[a]	100	99.2	96.0	95.7	100	100.1	94.4	92.5
gross	100	103.5	103.3	107.5	100	105.3	98.1	101.2
Income[b] as % of gross	24.0	27.2	29.4	32.4	28.9	32.4	31.5	35.0
Education:								
net[a]	100	98.3	91.8	91.3	100	99.4	92.3	91.3
gross	100	98.4	96.1	100.2	100	99.8	96.7	97.6
Income[b] as % of gross	13.4	13.5	17.2	21.0	13.4	13.7	17.2	18.9
Social services:								
net[a]	100	95.6	93.5	95.9	100	102.7	102.2	101.4
gross	100	94.6	96.8	99.7	100	105.8	106.8	107.9
Income[b] as % of gross	20.3	19.5	22.9	23.3	12.9	15.5	16.6	18.1
Housing revenue account:								
net[c]	100	125.6	123.8	142.1	100	57.9	53.0	63.5
gross	100	106.4	104.8	110.4	100	118.0	97.2	109.3
Income[b] as % of gross	83.2	80.1	80.1	78.3	91.6	95.4	94.9	94.5

Notes:
[a] Net expenditure met from local rates/rate support grant, thus excluding specific government grants
[b] Income from charges and specific government grants
[c] Net expenditure = rate fund contribution to Housing Revenue Account

Source: Labourville and Torytown Treasury Departments

Table 5.3 Changes in total local authority expenditure and spending on major programmes during the Conservative period of cuts, 1978/9–1982/3 in cost terms (1978/9 = 100: 1982/3 prices)

Expenditure	Labourville					Torytown				
	1978/9	1979/80	1980/1	1981/2	1982/3	1978/9	1979/80	1980/1	1981/2	1982/3
Total expenditure:										
net[a]	100	100.2	102.5	97.7	93.1	100	104.0	96.0	100.6	102.7
gross	100	101.2	101.5	104.4	96.2	100	95.6	95.0	99.8	100.9
Income[b] as % of gross	32.4	33.1	31.6	36.7	34.6	35.0	36.2	34.3	34.6	33.8
Education:										
net[a]	100	96.2	97.9	98.6	94.7	100	93.3	91.9	90.3	89.5
gross	100	97.0	99.0	98.3	96.1	100	92.8	89.3	88.7	85.7
Income[b] as % of gross	21.0	21.7	21.8	20.8	22.2	18.9	18.5	17.0	17.8	15.3
Social services:										
net[a]	100	102.8	106.1	107.0	107.5	100	99.4	98.6	99.4	100.8
gross	100	102.2	105.0	102.7	104.7	100	98.0	97.4	98.4	104.8
Income[b] as % of gross	23.3	22.9	22.6	20.1	21.3	18.1	16.9	16.8	16.5	18.1
Housing revenue account:										
net[c]	100	113.4	107.9	83.3	80.9	100.	94.4	98.2	39.5	44.8
gross	100	101.4	103.2	111.0	106.5	100	96.4	94.0	98.4	100.1
Income[b] as % of gross	78.3	75.8	77.3	83.7	76.0	94.5	94.7	94.3	97.6	97.6

Notes:
[a] Net expenditure met from local rates/rate support grant, thus excluding specific government grants
[b] Income from charges and specific government grants
[c] Net expenditure = rate fund contribution to Housing Revenue Account

Source: Labourville and Torytown Treasury Departments

per cent in Torytown. Local rates were thus not increased sufficiently to offset the decreased rate support grant. During this period, rate income declined in real terms by 14 per cent in Labourville and 21 per cent in Torytown.

At the same time, total gross expenditure was maintained in both districts through increased income from fees and charges and specific grants. This confirms Greenwood's findings that many local authorities maintained gross expenditure during this period by increasing charges (Greenwood 1981). Gross expenditure in 1978/9 was higher by 1.2 per cent in Torytown and fully 7.5 per cent in Labourville. There is partial evidence to suggest that both fees/charges and specific grants rose considerably over this period. Income from these two sources rose by 8.4 per cent in Labourville and 6.1 per cent in Torytown.

The overall level of net spending cuts for the era of Labour central government was thus significantly greater in Torytown than in Labourville. It is important to stress, however, that in real terms total gross expenditure was not reduced. Overall there were no real spending cuts other than during 1977/8 in Torytown. The maintenance of gross expenditure was markedly greater in Labourville than in Torytown.

Overall response to Conservative central government's cuts, 1978/9–1982/3

For the period of Conservative central government, both net and gross expenditure in Labourville were lower in real terms by 1982/3 than they were in 1978/9 (see Table 5.3). However, over the same period, Torytown's gross expenditure remained less than the 1978/9 figure until a recovery in 1982/3. The impact of Conservative-led spending cuts was more rapid in Torytown, where immediate real cutbacks occurred in 1979/80. By contrast, in Labourville both net and gross expenditure were maintained until 1981/2, when net expenditure decreased in real terms as central government control over local government was tightened; gross expenditure was cut only in 1982/3.

The decreased level of Labourville net expenditure by 1982/3 indicates that the district had not raised the local rates enough to compensate for reduced rate support grant. Of the ten districts in Greater Manchester County (GMC), Torytown rates had increased least since local government reorganization. The percentage increase (measured in cash terms) in rate levied between 1974/5 and 1982/3 was only 44 per cent for Torytown compared with 102 per cent for Labourville. Indeed, Labourville's much larger increase was itself the third lowest in GMC.

Torytown initially experienced real cuts in gross expenditure during this second period, whilst Labourville's gross expenditure continued to increase until 1982/3. This was achieved by a sharp increase during 1981/2 in income from fees and charges and specific grants. Total gross expenditure in 1981/2 was higher by 4.4 per cent in Labourville, compared with 0.2 per cent lower in Torytown. Substantial real cuts took place in Torytown over the first three years of Conservative central government. Labourville's overall cuts began to bite in 1982/3.

Selective cuts in major programmes

One of the spending cuts strategies which authorities may adopt is selectivity in social consumption spending. Evidence for selective cuts in services is provided by changes in spending on the three major local authority services: education, social services and housing. Details for the two periods of cuts are displayed in Tables 5.2 and 5.3 respectively.

For the period of Labour central government, net expenditure on education declined consistently in both districts to a level almost 9 per cent lower in 1978/9 than in 1975/6. The fall in gross education expenditure was less pronounced, indicating a rise in non-rates/RSG income. Specific education grants did in fact increase significantly over this period. In Labourville, gross expenditure recovered during 1978/9 such that the 1975/6 education spending level was attained. In Torytown, however, there was a real cut of 2.4 per cent in gross education expenditure compared with 1975/6.

Personal social services and housing reveal contrasting patterns in the two districts. Both net and gross social services expenditure fell in Labourville, gross less so than net owing to increased income from non-rate/RSG sources. On the other hand, Torytown's spending on social services rose in both net and gross terms. This finding is not consistent with the earlier local authority mediation literature, but it is relevant to point out that Torytown started from a very low level of social services provision (see Table 5.3).

Changes in net expenditure on housing offer a sharp contrast between the two districts. Whilst net expenditure increased by 42.1 per cent in Labourville, Torytown experienced a 36.5 per cent decrease in 1978/9 compared with 1975/6. The correlation between Labour control and housing expenditure in previous research is echoed here. Despite the huge net decrease, gross housing expenditure was maintained in Torytown, owing largely to a high rents policy and also a low level of housing provision to begin with (discussed later). By contrast, Lavourville's increase in gross expenditure was considerably less than the increase in net expenditure, owing to a low rents policy.

Both districts experienced reductions in net and gross education expenditure between 1978/9 and 1982/3 (Table 5.3). The level of real cuts in education was substantially greater in Torytown: gross expenditure declined by 14.3 per cent, as opposed to only 3.9 per cent in Labourville.

The contrast in social services policy was reversed compared with the first period of cuts. Both net and gross social services expenditure were maintained in Labourville, whilst decreasing in Torytown until a recovery in 1982/3. Net expenditure on housing fell in both districts, although in Labourville this occurred only in 1981/2. Labourville's gross housing expenditure was actually 6.5 per cent higher in 1982/3 than in 1978/9, whereas in Torytown there was a slight recovery to + 0.1 per cent after cuts up until 1981/2.

There is a clear difference between the two districts with respect to education, social services and housing for the second period of cuts under the Conservative administration. Torytown cut all three services in real terms during the early years of Thatcherism, whilst in Labourville only education experienced a reduction in gross expenditure. Even for education, the degree of cutback was four times greater in Torytown than in Labourville. The second period of spending cuts therefore corroborates previous research findings of a relationship between Conservative control and less expenditure on education, social services and housing.

Other expenditure and revenue strategies
Within expenditure programmes on particular services a possible option for reducing spending is to decrease the level of subsidization. The most controversial example has revolved around the legal battles over passenger transport subsidies. However, as revenue support for public transport in Greater Manchester was the responsibility of GMC and not the metropolitan districts, Labourville and Torytown cannot be differentiated on this item.

On the other hand, it is instructive to compare their respective policies on housing subsidies. Torytown markedly and consistently reduced its rate fund contribution (RFC) to the Housing Revenue Account (HRA), which in effect had to rely increasingly on income from rents. In 1975/6, 8.4 per cent of Torytown's total

HRA expenditure was accounted for by the RFC, but by 1981/2 the RFC had declined to a mere 2.4 per cent of total expenditure. On the other hand, Labourville maintained a consistently higher level of subsidy to the HRA – 17 per cent in 1975/6 and 16 per cent in 1981/2.

The strategy of reducing the number of local authority employees was pursued vigorously by Torytown: the total workforce was cut by 17 per cent between March 1975 and March 1982. Over the same period, Labourville actually increased its total workforce by 1 per cent. There was a particularly sharp reduction in Torytown's education staff. The number of teachers/lecturers declined by 25 per cent between 1975 and 1982 (Labourville, + 10 per cent) and other education staff fell by 22 per cent (Labourville, – 2 per cent). Whilst Labourville ranked second of the ten GMC districts with 34.32 full-time employees per 1,000 population, Torytown was tenth, having only 22.73

There were several specific examples of increased charges for services in both districts. The contributions of council house rents to total HRA expenditure rose substantially between 1980/1 and 1981/2 – in Labourville from 37 per cent to 53 per cent and in Torytown from 63 per cent to 76 per cent. The cost of home helps per hour rose in real terms between 1974/5 and 1978/9 by 9 per cent in Torytown and 4 per cent in Labourville.

Furthermore, the level of charges was consistently higher in Torytown for major chargeable items. In April 1981 Torytown had the fourth highest (out of nine GMC districts; missing data for the tenth) average weekly net unrebated rent for council housing, whilst Labourville was ranked eighth. This differential has been consistently evident since local government reorganization. Similarly, the two districts can be contrasted on the charge per resident week for elderly persons' homes. In 1975/6 Torytown's charges were the highest in GMC (out of nine districts with available data), whereas, in sharp contrast, Labourville's were the lowest. This pattern was virtually unchanged in 1980/1, with Torytown ranked second and Labourville tenth.

The most striking contrast in policy between Torytown and Labourville was over privatization. We suggest in Chapter 7 that it is its commitment to privatization which most distinguishes the Conservative administration from its Labour predecessor at the national level. In the field of local authority services, council house sales represented the most common form of privatization thus far and over which there had been numerous political struggles.

In February 1982, Torytown completed its one thousandth

council house sale since 1976. By contrast, Labourville had sold only 217 by April 1982 and in June 1982 the authority was criticized by the Environment Secretary for the slow pace of council house sales. The level of council house provision was much smaller in Torytown. In April 1982 Torytown possessed slightly fewer than 15,000 dwellings (ninth in GMC) as opposed to just over 45,000 in Labourville, which ranked second in GMC. In effect, Torytown was indulging in more rapid privatization of a smaller public housing base.

Torytown also exhibited a relatively stronger commitment to private education. The authority had the highest number of pupils at non-LEA schools in GMC. The total of 1,867 such pupils was more than six times larger than the second highest authority with 291. Not surprisingly, Labourville ranked tenth, with 24 non-LEA pupils.

Nursery education provides further evidence of this contrast in education policy. Torytown had by far the lowest percentage (16 per cent) of 3–4 year olds in state nursery education in GMC, whereas Labourville was ranked second on this indicator with 71 per cent.

Lastly, there is clear evidence of privatization of the school meals service in Torytown. Between 1978/9 and 1980/1 the proportion of pupils receiving meals fell from 71 per cent to 28 per cent. Over the same period, the proportion receiving meals in Labourville dropped by 6 per cent to 60 per cent.

The two districts thus differed widely in their adoption of the various spending cuts strategies. Torytown particularly was more inclined to decrease subsidies, reduce workforces and privatize services. The level of major charges also remained consistently higher in Torytown. And, lastly, in the second period of Conservative-induced cuts, all three major local authority services faced real cuts in Torytown.

Level of service provision per head

Not only did Torytown adopt the cuts mandate more vigorously, but it did so despite a lower level of public service provision to begin with. Evidence for this is available from CIPFA indicators of local authority service provision. There were marked differences in expenditure per head in total and on the three major services, as Table 5.4 shows.

Labourville's total net expenditure per head was higher in 1975/6 prior to the first round of cuts. Since then the differential has widened significantly. Similar patterns are evident for social

Table 5.4 Total local authority expenditure and spending on major programmes per head, 1975/6, 1978/9, 1982/3

Expenditure	1975/6 £	GMC ranking	1978/9 £	GMC ranking	1982/3 £	GMC ranking
Total net rate/grant-borne expenditure per head:						
Labourville	183.28	4	243.16	3	416.66	3
Torytown	180.52	6	207.57	8	334.54	9
Net education expenditure per head:						
Labourville	80.00	7	130.58	5	204.28	4
Torytown	88.08	3	123.47	7	161.39	10
Net social services expenditure per head:						
Labourville	16.85	3	26.31	2	51.05	3
Torytown	13.02	8	19.19	9	33.69	10
RFC contribution to HRA per head:						
Labourville	31.05	2	22.51	2	31.50	2
Torytown	6.01	10	2.48	8	0.55	8

Source: Finance and General Statistics, CIPFA

services expenditure and housing subsidies. For both of these Labourville was always ranked second or third in GMC, in sharp contrast to Torytown's ranking of between eighth and tenth. Only for education was net expenditure per head higher in Torytown in 1975/6, but by 1982/3 the level of service provision was much higher in Labourville.

It is relevant to state here that there are no significant variations in the age distributions of the two districts. An examination of net expenditure on education per pupil confirms the higher level of provision in Labourville. Net spending per pupil in Labourville was 26 per cent higher for nursery schools, 7 per cent higher for primary schools and 11 per cent higher for secondary schools.

It might be the case that low levels of provision reflect low resource levels. However, the consistently low ranking of Torytown service provision was inversely related to the average rateable value of the district, which was the highest in GMC. Labourville had the fourth highest actual rateable value per head.

Torytown council's own ideological justification for its policies was in terms of the priority of low-cost/value-for-money service for ratepayers rather than the actual level of service provision. This view was amplified in the local authority newsheet (the *Torytown Times*) and in press statements by Torytown councillors (*Torytown Echo* and *Manchester Evening News*).

Labourville's response is illustrated by the foreword to the 1982/3 budget estimates. It was stated that the central government determined target for 1982/3 could not be achieved without 'a seriously detrimental effect on the services provided'. As a result, Labourville had budgeted to exceed the target by £2.5 million, which would result in a grant penalty for 'overspending'.

Thus we can conclude that local political control is clearly a key factor in the explanation of the contrast between Torytown and Labourville with reference both to their relative level of service provision and to their differing responses to central government policies to reduce local authority expenditure.

Local press coverage of spending cuts

In order to assess the contrasting ethos of the two districts, we turn to our third source of data, that of coverage of the cuts by the local and regional newspapers. However, prior to presenting the data it is important to recognize that for a variety of reasons the local press typically provides an incomplete and uncritical coverage of local politics (Cox and Morgan 1973; Murphy 1976). For example, among the many external constraints on the local press are its dependence on local authorities for information and the need to report events quickly. Thus the local papers can be assumed to act as barometers or perhaps amplifiers of dominant opinion and provide a valid but not comprehensive index of official local authority policy.

We have examined differences in press coverage of Torytown and Labourville districts in both the local and regional press and have considered two specific hypotheses. The first hypothesis was that coverage in Torytown would be predominantly pro-cuts, whereas coverage in Labourville would be predominantly anti-cuts. Second, we surmised that the objective and subjective prominence of education cuts, demonstrated both above and in Chapter 6, would be reflected in the press data.

For both the *Labourville Bugle* and the *Torytown Echo*, all reports concerning spending on particular services were monitored initially for a 12-month period, commencing immediately before the interview survey. Table 5.5 reveals a higher scale of public spending coverage overall in the *Labourville Bugle*. Health and

Table 5.5 Number of items on particular services/issues in the local press, September 1980 to August 1981

Service	Labourville Bugle	Torytown Echo
Housing	34	16
Health	25	8
Local authority spending in general	15	8
Social services	14	4
Transport	6	8
All services except education	94	44
Education	22	39
All services	116	83

social service items were three times more frequent, and items on local authority spending in general and housing were twice as numerous compared with the *Torytown Echo*. The major exception was education, for which the *Echo* had roughly double the number of items compared with the *Bugle*. The second hypothesis is strongly supported by the Torytown data, with education accounting for almost half the items in the *Echo*. A subsequent analysis over a three-year period from April 1979 to March 1982 restricted to the *Echo*, revealed that 38 per cent of all reported protest items concerned education, in contrast to less than 10 per cent for any other single service/issue.

The different character of local press coverage in the two districts is amply confirmed. For instance, on local authority spending in general the Torytown paper cited a 'Mr Heseltine (the Secretary of State for the Environment)'; in the Labourville paper he was referred to less deferentially as 'the axeman'. The contrast in tone is unmistakable:

Echo	5 March 1981	'Wonderful news of Torytown poking into the black'
Bugle	2 January 1981	'MP calls for axeman to resign'
Bugle	12 June 1981	'Axeman's town hall battle'

A total of 15 out of the 39 education items in the *Echo* were concerned with school closures. By contrast, only 2 of the 22 education reports in the *Bugle* involved closures. Furthermore, whilst housing items in the *Echo* proclaimed the benefits and success of the council house sales scheme and reduced housing expenditure, the *Bugle* emphasized the council's resistance to both council house sales and housing cuts in general:

Echo	23 October 1980	'Council house sales nearly 1,000'
Echo	16 July 1981	'6,000 on waiting list'
Bugle	24 October 1980	'Housing chief warns buy own house and cripple Labourville'
Bugle	4 December 1980	'Housing chief steps up war on building cutbacks'

Regional press coverage of spending cuts

Table 5.6 summarizes material relevant to the spending cuts in the regional paper, the *Manchester Evening News (MEN)*, which was taken by 49 per cent of our panel sample. The news items were classified according to service (e.g. education, local authority spending in general, etc.) and area (e.g. Labourville, Torytown, North-West region or national).

Almost identical differences in both the overall pattern and contrasting tone emerged in the *MEN* as in the two local papers.

Table 5.6 Number of items on particular services/issues in the *Manchester Evening News*, September 1980 to June 1981

Service	Labourville	Torytown	North-West	National	Overall total
Housing	7	2	62	8	79
Health	0	1	27	9	37
Local authority spending in general	8	2	76	14	100
Social services	3	1	12	3	19
Transport	1	1	50	9	61
All services except education	19	7	227	43	296
Education	8	9	101	7	125
All services	27	16	328	50	421

Labourville had almost treble the number of non-education items as Torytown, with noticeably greater coverage of housing and local authority spending in general. The only service for which Torytown exceeded Labourville was yet again education. Education emerged distinctly as the service with the most reports for Labourville, Torytown and the North-West region. This evidence corroborates our second hypothesis, but more striking still is the predominance of education items for Torytown. Education accounted for over half of all reports on Torytown but less then a third of all reports on Labourville.

The low prominence given to social services cuts at all four area levels is also of importance. This finding is consistent with the distinct lack of knowledge of social services cuts expressed by survey respondents in both wards. The limited and negative coverage of welfare issues in the national media has been highlighted by Golding and Middleton (1982). In a more recent three-year analysis of the *Echo*, the social services category was distinctive in that a relatively high proportion of reported protests against spending cuts came from local state officials. Arguably this reflects the fact that those who are most affected by the cuts are least able to express their views. This may also be interpreted as evidence of professional radicalism (Offe 1975; Habermas 1976).

Once again there were differences in the nature as well as the extent of coverage for the two districts in the *MEN*. For Labourville, 5 out of the 8 education items concerned council opposition to government-imposed spending cuts:

19 March 1981	'Anguish at £2m school cuts'
18 June 1981	'Labourville fights teaching cuts'

By contrast, 8 out of 9 Torytown education items involved the effects of council spending cuts:

11 November 1980	'Cash caning for Torytown pupils' (Torytown bottom of spending league)
6 December 1980	'Only 4 old folk for nightschool' (previously 400)
13 February 1981	'School meals face the chop'
16 June 1981	'Schools will close despite protests'

Similarly with respect to housing, the only 2 items on Torytown were pro-council house sales:

9 October 1980   '50 per cent off home sales boom'
11 February 1981   'New home boost by councillors'

In the case of Labourville, no reports were pro-council house sales, but 4 out of 7 were anti-housing cuts/council house sales:

24 October 1980   'New homes ban protest'
                      (Labourville refuse to cut housing)
22 January 1981   'Storm over sales of homes claim'
                      (council house sales blocked)

Thus, the local and regional press data provide substantial support for both our hypotheses. Nonetheless, although presentation of Torytown's pro-cuts policy predominated in both local and regional press, reporting of action against the cuts accounted for 3 out of 9 items in the *MEN* and 7 out of 39 reports in the *Echo*. This would seem to indicate that, where active resistance is strong, the inherently partisan nature of the regional and local press can be broken.

The greater frequency of items on Labourville in both local and regional press as compared with Torytown may be a partial explanation of the higher levels of subjective knowledge of cuts exhibited in the survey (see Chapter 6). The explanation for both press and survey findings would seem to lie in the differing rhetoric and ethos of the two councils, the two local papers and implicitly the two local districts. The local press, on the whole, projected the local council view and this partial and selective reporting even extended to the regional press. Local councils were thus involved in a great deal of political impression management whereby, with the conscious or unconscious complicity of the local press, they attempted to shape rather than accommodate the views of the electorate.

However, there is evidence from research elsewhere that not all Labour authorities enjoy the support of their local press with regard to the spending cuts policy. Bristow's study of the 1980 local elections in Wolverhampton found that the local press did not adopt the Labour council's line of no cuts and higher rates (Bristow 1982).

Torytown extolled the efficiency and value-for-money of its services, whilst ignoring the extent of provision. On the other hand, Labourville vehemently denounced the spending cuts policy whilst continuing to make some cuts. Both Labourville and Torytown may be classified as fully partisan councils (Dunleavy 1980a). The only difference between them was which party was in control. The data presented here indicate similar information flow processes in both districts but the content of the information was highly dissimilar.

5   Conclusions

Our comparison of two districts in Greater Manchester has demonstrated that local political control was crucial during the first Thatcher government in determining the extent to which local government was an instrument of central control or an obstacle to it (Miliband 1969). The importance of local political control has been established with respect to both spending cuts strategies and pre-existing levels of service provision. The findings of the earlier literature on local authority mediation, although written during the period of public expenditure growth, retain validity in the current era of spending cuts and restructuring. The party effect was most salient when total expenditure was disaggregated into individual services or sub-services, most noticeably in the case of housing.

An additional facet of central–local relations to emerge from the case study is the pivotal significance of political control at both local and national levels. The reactions of a local authority to a central government call for spending cuts will vary according to the extent to which political control and policies are congruent at the two levels (see Figure 5.3). The Thatcherite ideal is what Butcher et al. (1990) call the contracting local authority. It is within this context that the local political dimension exerts an influence over the character of social consumption/investment policies. At the same time, it reflects the balance of local pressures for a particular pattern of public expenditure and revenue strategies.

		Central government	
		Conservative	Labour
Local authority	Conservative	Relative harmony	Relative friction
	Labour	Relative friction	Relative harmony

Figure 5.3   Central–local relations and the interplay of party at local and national level

The heuristic value of Saunders' ideal-type model to the local political process is readily apparent. There is ample evidence of the localization of conflict over social consumption policies, particularly in the case of the education cuts, which exhibited a high degree of visibility. The tension between economic and social priorities can be seen as an important element in the deterioration of central–local relations. The other half of Saunders' model – the degree to which social investment policies are resolved at the central/regional level by a corporatist mode of interest mediation – was not tested in this research.

Saunders contended that non-capitalist interests can win at the local level, which highlights both the existence of local autonomy and the importance of political control. There are indeed sharp variations between authorities in their degree of commitment to social consumption. The different patterns of retrenchment in Labourville and Torytown were expressed at the political/ideological level by a clear contrast between the pro-cuts and anti-cuts rhetoric of the two districts. Whereas Labourville was ideologically committed to the welfare state, Torytown could be regarded as ripe for privatization.

The contrasting political control, the variations in spending cuts strategies and the highly dissimilar content of the information flow processes may also be interpreted in terms of the mix of dominant and radical values in the two districts (Parkin 1971). Thus the local press seemed passively to accept local authority impression management and public relations information. It is significant that identical patterns were also evident in the regional press. Elcock (1986) has confirmed the importance of local political cultures. Urry (1981) has stressed the increased diversification of local class structures and also the growing importance of political struggles centred around the locality. Further research is required into the local balance of class forces.

In the period under study (1975–83) there existed considerable local autonomy in the mediation of central government requests for spending cuts. Recent legislation has been seen by many as shifting the balance of influence towards central government. However, the situation is far from clear-cut: Conservative government policy has combined elements of increased central control (e.g. total expenditure and subsidies) with measures designed to increase local autonomy (e.g. privatization and charges).

Nonetheless, the new community charge framework (as of June 1990) moves local authorities closer to a position of merely delivering the level of service central government wants at a given level of expenditure. Local authorities are increasingly prevented from operating policies they want to and forced to operate policies they do not want to (Duncan and Goodwin 1988). The rhetoric meanwhile is of increased freedom of choice for the consumer and rolling back the state. In practice, Thatcherism has proved highly interventionist in local affairs and consequently has undermined local democracy (Stallworthy 1989).

By using Saunders' model, it is possible to identify a fundamental contradiction in the Conservative central government policy towards the local state. The escalating (on balance) degree of central control is eroding the specificity of the local state function by attempting to limit even an authority's power to influence social consumption. Yet it has been argued that it is the very separation of social investment policies from the need for legitimation that is advantageous for monopoly capital (Jessop 1978). Thus erosion of social consumption threatens the legitimacy of the political system, which in turn threatens social investment.

The single most important theoretical contribution of Saunders' dual-state model is in relation to the problematic of the relative autonomy of the state. The relative autonomy of the state as a whole is resolved with reference to the existence of different processes (corporatist/competitive) involving different functions (social investment/consumption) at different levels of government (central/local). Whereas current Conservative government policy can be seen in general terms to be cutting social consumption at the local level whilst increasing social investment (and social expenses), problems remain in the more specific operationalization of the three dichotomies in the model.

The Saunders' model has been criticized for inherently playing down the class nature of the local state. Each consumption issue is seen as involving a different social base, which cannot be defined in class terms. Thus Saunders stresses the necessary non-correspondence between class struggles and sectoral struggles. However, local conflicts cannot be fully understood without reference to the wider capitalist state.

The class nature of the restructuring of the welfare state was in fact stressed by Gough in his prescient contribution. His analysis and our study both show that what is taking place is a rolling back of the welfare state rather than a rolling back of the state per se. Gough's interpretation of restructuring as an attempt to alter the balance of class forces is vindicated by the attack on trade union power by both government legislation and economic recession. Duncan and Goodwin (1982), too, have stressed that the restructuring of central–local relations and that of capitalist social relations are part of the same process. In addition to trade union regulation, they cite the policy proposal of returning women to the home.

Lastly, this case study identifies the problems as well as the benefits of operating with a neat dualistic model of the local political system. Above all, we would wish to stress the key variable of local political control in influencing the extent to which a local authority gives priority to social consumption and need rather than to social investment and profit.

CHAPTER 6

The Social Impact of Thatcherism

1 Introduction

A further aspect of our case study research design involved an attempt to measure the social impact of government policy in our two districts in Greater Manchester. In this exercise we wanted to go beyond the usual presentation of official statistics on changes in government/local authority spending (see Chapter 5). As part of the panel survey, respondents were asked directly whether (and in what way) their family or household had been affected by government policy. These data constitute a measure of the *perceived* impact of government policy. When combined with the objective official indicators, a more complete picture of the social impact of Thatcherism is revealed.

It is important to bear in mind the historical context of the two panel interviews when the social impact data were obtained (see Chapter 1). At the time of the first interview in 1980–1, spending cuts dominated the local political agenda. By the second interview in 1983–4, unemployment had become the dominant issue, locally and nationally. Furthermore, privatization was growing constantly in importance during the period of research (see Chapter 7).

2 Inequality and Government Policy

One of the major tasks of social policy analysis is to 'evaluate the distributional impact of existing policies' (Walker 1981: 225). According to this view, therefore, inequality is the central issue raised by the expansion of social expenditure that the term welfare state summarizes. Although the basic structure of inequality in Britain has not been altered by the development of the welfare state (Wedderburn 1974; Westergaard and Resler 1975; Townsend 1979), it is within this context that we will be considering the social impact of the cuts in public spending between 1980/1 and 1983/4.

Historically the distributional impact of the development of the welfare state has been analysed in terms of class, often in combination with need arising from the patterning of dependence over the family life cycle (Rowntree 1901). Of these two dimensions, class inequality is by far the most dominant theme in the literature (Tawney 1952; Titmuss 1962; Le Grand 1982; George and Wilding 1984). Arguably, this dominance reflects its explanatory significance and the extent of its documentation in official statistics and social policy research. In this tradition, changes in welfare state services and benefits are usually examined with reference to occupational and/or income classes.

Recent analysis of the winners and losers during the period of restructuring public expenditure has concluded that Conservative spending patterns tend to favour the middle class (Le Grand and Winter 1986). Similarly, taxation policy has favoured those on above-average earnings. Hogwood (1989) has stressed the important distributional effects of tax expenditures that involve tax reliefs or exemptions. Thus mortgage tax relief for owner-occupiers rose sharply in real terms during the mid 1980s, while subsidization of council house rents fell substantially.

Unemployment has become a major force for inequality and is closely related to social class (Wicks 1987). More recent research has been conducted on the impact of unemployment than on any other aspect of government policy. For instance, unemployment has been considered in relation to health (Whiteside 1988), early retirement (Laczko *et al.* 1988) and local polarization (Morris 1987) in Britain; as well as being studied in other countries (e.g. Rowley and Feather 1987, in Australia).

The recognition that need varies over the life cycle is a minor though persistent theme in the study of social policy outcomes (Titmuss 1958; Whiteley 1981; Taylor-Gooby 1983). Prior to the large increase in unemployment at the beginning of the 1980s, the elderly constituted the largest group in poverty. Furthermore, class inequalities among pensioners widened during the 1980s (Taylor-Gooby 1988).

The gender dimension of the welfare state has belatedly attracted more attention, despite the limitations of available data (Wilson, 1977; Rose 1981). Our own earlier work concluded that the initial period of spending cuts hit women first and foremost (Edgell and Duke 1983). The restructuring of the welfare state affects women more than men in three ways: first, as producers – three-quarters

118

of welfare state workers are women; second, as consumers – women are the main users of collective social provision, e.g. women are significantly more dependent on public transport; and, third, as the major providers of care in the family – the less the welfare state does, the more is done by women.

Whereas there is considerable agreement regarding the social policy significance of class, life-cycle and gender inequalities, there is some controversy concerning the exact relationship between political–geographic areas and the patterning of social expenditure. Until quite recently this debate had, of necessity, been conducted solely in the context of the expansion of welfare state spending, rather than in the context of retrenchment (see Chapter 5).

The racial and ethnic dimension of inequality and the welfare state has become a major social research specialism of great political importance in Britain, with particular emphasis on education and housing (Rex and Moore 1967; Rex and Tomlinson 1979; Husband 1982; Cashmore 1989). Divided Britain is an increasingly prominent research theme under Thatcherism and includes also the spatial dimension of inequality typically conceptualized in terms of north–south regional differences (Smith 1989).

Lastly, it has been suggested that the distributive consequences of changes in public spending are best understood by a sectoral cleavage model (Cawson and Saunders 1983; Duke and Edgell 1984; Dunleavy, 1980a, b and c; Saunders 1981). Sectoral cleavages refer to divisions between those who are dependent upon the public or private sector for their employment (i.e. as producers) or for certain services (i.e. as consumers). Production and consumption sectoral cleavages cut across class divisions and are thought to have become increasingly important in recent years in relation to both social inequality and political alignment (see Chapters 2 and 3).

Our surveys on the social and political effects of the public expenditure cuts were designed to cover each of these seven possible sources of inequality in welfare state services (class, life-cycle stage, gender, political area, race/ethnicity, region and sector), except race/ethnicity and region. Race/ethnicity was excluded to avoid the possibility of 'contaminating' the class data (Edgell and Duke 1981, 1985) and region was an inappropriate dimension given our Greater Manchester research design. Gender has been considered separately in its own right (Edgell and Duke 1983) and political area is examined at length in Chapter 5. The main focus of the analysis in this chapter is to assess the relative merit and demerit of class, stage in the life cycle and sectoral dimensions of the perceived impact of the cuts in public spending between 1980–1 and 1983–4. The impact of privatization policy is treated separately in Chapter 7.

Prior to examining the perceived impact of the cuts it is necessary to establish the validity of our data. This will be done by presenting evidence of the levels of knowledge of changes in public spending displayed by our sample.

3 Knowledge and Perceptions of Spending Trends

At the time of the first interview in 1980–1, 96 per cent of the respondents had heard of the cuts in public spending. Of that 96 per cent, only 7 per cent failed to give a satisfactory explanation as to what they understood by the spending cuts. Subsequent questioning of the apparently ignorant 11 per cent (4 per cent 'not heard' and 7 per cent 'unsatisfactory') about cuts in specific services left a residue of 4 per cent of the sample who did not display any knowledge of the spending cuts during the first interview. This residue comprised only 2 per cent of the panel sample (owing to the disproportionate loss of the less knowledgeable old and frail) and of these only a quarter (0.5 per cent of the panel sample) expressed no knowledge at the second interview in 1983–4. These high levels of knowledge suggest that the vast majority of our respondents were aware of public spending cuts at both stages of the research.

The extent of respondents' more detailed knowledge of changes in public spending was investigated in both surveys with reference to four services: education, health, transport and social services. This was achieved using an open-ended question on each of the four services. The answers were categorized into those with no knowledge of cuts, those with general knowledge only (i.e. there have been cuts but cannot give any specific details) and those with specific knowledge of the cuts in the service. Examples of the most frequent specific-knowledge items mentioned are provided in Table 6.1.

At the first interview, the panel overall exhibited most knowledge on cuts in education (over two-thirds with specific knowledge), though more emphatically in Torytown. The first stage followed a prolonged teachers' strike and dispute over school closures in Torytown, which accounts for education's relative prominence there. Of the other services, there were majorities with specific knowledge on transport and health, but a distinct lack of knowledge of any cuts emerged for the personal social services. Indeed, there was evidence of considerable confusion among a minority of the sample as to what constituted these services.

Labourville displayed significantly greater knowledge on health and transport cuts than Torytown in 1980–1. These differences

Table 6.1   Specific knowledge of spending cuts in education, health, transport and social services by area

Service	Labourville (n = 334)			Torytown (n = 351)		
	GMS1	GMS2	Change	GMS1	GMS2	Change
Education:						
% specific knowledge	67	50	– 17	70	52	– 18
Most frequent mentions at GMS2	fewer staff school closures universities		72 36 35	fewer staff school closures school books		91 69 47
Health:						
% specific knowledge	61	66	+ 5	46	50	+ 4
Most frequent mentions at GMS2	fewer staff privatisation hospital closure		122 74 52	fewer staff hospital facilities waiting lists		94 41 30
Transport:						
% specific knowledge	68	49	– 19	59	32	– 27
Most frequent mentions at GMS2	fewer services increased fares fewer staff		100 65 34	fewer services increased fares fewer staff		78 40 15
Social services:						
% specific knowledge	31	26	– 5	27	29	+ 2
Most frequent mentions at GMS2	home helps elderly facilities meals on wheels		23 18 15	home helps fewer staff fewer visits		59 23 22

Sources: GMS1 and GMS2 panels.

were maintained at the second interview and possible explanations for this will be taken up later after considering the impact data.

In both areas the proportion of respondents with no knowledge whatsoever declined in all four services at the second stage, the decline being quite substantial in the case of health and social services. Other changes over time were consistent in the two areas. Health was the only service whose level of specific knowledge increased in both areas, in fact taking over from education as the service with the most knowledge overall in Labourville. Specific knowledge of cuts in education and transport decreased significantly for both areas at the second interview. These figures are explicable in terms of particular events prior to the first interview, such as disputes over education cuts in 1980–1 and a reduction in bus services and an increase in bus fares by Greater Manchester Transport during 1980. Personal social services remained the lowest on specific knowledge, though increasing slightly in Torytown.

At the second interview stage, questions on four additional services were included: defence, police, housing and social security. Thus, in all, questions about changes in the patterning of public spending were directed at eight services. In 1983–4, not only the level of knowledge on each service was ascertained but also respondents' perceptions as to whether spending on the service had been cut, had stayed the same or had increased.

Table 6.2 shows that Labourville respondents were generally more knowledgeable than Torytown respondents on six of the services in terms of the ability to mention specific service items. Moreover, the percentage of respondents in Torytown who revealed no knowledge of specific services was higher for all the eight services investigated. Of the four additional services, none matched the high levels of specific knowledge for health and education. Housing, welfare benefits and defence were on a par with transport, at just over 40 per cent specific knowledge, whilst the police evoked low specific knowledge at around 30 per cent, equivalent to the personal social services. The only significant difference between the two areas on these four services was the higher level of knowledge on welfare benefits in Labourville. This point will be taken up again later.

Respondents' perceptions of the direction of spending changes reveal some interesting patterns and a large degree of consensus. An overwhelming majority (in excess of 80 per cent) were of the view that spending on health and education had been cut. These were, of course, also the two services with high levels of specific

Table 6.2 Perception of spending trends and specific knowledge of spending cuts and proportion local specific knowledge for eight services by area

| Service | Perception of spending trends at GMS2 | | | | |
	% cut	% same	% increase	% specific knowledge	% of the specific knowledge which is explicitly local
Labourville (n = 334)					
Health	93	2	2	66	15
Education	84	8	1	50	37
Transport	66	14	2	49	80
Housing	50	14	6	44	29
Social services	47	16	3	26	27
Welfare benefits	49	14	20	47	0
Defence	19	11	57	44	1
Police	10	30	43	31	6
Torytown (n = 351)					
Health	85	2	4	50	29
Education	83	4	2	52	52
Transport	52	15	2	32	70
Housing	54	10	3	40	26
Social services	52	9	4	29	32
Welfare benefits	36	14	19	38	0
Defence	20	9	52	40	1
Police	9	21	46	29	18

Source: GMS2 cross-section.

knowledge. For three other services (transport, housing and social services) marginal majorities (50 per cent and just over) perceived a reduction in spending. Slightly less than half of the sample (42 per cent) stated that welfare benefits had been cut, but it is clearly the modal answer.

There were thus six services which our sample perceived as having been cut. In stark contrast, the remaining two services were seen as experiencing increased expenditure – by a majority in the case of defence and by just under half (46 per cent) in the case of the police. On the basis of our survey data collected from the same respondents at two points in time, we can confidently state that our

Greater Manchester sample were clearly aware of cuts in 1980–1 and had become even more so 1983–4. Given the clear patterning of relative spending perceptions, it is instructive to compare these subjective appraisals with the 'objective' statistics published by both central government and the two local authorities.

4 Official Data on Spending Trends

First, it is necessary to consider briefly the definition of a 'cut in spending'. There are basically three ways of measuring changes in public expenditure:

(a) In cash terms, which is the method favoured by the Conservative government since the Public Expenditure White Paper of 1982 on the grounds of cost! It is the least instructive for historical comparisons and recognized to be so by the Treasury and Civil Service Committee (Fifth Report 1981–2).

(b) In cost terms, controlling for the general level of inflation using the GDP deflator. This is the most commonly used definition and that employed in Table 6.3.

(c) In relative cost terms within services, which is the most difficult definition to operationalize, but it has the virtue of taking into account relative price changes and the growth of demand for particular services; for example, increasing numbers of old people. This method formed the basis of the volume figures used in the Public Expenditure White Papers prior to 1982.

A further complication arises in that the subjective appraisals may be based on differing frames of reference. Thus it is perfectly possible for a service which has been increased nationally to have been cut in the local area. For many of our respondents, local knowledge was paramount. Table 6.2 lists the proportion of specific knowledge which was explicitly local for both areas. These data should be interpreted as the minimum level of local knowledge, in that many respondents may have based their knowledge on local experience without explicitly stating a local example (which was our criterion for inclusion). The proportion of local knowledge was highest for transport and education, and was also significantly higher in Torytown than in Labourville for four of the services. Lastly, even within overall programmes which may have experienced increased spending both nationally and locally, there can be specific cuts in particular items which may be of importance to the respondent.

Despite these problems, there are clear links between the subjective perceptions in Table 6.2 and the 'objective' cuts in Tables 6.3 and 6.4. The perceptions of increased defence and police expenditure are clearly mirrored in the consistent upward trends in Table 6.3. Equally, the perceived cuts in transport and housing can be located in the official data, although the extensive 'objective' cuts in housing are not similarly outstanding in the subjective data.

The remaining four services, however, require closer examination because there is a marked disjuncture between the perceived and actual patterns. In the case of education, the discrepancy is readily explicable in terms of local cuts within the context of a slight national increase (although education spending did drop nationally between 1980/1 and 1981/2). There were real cuts in Labourville and Torytown education spending during this period and specific items were cut (see Chapter 5 and Table 6.4).

Health expenditure increased consistently in cost terms according to Table 6.3, which sharply contrasts with the 89 per cent of respondents perceiving cuts in Table 6.2. The explanation here would appear to lie in a combination of: (a) adopting a relative cost framework, which perceives volume cuts in the National Health Service (NHS); and (b) knowledge of local cuts in specific items. Both wards have large general hospitals on their boundaries and thus contain a substantial number of NHS producers (16 per cent of households had one). The disparity between Tables 6.2 and 6.3 as regards the personal social services can also be accounted for

Table 6.3   Actual central government spending trends on eight services in cost terms, 1979/80–1982/3 (1979/80 = 100: 1982/3 prices)

Service	1979/80	1980/1	1981/2	1982/3
Health	100	108.1	110.5	112.3
Education	100	102.7	101.5	102.0
Transport	100	102.8	100.0	96.4
Housing	100	83.1	53.1	42.0
Personal social services	100	104.4	104.8	107.1
Welfare benefits	100	101.7	112.8	120.1
Defence	100	102.0	104.7	112.3
Police	100	100.3	110.5	115.0

Source: HMSO 1984.

125

Table 6.4 Actual local authority spending trends on three services in cost terms,[a] 1978/9–1982/3 (1978/9 = 100: 1982/3 prices)

Service	1978/9	1979/80	1980/1	1981/2	1982/3
Labourville District Authority:					
Education	100	96.2	97.9	98.6	94.7
Personal social services	100	102.8	106.1	107.0	107.5
Housing	100	113.4	107.9	88.3	80.9
Torytown District Authority:					
Education	100	93.3	91.9	90.3	89.5
Personal social services	100	99.4	98.6	99.4	100.8
Housing	100	94.4	98.2	39.5	44.8

Note:
[a] Adjusted for inflation by the Gross Domestic Product deflator.

Source: Adapted from Torytown and Labourville treasury department figures.

by the application of a relative cost framework (particularly with regard to the increasing ranks of the elderly in need of such services) as well as by actual cuts in Torytown (see Table 6.4).

The least consensus on the direction of spending changes in Table 6.2 was over welfare benefits. This accurately reflects the reality of increased social security expenditure overall (because of rising unemployment), but at the same time the value of specific benefits had often not kept up with inflation (e.g. unemployment benefit) and some benefits had been abolished altogether (e.g. the earnings-related supplement paid for the first six months of unemployment). Clearly, respondents varied in which part of this paradox they emphasized.

5 Overall Social Impact of the Public Spending Cuts

Measuring the impact of the spending cuts is far from straightforward. For example, in objective terms it may be possible to document that hospital X has been cut and therefore argue that both NHS users of, and NHS workers in, that hospital have been affected. However, it has already been suggested that the consumers and producers of state services may perceive the situation differently. Thus our strategy was to measure the subjective impact of the cuts according to the respondents' definition of the situation.

The only subsequent study to adopt a similar approach was that of Hyde and Deacon (1986) in Plymouth.

Following on from the knowledge questions outlined above, we asked our respondents an open-ended question about whether they or anyone else in the household had been affected by the spending cuts in the preceding period. Interviewers were instructed to probe fully on this question and record all details. The answers were coded according to who in the household was affected, whether this was as a consumer or producer of services, and which service or sector was involved.

It is clear from Table 6.5 that the overall perceived impact of the cuts was quite similar in both areas and remained fairly constant over time at just over 50 per cent. Moreover, a large minority (one-third) of panel respondents in both areas considered that they had been affected by the cuts in public spending in the period prior to both interviews. In fact, only 26 per cent of the panel sample stated no impact at both interviews. The Torytown panel proclaimed a significantly higher level of multiple impacts on the household at both interviews, which squares with the picture obtained from local authority data of more substantial cuts in Torytown than in Labourville over this period (see Chapter 5 and Table 6.4).

There is considerable evidence to suggest that our subjective measure of impact is an understatement. Many respondents in both interviews responded to later questions on particular services by clearly outlining cuts which had affected them that they had not mentioned in response to the impact question. For instance, later in the second interview we obtained two indicators of understatement of education cuts impact: (a) of those households resorting to private tuition (e.g. music lessons) specifically because of local cuts, only 31 per cent had mentioned it previously under impact; (b) of those using private nursery facilities specifically because of local cuts, only 27 per cent had given this answer earlier. Interestingly, Hyde and Deacon found majorities who considered the impact of policy on them (or their family) a bad thing for health, housing and unemployment benefit.

The reported impact on panel respondents as consumers declined by 7 per cent between 1980–1 and 1983–4, in contrast to producer impact, which increased by 8 per cent. Nonetheless, quite high levels of consumer impact were reported at both interviews, especially in Torytown (44 per cent in 1980–1), which remained higher than Labourville despite the decline over time. Consumer impact remained significantly greater than producer impact in

Table 6.5 Perceived impact of spending cuts on households as consumers and producers by area

	Labourville (n = 334)			Torytown (n = 351)		
	GMS1	GMS2	Change	GMS1	GMS2	Change
General:						
% reporting any impact	55	49	− 6	55	55	0
Consumer:						
% affected as consumer	35	27	− 8	44	37	− 7
% education	16	9	− 7	24	17	− 7
% transport	6.5	0.5	− 6	5	2	− 3
% welfare benefits	4	12	+ 8	2.5	9	+ 6.5
% health	3.5	2.5	− 1	2.5	4	+ 1.5
% social services	1	0.5	− 0.5	1.5	1	− 0.5
% housing	1	2.5	+ 1.5	1	0.5	− 0.5
Producer:						
% affected as producer	23	28	+ 5	16	26	+ 10
% redundancy	7	17	+ 10	3	12	+ 9
% private sector	10	17	+ 7	5	11	+ 6
% local authority	9	6	− 3	6	6	0
% education	6	2	− 4	3	4	+ 1
% health	1.5	3	+ 1.5	2	5	+ 3
% central government	1.5	3	+ 1.5	2	2.5	+ 0.5

Sources: GMS1 and GMS2 panels.

Torytown at the second interview, whereas in Labourville the level of producer impact surpassed that of consumer impact.

Education was clearly the main consumer impact at the first interview, accounting for over half of all such impacts. The distinctiveness of the impact of education cuts in Torytown was apparent at both interviews (24 per cent and 17 per cent). The proportion mentioning consumer impact in transport decreased substantially, which matches the knowledge pattern described previously. The only consumer impact to increase significantly was welfare benefits, which trebled in both areas and indeed overtook education as the leading consumer impact in Labourville. This finding is of greater concern regarding benefits, which is directly related to increased employment, in line with the general tendency for producer impact to increase and for consumer impact to decrease over the three-year period between the two interviews. In other words, it reflects the dramatic increase in and concern over unemployment during the period of this study.

The level of reported household unemployment was almost identical in both areas at both interviews, doubling overall from 18 per cent to 36 per cent in three years. An incredible 43 per cent of the panel claimed that someone in the household had been unemployed at some time, and this in a socially mixed, not a deprived, milieu. Of those unemployed at the first interview, 65 per cent of households remained so at the second interview. Further confirmation of the steep rise in unemployment over the period of the research is indicated by the trebling of mentions of unemployment by panel respondents when questioned about the producer impact of the public spending cuts. Virtually all the increase in producer impact is accounted for by redundancy in the household. The level of redundancy impact in Labourville was significantly higher than in Torytown at both interviews.

Perceived producer impact of the cuts may be either direct in the form of public sector workers, or indirect in the form of private sector workers. Producer impact among those employed in the private sector increased by 7 per cent in Labourville and by 6 per cent in Torytown. Taken together this amounts to a doubling of reported producer impact among this sector. The level of private producer impact was significantly higher in Labourville throughout. Of the public sector producers, the only significant increase between the two interviews was the doubling of reported impacts by NHS workers. The overall level remained low however.

Having examined the changing profile of perceived impact, with a marked shift towards producer impact, we turn now to an examination of the three theories of the impact of the cuts outlined in the introduction – namely, social class, stage in the life cycle, and sectoral location. As our dependent variable was perceived impact on the household, we measured all three independent variables at the level of the household. A justification for utilizing household social class and sector is presented in Chapter 2.

6 Dimensions of Inequality

Social impact and social class

The class impact of social policy is typically examined with reference to occupational class (Le Grand 1982; George and Wilding, 1984). This type of classificatory scheme tends to assume that the key distinction in the class structure is between manual and non-manual occupational classes. The alternative operationalization of social class is to adopt a neo-Marxian conceptualization that emphasizes the importance of ownership and control, or the lack of them (see Chapter 2). Table 6.6 presents cross-sectional data on impact using social class, and an interesting class pattern emerges.

Most revealing is the distinctiveness of the employers, who reported a considerably greater decline in impact over the period of the study. At the time of the first interview, this social class was the most affected, largely owing to a higher level of perceived producer impact (i.e. own business affected); at the second interview stage three years later, they were the least affected in terms of

Table 6.6 Perceived impact of spending cuts on households by household social class

Social class	GMS1	GMS2	Change
% reporting any impact:			
Employer	62	43	− 19
Petty bourgeois	54	44	− 10
Controller	53	53	0
Worker	53	54	+ 1
% affected as consumer:			
Employer	40	32	− 8
Petty bourgeois	43	29	− 14
Controller	37	32	− 5
Worker	41	34	− 7
% affected as producer:			
Employer	27	18	− 9
Petty bourgeois	13	21	+ 8
Controller	22	31	+ 9
Worker	17	26	+ 9

Sources: GMS1 and GMS2 cross-sections.

overall perceived impact. In 1980–1 the other three social classes were identical in perceived overall impact.

By 1983–4, however, a distinct pattern consistent with the class interpretation of the public expenditure cuts had emerged for overall impact: the employer and petty bourgeois classes were less affected than the controller and worker classes. Thus whereas our data at the first interview did not lend support to theorists who argue that the spending cuts are intended to alter the balance of class forces in favour of capital (e.g. Gough 1979, Hall 1983), the data at the second interview most certainly did.

Social impact and life-cycle stage

Four life-cycle stages were distinguished at the first and second interviews: (1) households with retired persons only, (2) households with a combination of retired persons and those in full-time employment, (3) households with non-retired adults and children, and (4) households with non-retired adults but no children.

At the first interview, the non-retired plus children group

Table 6.7 Perceived impact of spending cuts on households by life-cycle stage

Life-cycle stage	GMS1 %	GMS1 No.	GMS2 %	GMS2 No.	Change
Reporting any impact:					
Retired	38	191	46	164	+8
Retired + full-time work	52	27	57	23	+5
Non-retired + children	65	422	60	265	−5
Non-retired − children	48	308	49	233	+1
% affected as consumer:					
Retired		36		38	+2
Retired + full-time work		44		39	−5
Non-retired + children		49		38	−11
Non-retired − children		27		22	−5
% affected as producer:					
Retired		3		9	+6
Retired + full time work		7		30	+23
Non-retired + children		24		31	+7
Non-retired − children		23		35	+12

Sources: GMS1 and GMS2 cross sections.

Table 6.8 Perceived impact of spending cuts on households by life-cycle stage and household social class

	Social class											
	GMS1						GMS2					
	E/PB		C		W		E/PB		C		W	
Life-cycle stage[a]	%	No.	%	No.	%	No.	%	No.	%	No.	%	No.
Reporting any impact:												
Retired	35	17	38	76	38	94	50	16	45	69	46	79
Non-retired + children	66	61	67	161	62	197	53	51	58	107	65	107
Non-retired − children	53	38	45	130	51	136	23	30	53	98	51	105
Affected as consumer:												
Retired	35		34		37		44		36		39	
Non-retired + children	51		51		47		39		33		42	
Non-retired − children	29		20		35		3		26		23	
Affected as producer:												
Retired	0		7		1		6		12		6	
Non-retired + children	21		27		22		25		38		27	
Non-retired − children	24		25		19		20		35		40	

Notes:
[a] Retired + full-time work households have been excluded from the control table because of low numbers.
[b] E/PB = employer/petty bourgeois household
C = controller household
W = worker household
The employer and petty bourgeois categories have been merged because of low numbers.

Sources: GMS1 and GMS2 cross-section.

reported the highest level of perceived impact and this rank position was maintained over time, despite a small decline (see Table 6.7). This decline can be linked to the decline in salience of education cuts over the three years. The same explanation accounts for the drop in perceived consumer impact among this category.

The retired group reported the greatest increase in impact over the period of the study, owing partly to an increase in consumption impact (i.e. welfare benefits), but mainly to the unemployment impact (i.e. forced early retirement).

The overall pattern of impact in terms of the life cycle did not basically change over time and confirmed that the two most vulnerable life-cycle stages are the ones identified by Rowntree at the end of the last century, namely 'early middle life' before children begin to earn, and in terms of consumption in old age following retirement (1901: 169–72).

When a control for household social class is introduced, the influence of life cycle is largely confirmed (see Table 6.8). Perceived impact among the retired was remarkably stable across the three classes at both interviews. The non-retired with children consistently displayed the highest level of overall impact in all classes. There was, however, a hint of class influence within this category at the second interview in that 65 per cent of worker households with children had been affected by the cuts, compared with 58 per cent of similar controller households and 53 per cent of employer/petty bourgeois households.

Social impact and sectoral location

The government's affirmed policy of 'rolling back the state' may be expected to affect public sector producers and consumers disproportionately. The point at issue here is to what extent did they feel themselves affected by the spending cuts? The analysis by sector was divided into perceived consumer impact in different consumption locations and perceived producer impact in different producer locations.

The influence of overall consumption location on perceived consumer impact was slight at the first interview, but three years later there was a clear pattern consistent with sectoral expectations (see Table 6.9). Indeed, the only consumption location to register an increase in perceived consumer impact was that of totally public households (to fully 56 per cent). Thus public spending cuts were increasingly affecting those consumers most reliant on state services.

Perceived producer impact was significantly higher among

Table 6.9 Perceived impact of spending cuts on households by household consumption and production sectoral locations

Sectoral location	GMS1	GMS2	Change
% affected as consumer:			
Totally private	36	35	− 1
Predominantly private	39	27	− 12
Predominantly public	41	39	− 2
Totally public	42	56	+ 14
% affected as producer:[a]			
Self-employed	19	22	+ 3
Private sector	13	21	+ 8
Public sector	26	37	+ 11
Self-employed and public sector	14	13	− 1

Note:

[a] Self-employed and public sector are the two polar defining characteristics of production sectoral location. Thus if either the respondent or spouse was employed in one of these sectors, the household was so classified. (This method produced a small category of contradictory locations, i.e. self-employed *and* public sector, which is included above in the interest of completeness.) The private sector household was residual in the sense that it was private only, i.e. nobody was self-employed or public.

Sources: GMS1 and GMS2 cross-sections.

public sector households at both interviews (see Table 6.9). Moreover, the largest increase in producer impact over the three years was also in this category. Increasingly the spending cuts are affecting public sector producers rather than those working in other sectors.

In order to appraise the salience of the spending cuts to various *specific* consumer and producer locations, we also examined what proportion of each location perceived themselves affected by cuts in their service/sector (rather than by any cuts), a measure we labelled 'cuts consciousness'. By far the highest level of consumer cuts consciousness was associated with state education users. Overall at the first interview the level of cuts consciousness among state education consumers was just under half (47 per cent), largely owing to the 63 per cent of Torytown respondents who attributed changes in their educational provision to cuts in education spending. Although education consumer cuts consciousness decreased at the second interview, it was relatively high compared with all other services, with the area differential remaining as large as ever (Torytown 56 per cent and Labourville 24 per cent). Significantly, in Torytown the highest level of producer cuts consciousness at both interviews was among education producers, rising from 27 per cent to 35 per cent at the second interview. The persistent distinctiveness of education, where there was a lengthy industrial dispute during the first fieldwork stage, has been apparent since the start of this project (Edgell and Duke 1982).

When controlling for household social class, the relationship between overall consumption location and perceived consumer impact changes over time. At the first interview there was clear evidence of the sectoral effect among controller households but not among worker households (see Table 6.10). By the second stage of the research, the sectoral effect was also apparent among workers, with public consumers markedly more affected than private consumers.

Table 6.10 Perceived impact of spending cuts on households by household consumption and production sectoral locations and household social class

| | Social class[a] | | | |
| | GMS1 | | GMS2 | |
Sectoral location	C	W	C	W
% affected as consumer:				
Totally private	30	44	44	33
Predominantly private	36	40	28	26
Predominantly public	46	39	33	44
Totally public	46	44	67	50
% affected as producer[b]				
Private sector	14	13	21	22
Public sector	31	22	40	34

Notes:
[a] C = controller household
W = worker household
The employer and petty bourgeois classes were excluded from the upper half of the table (consumer impact) because of low numbers in the public sector categories, and from the lower half (producer impact) because they are, of course, in the self-employed sector.
[b] If either the respondent or spouse worked in the public sector, the household was classified as public.

Sources: GMS1 and GMS2 cross-sections.

When the relationship between production sectoral location and perceived producer impact is re-examined controlling for household social class, two significant conclusions may be drawn. First, the sectoral effect was strongly evident among both controller and worker households at both interviews. Second, within public sector households it was controllers who were more likely to feel affected at both interviews. Thus both sectoral and class effects are in evidence here.

In concluding this section it is pertinent to return to the differences in significant knowledge between the two areas with respect to health, transport and welfare benefits, and to examine, first, whether these differences are repeated in terms of perceived impact and, second, whether they may be due to significantly larger numbers of service users or producers in the area. Labourville's greater knowledge levels on health and transport were not reflected in higher perceived impact, but in the case of welfare benefits the level of perceived impact was markedly higher in Labourville.

Labourville's superior health knowledge cannot be attributed to having more state health consumers as the level of NHS usage was identical (96 per cent in both areas in 1980–1). Part of the explanation may lie, however, in a significantly larger proportion of households in Labourville containing NHS workers (19 per cent compared with 13 per cent).

On transport there is clear evidence of more frequent public transport usage in Labourville: at the second interview, 49 per cent used public transport in the previous week compared with only 29 per cent in Torytown. The explanation here is clearly one of differential consumption of state services.

The greater knowledge and perceived impact of welfare cuts in Labourville cannot be linked to either high usage or more producers in the area, so the explanation must lie elsewhere. Similarly, the greater frequency of perceived impact on redundancy and private sector producers in Labourville cannot be accounted for by differential rates of household unemployment or private sector employment. In Chapter 5 we suggested that the most likely explanation of these local differences was ideological.

7 Conclusions

The panel exhibited impressively high specific knowledge of the cuts in public expenditure at both interview stages. Given our

136

broad definition of the term 'spending cuts' (outlined in Duke and Edgell 1984) as an umbrella of interrelated strategies, we could readily incorporate respondents' own views into this framework. Relevant knowledge embraced fewer services, fewer staff, increased charges, cash limits and privatization.

Health overtook education as the specific service of greatest knowledge, although the distinctiveness of education in Torytown continued to be revealed over time. Interestingly, both these services are predominantly public in their consumption and thus used by all social classes. By contrast, those state services used mainly by workers (e.g. housing, transport and means-tested welfare benefits) were less prominent in public perceptions, notwithstanding greater cuts in some of these services.

Changes in the patterning of knowledge and perceived impact of the spending cuts were clearly linked to actual events, especially local ones, prior to the two interviews. This congruence between local events and local perceptions indicates that the mass of consumers/citizens did indeed know what was going on.

In 1980-1 the major perceived impact of the cuts in public spending was on respondents as consumers (especially education in Torytown). Corresponding to the steep rise in unemployment, at the second stage in 1983-4 there was a clear shift towards producer impact (especially unemployment in Labourville). Our panel data have shown the importance of distinguishing between perceived producer and consumer impact.

The dramatic rise in unemployment during the period of the study was clearly reflected in all the data, however they were analysed and presented. The extent to which there was a direct link between government policy and job losses was less important than the fact that many of our panel clearly perceived such a link. This confirms the famous 'Thomas Theorem': 'if men define situations as real they are real in their consequences' (Thomas 1928: 572).

There was some empirical support for the relevance of all three theories of social inequality utilized to examine the perceived impact of the public spending cuts between 1980-1 and 1983-4, thus confirming the view that social inequalities have increased under Thatcherism (Walker and Walker 1987; Wicks 1987).

(a) The class patterning of the perceived impact of the cuts became more marked over time, to the relative disadvantage of employees (controller and worker households) compared with employer and petty bourgeois households. In the case of producer impact, employers were especially distinctive, being the only social class to report a decline in this type of impact over time.

(b) At the first interview, households with children reported the greatest impact and this pattern declined slightly over time. Households with retired persons reported an increase in overall impact during the period of the study, and were the only group to report an increase in consumer impact.

(c) Both production sectoral cleavages and consumption sectoral cleavages increased in importance over time. In other words, the cuts increasingly affected public sector producers and public sector consumers.

The application of these theories of social inequality to our cross-sectional and panel data on the cuts revealed in each case interesting changes in social impact over time, changes that might not have become apparent in a non-longitudinal research design. With the relentless advance of the policy to restructure public spending, social class and sectoral location influences appeared to have grown stronger. Thus, in addition to traditional social class inequalities, Britain in the 1980s was increasingly experiencing new inequalities based on sectoral cleavages.

The perceived impact of the cuts was fragmentary, and arguably this reflects the highly selective nature of the restructuring of public spending. Thus different households were affected in different ways at different times. It may be that these two factors, the selective nature of the policy and the fragmentary experience of the cuts, together explain the lack of a successful opposition to the new right policy in Britain.

CHAPTER 7

Privatization: Progress and Prospects

1 Introduction

The increasingly important role of privatization in overall government policy has been emphasized already in Chapter 1. Privatization in its various forms can be seen as contributing to some of the Thatcher administrations' main aims: (a) reducing the role of the state and expanding the role of the market; (b) lowering (or more recently stabilizing) the level of public expenditure; (c) undermining the power of the trade unions, especially public sector trade unions; (d) increasing productivity and profitability; and (e) spreading share ownership wider.

The first hint of privatization policy was subsumed initially under the heading of nationalization in the 1979 Conservative manifesto. By contrast, the term appeared in its own right in the 1983 manifesto. Evidence of the ideological success of Thatcherism in changing the nature of politico-economic debate is provided by the switch from discussions of more/less nationalization in the 1970s to more/less privatization in the 1980s. Interestingly, there is as yet no separate heading for privatization in the *Times Index*. It appears as a sub-category under nationalization, and even the sub-category dates only from 1985.

Since 1983 this increased momentum has been more than maintained. Table 7.1 documents the proceeds from central privatization for the period 1979/80–1986/7: net receipts in cash terms increased from under £0.5 billion per year during the first Conservative administration to over £2 billion in 1984/5 and 1985/6, and to over £4 billion in 1986/7. Even in real terms it is apparent that the level of privatization during the second Conservative administration was qualitatively distinct from the first. It is noteworthy that with the 1986 Public Expenditure White Paper (HMSO 1986a) the more ordinary term 'central privatisation proceeds' replaced the previous label '*special* sales of assets'.

Table 7.1 Central privatization proceeds, 1979/80–1986/7 (£m)

	1979/80	1980/1	1981/2	1982/3	1983/4	1984/5	1985/6	1986/7
In cash terms	377	405	493	488	1,142	2,132	2,707	4,422
In real terms[a]	627	569	630	582	1,302	2,329	2,789	4,422

Note:
[a] The real figures are calculated using the GDP deflator at 1986/7 prices.

Sources: HMSO 1986b, 1987, 1988.

The figures in Table 7.1 do not cover proceeds from local authority privatization, the most notable contribution to which is from housing. Table 7.2 lists the annual and cumulative sales of public sector dwellings between 1979/80 and 1986/7. By early 1988, over 1 million public sector dwellings had been sold since 1979. Receipts from sales of local authority housing exceeded £1 million each year between 1981/2 and 1986/7 (HMSO 1987, 1988).

By the 1987 Public Expenditure White Paper the government was able to state that the 'privatization programme is moving forward strongly'. It could also claim that the number of shareholders had trebled since 1979 from 7 per cent in 1979 to 20 per cent at the beginning of 1988. Of shareholders in 1988, approximately one-third owned only shares in privatized companies (*Economic Progress Report*, No. 195, 1988).

Privatization in relation to the welfare state and local authorities has taken many forms (other than those covered in section 3 below). For instance, the Social Security Act 1986 established new incentives to use private pension schemes; the private sector share of residential places for the elderly in England and Wales increased from 29 per cent in 1979 to 43 per cent in 1984 (Biggs 1987) and to around 50 per cent in 1988 (Day 1988); some local authorities have been more eager to contract out services than others (Stoker 1988).

Table 7.2 Sales of public sector dwellings, 1979/80 – 1986/7 ('000)

	1979/80	1980/1	1981/2	1982/3	1983/4	1984/5	1985/6	1986/7
Annual sales	55.3	71.8	141.4	204.6	144.2	105.2	95.3	101.5
Cumulative sales	55.3	127.1	268.5	473.2	617.3	722.5	817.8	919.3

Source: HMSO 1987.

It has been argued that the privatization policy has been a considerable ideological success in the sense that since 1979 market values have been successfully reasserted throughout the economy (Gough 1982; Hall 1983), witness the replacement of nationalization by privatization in debates about the public/private mix. Moreover, this move to the 'right' has been emulated abroad (*Economic Progress Report*, No. 183, 1986) and has led the Labour Party to 'modernize' its traditional commitment to nationalization in particular and the market economy in general.

Riddell (1985: 182), in his review of the first Thatcher administration, suggested that 'the privatization and liberalisation programmes may turn out to be the most lasting achievement of the Thatcher administration'. Certainly it is privatization more than anything else which differentiates the Thatcher austerity policies from those of the previous labour administration (Duke and Edgell 1984). Heald and Thomas (1986) referred to privatization as the dominant political development of the decade.

More recently, McAllister and Studlar (1989) described privatization as the centrepiece of the three Thatcher governments. They argued that the privatization policy stemmed from the government rather than from popular demand, but they demonstrated small electoral gains for the Conservatives from increased share and house ownership.

Assessment of this ongoing policy is highly problematic. First, much of the literature that has developed is partisan (see Halford 1985). Second, there seems to be little agreement on the meaning of the term privatization. Prior to looking at our data on privatization, it is pertinent briefly to review the different definitions of privatization, plus the previous evidence on the extent of, and attitudes to, privatization. Following on from this, the remainder of the chapter will examine two main themes: first, the progress of and potential for privatization in four essential services (housing, transport, health and education); and, second, attitudes to both welfare state and non-welfare state privatization.

2 Scope and Definitions of Privatization

The first official government statement on privatization appeared in the *Economic Progress Report* of May 1982 (No. 145). As highlighted in Chapter 1, the six ways of opening up the public sector to market forces concentrated on withdrawal from production of industries rather than welfare services.

141

As sociologists, it is important to stress that the current government policy should be distinguished from the privatization of family life style documented in the affluent worker study in the 1960s (Goldthorpe *et al.* 1969) and reappraised more recently by Procter (1990) and Saunders (1990). We noted in Chapter 1 that the government policy should be referred to as *economic privatization* of production and consumption, in contrast to the *social privatization* of affluent workers identified by Goldthorpe. The notion that the two types of privatization are related, especially in connection with the economic privatization of housing and transport, must await further research investigations (see Flynn 1988).

Academic authors on privatization vary in adopting a broad or a narrow definition – whether to include funding and regulation of a service as well as provision, and whether to include or exclude consumption of welfare state services.

An example of a narrow definition of privatization is found in the work of Dunleavy. In his view, privatization is restricted to the 'permanent transferring of service or goods production activities previously carried out by public service bureaucracies to private firms or to other forms of non-public organisation such as voluntary groups' (Dunleavy 1986). Privatization is not therefore cutting the scope of public policy responsibility, selling equities or assets, or encouraging private sector initiatives. Many articles on privatization are concerned narrowly with its effects on a particular service or organization – for instance, Birch (1986) on health, Forrest and Murie (1986) on housing, Evans (1985) on local authorities, and Heald (1985) on nationalized industries.

A broad view of privatization as 'strengthening the market at the expense of the state' was proposed by Heald (1983: 298). As noted in Chapter 1, he cited four components to the policy of privatization: (1) *increasing charges*, that is, the privatization of the financing of a service produced by the public sector (this component is noticeably absent from the official definition); (2) *contracting out*, that is, the privatization of the production of a service financed by the public sector; (3) *denationalization* (and load shedding), that is, transfers of activity from public sector to private sector; and (4) *liberalization*, that is, the removal of formal obstacles which inhibit the private sector from competing against the public sector. Other proponents of a broad view, though varying in terms of detailed categories include Hastings and Levi (1983), Whitfield (1983) and Young (1986).

As indicated in Chapter 1, our own preference is to adopt a broad approach on the grounds that it more accurately reflects the diversity and historical significance of the privatization policy. We would suggest, however, a fifth component to the privatization policy in addition to Heald's four: the *encouragement* of private sector consumption. This is achieved by a combination of financial incentives to consume privately (for example, housing and health) and allowing the quantity and quality of public sector provision to deteriorate (through selective cuts in spending), which in itself encourages privatization (see Duke and Edgell 1984).

A common analytic distinction is to subdivide state intervention (and ensuing privatization) according to whether the state merely pays for the industry/service or whether the state also employs workers who run the industry/service. Glennerster (1985), writing on the welfare state, dichotomized between state *finance* and state *provision* of a service. Thus he suggested that privatization introduces an element of either private funding, or private provision, or both. Similarly, Leat (1986) distinguished between funding, regulation and provision of welfare state services; Le Grand and Robinson (1984) talked of provision, subsidy or regulation; and Savas (1982) concentrated on arranging, producing or financing.

In a review article on privatization, Kolderie (1986) stressed the need to separate the primary policy to *provide* a service from the secondary decision to *produce* a service. Contracting out and liberalization are thus *privatization of production*, i.e. the state still pays. The 'real' privatization is seen as *privatization of provision*, i.e. the state withdraws, as in denationalization and load shedding. Increasing charges Kolderie viewed as a form of creeping privatization of provision.

Interestingly, Kolderie's use of the term *production* of a service is the same as Glennerster and Leat's *provision* of a service. On the other hand, Kolderie's *provision* of a service is equivalent to Glennerster and Leat's *financing* of a service. We find Kolderie's conceptual terminology more useful, in that *production* of a service/ industry suggests that the state directly employs workers to do this. This version is more congruent with recent theoretical developments in the field of production sectoral cleavages (Dunleavy 1980b; Edgell and Duke 1983).

Lastly, a wider theoretical framework into which the privatization of consumption can be located is *consumption sectoral location*. This refers to whether the household consumption of services is totally private, predominantly private, predominantly public or totally public in relation to housing, transport and health (see Chapter 2). Each household was classified according to the degree of private or public consumption. Privatization of household consumption for one of the three services thus results in a shift of consumption sectoral location.

3 Previous Evidence on the Level of and Potential for Privatization of Consumption

The extent of private consumption in our four essential services is presented in Table 7.3. In each case there was further privatization from the beginning of the first Thatcher administration in 1979, ranging from a further 8 per cent of households in the case of housing to only 1 per cent more of school pupils. Housing and transport were predominantly private services in terms of consumption, and this tendency was reinforced, especially in the case of housing. By contrast, health and education were predominantly public services, with only small minorities consuming privately. It is noteworthy, however, that the proportion of the population covered by private health insurance almost doubled between 1979 and 1986.

The political significance of growth in private consumption of services has been analysed in Chapters 2 and 3. Predominantly private services produce greater fragmentation within the 'working class', whereas predominantly public services produce greater fragmentation within the 'middle classes'. There is also a strong link between consumption sectoral location and party support: the more private the consumption, the greater the support for the Conservative Party (Duke and Edgell 1984; Dunleavy and Husbands 1985).

Table 7.3 Growth in private consumption of four essential services, 1979–89

Service	1979	1989	Growth
Housing: % owner-occupation	55	63	+ 8
Transport: % car ownership	58	64	+ 6
Health: % private insurance	5	9	+ 4
Education: % private school	6	7	+ 1

Source: Social Trends (HMSO).

Housing

The level of sales of public sector dwellings has been documented already in Table 7.2. This is a clear example of our fifth component in privatization policy, that of state encouragement of private consumption of services. The 1970 Housing Act offered a discount of up to 50 per cent on the sale of local authority dwellings. In 1984 the maximum discount was raised to 60 per cent and in 1986 further raised to 70 per cent. Furthermore, the Housing Planning Act 1986 gave local authorities the power to evict tenants in order to ensure that estates can be sold to private developers.

Another longstanding form of subsidy to private housing (dating back to the Second World War) is mortgage interest tax relief. In 1980/1, this subsidy was five times higher in real terms than in 1970/1 (Ball 1983). The encouragement to consume housing privately in Britain is thus considerable. There is also no capital gains tax on first home sales.

Several other studies have examined the potential for further privatization of housing. Both the *General Household Survey* (1985) and a more localized study in Aberdeen (Williams *et al.* 1986) inquired whether local authority tenants had considered buying their dwellings. This question was repeated by the *General Household Survey* in 1981, 1982 and 1983 and produced remarkably consistent answers. The proportion who had considered privatization and taken active steps ranged between 9 and 10 per cent over the three years. Those who had considered buying but taken no action ranged from 11 to 13 per cent. However, the overwhelmingly consistent majority had not considered privatization (77–79 per cent). The Aberdeen findings were very similar, with 9 per cent seriously considering, 22 per cent considering and 70 per cent not considering buying.

A slightly different form of question wording was used in the *British Social Attitudes* series (Jowell and Airey 1984; Jowell *et al.* 1986) and a Building Societies Association survey (Boleat 1983). Here, local authority tenants were asked how likely they were to buy their present home. Again the responses were almost identical in the three surveys: 13–15 per cent were very/quite likely to privatize, 4–8 per cent were quite unlikely and a dominant 70–80 per cent were very unlikely.

Taken together, these findings provide little evidence of much further potential in the privatization of housing via tenants buying their homes. In a slightly different context, Brindley and Stoker (1988) concluded that there were limitations to the prospects for further privatization of housing renewal.

More qualitative investigation into the reasons for not buying their local authority dwellings was undertaken by two of the studies. The *British Social Attitudes* 1985 survey asked those tenants who would like to buy but didn't expect to why this was the case. Three of the four most frequently cited reasons were financial (low income, 64 per cent; economic position, 13 per cent; can't afford mortgage, 11 per cent), whilst the other was old age (22 per cent). Only 3 per cent disagreed in principle about buying local authority housing. The Aberdeen study produced similar results, with non-purchasers citing finance, age and house type as the main reasons. Again, a mere 6 per cent of tenants would not buy on principle. The overwhelming majority in both studies gave pragmatic reasons for not privatizing their housing.

These studies also shed light on which households are most likely to privatize. The *General Household Survey* found that likelihood to buy was associated with non-manual socioeconomic groups, high-income households, economically active households and large households. Purchasers in the Aberdeen study exhibited different socioeconomic characteristics from non-purchasers. The relevant variables were income, number of wage-earners, employment status, occupational class, age and household type. Boleat showed that the likelihood of local authority tenants buying their present home was related to age.

In a recent study of three English towns, Saunders (1990) concluded that there is an overwhelming preference to buy rather than rent housing. However, his question wording offered a completely free choice, irrespective of financial constraints and other pragmatic restrictions mentioned above.

The growth in owner-occupation since 1979, much of it owing to the government's 'Right to Buy' policy, has been accompanied by even more rapid growth in the level of repossessions and mortgage arrears. Repossessions per 100,000 loans increased from 48 in 1979, to 123 in 1983, and to 319 in 1987 (*Labour Research*, February 1989). Similarly, the number of mortgages 6–12 months in arrears per 100,000 loans rose from 160 in 1979, to 430 in 1983, and 670 in 1987.

Transport

Transport consumption has been predominantly private in Britain for longer than housing, dating back to the 1960s. As such, car ownership has been accepted as the norm and there has been no recent work on the likelihood of further transport privatization. It remains the case, however, that women are far more restricted than men in their access to a private car (*National Travel Survey 1978–9*). The growth of private consumption of transport is confirmed by the fact that, in 1985/6, two-thirds of journeys to work were in private cars compared with only one-third in 1965 (*Social Trends*, 1988).

As with housing, in recent times transport has experienced the combination of state encouragement of the private sector at the same time as subsidies to public transport were cut. Bus deregulation in October 1986 (a classic example of liberalization) resulted in 85 per cent of services running commercially without subsidy by late 1987 (HMSO 1988). On the other hand, between 1982/3 and 1986/7 the Public Service Obligation subsidy (mostly to British Rail) decreased in cash terms by £90 million. In real terms this represents a 25 per cent decrease.

Health
The period of the first two Conservative administrations witnessed a massive growth in private health. In 1979, 2 million people (around 5 per cent of the population) were covered by private medical insurance. By 1986, this had risen to 5 million people (9 per cent of the population) (*Social Trends*, 1988). More recently, *British Social Attitudes*, 1988, found that the proportion of their respondents covered by private schemes was 14 per cent (8 per cent paid for by employers). British United Provident Association (BUPA) accounted for 60 per cent of all policies and, together with Private Patients Plan (PPP) and Western Provident Association (WPA), the big three accounted for 92 per cent.

Impressive though the rise of private health insurance is, five qualifying factors need to be taken into account. First, the boom in private insurance was mainly in 1980 (+ 26 per cent) and 1981 (+ 13 per cent). By 1983 the rate of growth had slowed to 2 per cent (*Social Trends*, 1985). Second, the bulk of the growth was in company schemes rather than individual subscriptions. This is because tax incentives are available to employers for private health. Third, coverage of private health insurance is very low outside professional and managerial groups (over 20 per cent coverage). Fourth, subscription to private health insurance does not preclude continued usage of the NHS. Fifth, expansion of private health care has been geographically uneven (Mohan, 1986, 1988).

Two studies have examined factors influencing access to private health. The *General Household Survey* in 1983 found that 7 per cent of the population were covered by private medical insurance. Coverage was related to age, economic activity, socioeconomic group and income. Significantly, policy holding (as opposed to coverage) was more common for men than for women. The *British Social Attitudes* 1983 survey confirmed that coverage was related to occupational class, income and employment status.

Most of the recent work on health privatization has concentrated on private insurance schemes. However, it is important to recognize that other components of privatization are occurring in the form of contracting out (see Ascher 1987; Ranade and Haywood 1989) and increased charges (see Radical Statistics Health Group 1987). The percentage of National Health Service expenditure derived from charges to patients stood at 2 per cent in 1979/80, 3 per cent in 1985/6 and 4 per cent in 1987/8 (HMSO 1988). Other indicators of note are that private sector beds have increased by over 50 per cent since 1979 (Laing 1987), and the number of private hospitals increased by one-quarter in the period 1979–85 (Rayner 1986).

Education
The level of private education has fluctuated between 6 and 8 per cent of all schoolchildren in the post-1945 period (Independent Schools Information Service). More recently, pupils in private schools constituted 5.8 per cent of all pupils in 1979, 6.2 per cent in 1983 and 7.0 per cent in 1988 (*Social Trends*, 1990). A steady growth in private education is taking place, with the largest increase among the 16 and over group. The proportion of pupils in private schools increases with age: in 1987, 5 per cent of the under-11s, 8 per cent of the 11–15s and 19 per cent of the 16 and over group were in private schools. The *British Social Attitudes* 1985 survey reported that 11 per cent of adult respondents had attended private schools.

State encouragement of private education was furthered by the 1980 Education Act. The Assisted Places Scheme offers full or partial subsidy of fees for private schools. By 1987/8 the take-up rate was 98 per cent with 33,200 places (HMSO 1988). Evidence suggests that the 'middle classes' have benefited most from the Assisted Places Scheme (Tapper and Salter 1986; Whitty *et al.* 1986): only 9 per cent of fathers and 4 per cent of mothers of pupils on the scheme were from working-class manual occupations. Tapper and Salter also found that the scheme costs more than the state provision it replaces.

Most recently, the Education Reform Act 1988 allows individual schools to opt out of local authority control, thereby creating a new category of quasi-private schools directly funded by central government. For details on this see the special issue of *Local Government Studies* in January 1988.

4 *Attitudes to Privatization: Previous Research*

Attitudinal data on the many forms of privatization are less than comprehensive. This is partly owing to the recent appearance of privatization on the political agenda (see Leat 1986). Earlier work was more concerned with the general nationalization/denationalization debate in the industrial sphere (Butler and Stokes 1974). Given that the focus here is on attitudes to privatization, another more empirically based division is called for, namely that between privatization of welfare state services and non-welfare state privatization. The historical motives behind state involvement in the two spheres are quite different. Basically, welfare state services were provided to meet social need, whereas many non-welfare state services were provided in order to achieve economies of scale. Correspondingly, attitudes to privatization in these two spheres may be different. Even among more recent work, no study systematically compares attitudes to welfare state privatization (WSP) and non-welfare state privatization (NWSP). Nor has there been any attempt to compare the attitudes to the privatization of one industry or service with attitudes to the privatization of another industry or service.

With regard to NWSP, previous work has concentrated on nationalization/denationalization of industry. Attitudes to the state ownership of industry have been surveyed regularly as part of the British Election Studies (BES) since 1963 (Butler and Stokes 1974; Sarlvik and Crewe 1983; Heath *et al.* 1985). Heath *et al.* (1985, Table 9.1) summarized the responses to an identical question on nationalization for each of the election studies since 1964. From the 1964 election to the October 1974 election, further nationalization received more support than privatization, although the status quo was the most popular option. In 1979, however, privatization was significantly more favoured than nationalization (40 per cent to 17 per cent) and in 1983 even surpassed the status quo as the most popular option (42 per cent to 40 per cent).

The increased level of support for privatization of industry in the early 1980s was confirmed by the *British Social Attitudes* (BSA) reports (Jowell and Airey 1984; Jowell and Witherspoon 1985). The authors of the second report suggested that 'the argument has shifted since 1979 from being concerned with more or less nationalisation to being concerned with more or less privatisation' (Jowell and Witherspoon 1985: 22). They went on to show that attitudes to the privatization of industry were influenced by production sector, occupational class and partisanship. Similarly, Heath *et al.* (1985) demonstrated that attitudes were related to social class and partisanship.

However, by the BSA 1988 report, attitudes to the privatization of industry had reversed direction: only 30 per cent wanted less state ownership in 1987, compared with 49 per cent in 1983. In the interim period there was significant privatization of industry, most notably British Telecom and British Gas. Nonetheless, the tide had turned against any further denationalization.

Attitudes to WSP were first surveyed for the Institute of Economic Affairs (IEA) by Harris and Seldon (1979), and more recently by Taylor-Gooby (1985, 1986). Unsurprisingly, given the loaded wording of their questions, Harris and Seldon found strong support for the freedom to go private and around 50 per cent in favour of voucher systems to buy private health and education. Judge *et al.* (1983) reanalysed the IEA data to reveal that this support for private welfare coexisted with strong support for state welfare.

In a small-scale case study in Medway, Taylor-Gooby (1985) confirmed the high level of tolerance for contracting out of state health and education services, and the majority preference for private rather than state health and education ('if the cost were the same'). Subsequently Taylor-Gooby achieved similar results using a national sample, but he concluded that 'sentiments that support privatisation of the welfare state coexist with countervailing sentiments of collectivism' (Taylor-Gooby 1986: 244). Elsewhere, Hyde and Deacon (1986) found little support for the privatization of health and housing when a full range of alternatives was presented to respondents.

The first BSA report in 1984 provided somewhat mixed and partly conflicting evidence on WSP. Whereas there was a clear majority in favour of housing privatization (54 per cent), only minorities supported privatization of health (20 per cent generally, 26 per cent outside NHS hospitals) and education (11 per cent) (Jowell and Airey 1984). All three of these attitudes were linked to partisanship and housing and education were related to occupational class. In the 1983 BES, Heath *et al.* (1985) found majorities in favour of privatizing both housing and health. By BSA 1987, support for council house sales had risen to 61 per cent but the proportion wanting more private schools remained at 11 per cent.

This brief review of existing evidence indicates the complexity and dynamic nature of attitudes to privatization, and confirms the importance of distinguishing welfare state from non-welfare state privatization. The summary of previous findings, in conjunction with theoretical considerations, provided the basis for selecting the hypotheses to be tested on the Greater Manchester Study data.

For the purposes of this chapter on the progress/potential of and attitudes to privatization, the data for Labourville and Torytown were combined, because our concern here is with appraising general trends and theories in relation to privatization. The next two sections present our operationalization of the two sets of dependent variables: first, private/public consumption locations for our four essential services (housing, transport, health and education) and the potential for future privatization; second, attitudes to privatization – both welfare state and non-welfare state.

5 Operationalizing the Dependent Variables

Private and public consumption locations: housing, transport, health and education

Consumption of all four services was measured at the level of the household. This was because it is the household as a whole that usually has access to consumption (see Chapter 2). Most obviously, the household as a whole consumes either private or public housing. Private health insurance also tends to cover all members of a household.

The sectoral cleavage in *housing* was between owner-occupiers (private) and local authority tenants (public). A small residual group of housing association tenants and those renting from a private landlord was classified as neither public nor private. This group amounted to 7 per cent of the panel sample and was excluded from the analysis.

Transport was dichotomized straightforwardly on the basis of car ownership. Car owners consume private transport, whereas non-car owners must rely on public transport. There is, however, an additional complication to bear in mind. Although the whole household has access to a private car, the frequency of use by individual members of the household may be uneven. As noted above, the male is typically more likely to use the car than the female (*National Travel Survey 1978–9*). Further questions on respondent and household use of public transport were asked.

A simple dichotomy was employed in the case of *health* also.

Households with private health insurance were regarded as private, whereas those without had to rely exclusively on the National Health Service. Private health insurance was defined as membership of one of the big three schemes (BUPA, PPP, WPA). This meant that Hospital Saturday Fund and other small-scale intermediate schemes were excluded. As it is possible to purchase private health care without private insurance, a further question was asked about whether the household had ever received private medical treatment. Lastly, a measure of household use of the NHS was obtained by recording visits to doctor, dentist and/or hospital.

In the case of *education*, households were categorized according to whether the children attended private or state schools. Unlike the other three services, education is not consumed continuously by all households. This meant that over two-thirds of households had no children of school age at the time of the study and were therefore unclassified. In order to obtain a more complete picture, a further question was asked about whether anyone in the household had ever attended a private school.

A measure of potential further privatization was obtained for each of the four services. In each case, public sector consumers were asked how *likely* it was that they would privatize, that is, buy their home, buy a car, join a private health scheme or send their children to a private school. The answers available were 'very likely', 'quite likely', 'not likely' and 'definitely not'.

The final stage in the questioning was to follow up the question on likelihood with an open-ended 'why?' After examining all the replies, the *reasons* for privatizing or not were coded into various categories of pragmatic (e.g. cost, age) or principled response.

Attitudes to privatization: welfare state and non-welfare state

As outlined earlier, our coverage encompassed both WSP and NWSP. We examined knowledge of and attitudes to privatization at the second interview of the panel in 1983–4. This was because privatization increased markedly in importance between the first and second stages of the project (see Table 7.1). We included three attitudinal items on WSP and two on NWSP. Table 7.4 summarizes the five items in terms of: which component of privatization they involve; whether the privatization is of production or provision; whether the service is predominantly private or predominantly public (for WSP only).

Most WSP takes the form of privatization of provision, that is, increased consumption of private sector services at the expense of

Table 7.4 Attitudinal items on privatization

Nature of service/ industry	Component of privatization	Privatization of production or privatization of provision	Predominantly private or predominantly public
WSP			
1 Private health	encourage private consumption	provision	public
2 Voluntary social services	encourage private consumption *and* contracting out	provision/production	public
3 Council house sales	load shedding	provision	private
NWSP			
1 Nationalized industries	denationalization	provision	—
2 Local authority services	contracting out	production	—

Source: GMS2 panel.

state services. Two of our three WSP items were of this type, namely the growth of private health and council house sales. The possible exception was the voluntary sector's contribution to social services. This frequently takes the form of voluntary production of the service with continued state financing (provision) of the service.

An important distinction in relation to welfare state services is that between predominantly private and predominantly public services (see Dunleavy 1980a; Duke and Edgell 1984). Predominantly private services are those that the majority of households consume in the private/market sector. For instance, both housing and transport are now over 60 per cent private (*Social Trends*, 1986). By contrast, health and education are examples of predominantly public services, which the majority of households consume in the public/state sector (*Social Trends*, 1990). We would expect privatization to be more popular in predominantly private services than in predominantly public services.

The two NWSP items comprised one of provision and one of production. The first concerned selling off profitable nationalized industries, and the second contracting out of local authority services. We would expect limited privatization of production to be more popular than total privatization of provision.

In the later stages of the ensuing analysis the five items were combined into an index of attitude to privatization. Each item was deemed to have a pro-privatization response and an anti-privatization response (see Table 7.5). The baseline score on the index was 0, to which pro-privatization responses were added and from which anti-privatization responses were subtracted. Thus a respondent giving pro replies to all five items would score +5; a respondent giving five mixed answers (neither pro nor anti) would remain on a score of 0. This approach is akin to Wright's class-consciousness scale (Wright 1985: 147).

The index of attitudes to privatization possessed both internal and external validity. Each item was significantly intercorrelated with all other items on the index at the 0.001 significance level. Three was no tendency for WSP items to be more strongly associated with other WSP items than with NWSP items, or vice versa. This confirmed the presence of a single dimension on attitudes to privatization rather than separate dimensions for WSP and NWSP.

External validity for the index is demonstrated powerfully in Table 7.6, which cross-tabulates the index with two attitudinal items framed in terms of nationalization – one welfare state (private schools) and one non-welfare state (industry). Those classified as pro-privatization on the index were overwhelmingly

Table 7.5 Index of attitudes to privatization (base = 0)

Item[a]		Pro-privatization +1-5	Anti-privatization -1-5
WSP			
1	(Q18f) Encourage private medicine	government should	government should not
2	(Q18b) Encourage voluntary social services	government should	government should not
3	(Q19) Council house sales	government should should be allowed	government should not should not be allowed
NWSP			
4	(Q18j) Sell off nationalized industries	government should agree	government should not disagree
5	(Q20) Contract out local authority services		

Note:

[a] Detailed question wordings as follows:

Q.18 Do you think the government *should* or *should not* do each of the following or doesn't it matter either way?

(b) encourage the voluntary provision of social services in place of state provision
(f) encourage the growth of private medicine
(j) sell off/privatize profitable parts of nationalised industries.

Q.19 Which of these views comes closest to your own on the sale of council houses and flats to tenants?

(a) council house tenants *should not* be allowed to buy their houses or flats
(b) council tenants *should be* allowed to buy *but* only in areas of no housing shortage
(c) council tenants *should generally* be allowed to buy their houses or flats.

Q.20 Some people think that certain services should be taken away from local councils and handed over to private contractors: do you agree or disagree with this idea?

Source: GMS2 panel.

155

Table 7.6 Validation of index of attitudes to privatization

Index	*n*	% govt should not abolish private schools[a]	% favouring less nationalization
+ 5	22	100	91
+ 4	14	93	93
+ 3	64	91	70
+ 2	29	86	62
+ 1	56	95	61
0	55	72	60
− 1	79	71	38
− 2	52	69	31
− 3	56	64	29
− 4	64	55	16
− 5	47	38	6

Note:

[a] Detailed question wordings as follows:

Q.18   Do you think the government *should* or *should not* do each of the following or doesn't it matter either way?
(a)   abolish the private schools which are outside the state education system.

Q.21   Do you think there should be more nationalization of industry, less nationalization or stay as it is?

Source: GMS2 panel.

against the abolition of private schools, to the point where those most pro (+ 5) were 100 per cent against. The only sub-group not to have a majority against were those totally anti-privatization on the index (− 5), of whom 53 per cent thought the government should abolish private schools.

Similarly, regarding the nationalization of industry, all those pro-privatization on the index had majorities favouring less nationalization; by contrast there were minorities in favour for those anti-privatization on the index. The range extends from fully 91 per cent of the + 5's wanting less nationalization to only 6 per cent of the − 5's.

6   *Operationalizing the Independent Variables*

In this section we outline the operational definitions for all the independent variables utilized in the two sets of analyses. The first analysis was concerned with factors influencing the level of and potential for privatization, and the second with factors affecting attitudes to privatization.

Previous research into factors influencing private sector consumption and privatization of services had stressed the importance of occupational class. The extensive discussion of class operationalization in Chapter 2 indicated our preference for neo-Marxist social class categories based on the social relations of production rather than conventional occupational class categories based on the technical relations of production. In the light of this conclusion, we employed social class in both analyses based on Wright's original formulation (Wright and Perrone 1977).

Furthermore, it was argued in Chapter 2 that, for studies of consumption behaviour and attitudes, a household-based measure of class inclusive of the economically inactive is appropriate. Accordingly this type of measure was used for both analyses. A respondent-based measure of class covering the economically active only would have been particularly inappropriate here because consumption sectoral locations were measured at the level of the household.

For the analysis of factors influencing attitudes to privatization, the preliminary bivariate analysis of class was performed using household social class. However, the subsequent fuller multivariate analyses entered the class positions of *both respondent and household* into the regression model. This solution allowed the influence of either or both to be displayed in the model. In practice, the influence of others in the household was measured by a set of dummy variables indicating the presence or not of a particular class category, for example, the presence of an employer in the household other than the respondent.

The other variables included in the first analysis all figured in the previous literature as relevant influences on private consumption and privatization. All of them were measured at the level of the household, with the exception of *age*, which was asked only of respondents. Gender was not included precisely because the consumption indicators were household measures.

Household *income* was asked only at the first interview. Therefore it was not an ideal measure in relation to the level of private consumption of services at the second interview. Nonetheless, it was included because of its importance in previous studies.

The household *economic activity* indicator was based simply on the number of economically active adults. Household *unemployment* was a dichotomous variable indicating whether or not anyone in the household was employed at the time of the second interview.

For the second analysis, additional independent variables of sectoral location and partisanship were relevant. There are two aspects to sectoral location. First, *production sectoral location* refers to whether the individual being classified works in the private sector, in the public/state sector or in the self-employed sector. Secondly, *consumption sectoral location* refers to whether the household consumption of services is private, public or mixed (see Chapter 2).

The same procedural decisions apply to production sector as were outlined for class. Thus both respondent and household measures were entered into the full model and the economically inactive were classified according to the previous sectoral location. The self-employed were automatically employers or petty bourgeois, thus only the controller and worker classes were split into public and private sectors.

Consumption sectoral location was less problematic operationally in that measurement tends to be inherently at the household level. For instance, the household as a whole consumes either private or public housing (see section 5 above for details on all four services). *Overall* household consumption sectoral location was based on three services – housing, transport and health. Each household was classified according to the degree of private or public provision of the three services (see Chapter 2 for details). It is pertinent to point out that for the first analysis the consumption sectoral locations of the four essential services were dependent variables, whereas for the second analysis *overall* household consumption sectoral location was an independent variable.

The literature review highlighted the influence of partisanship on attitudes to privatization. Previous authors of BES data have stressed the importance of measuring (a) strength of party identification rather than just direction (Crewe *et al.* 1977; Sarlvik and Crewe 1983) and (b) negative as well as positive partisanship (Sarlvik and Crewe 1983). Our approach incorporated both of these elements.

The interview schedule included a sequence of questions on *partisanship*. Respondents were asked for their party identification and whether this was 'very strong', 'fairly strong' or 'not very strong'. Negative partisanship – ranging from 'very strongly against' to 'not really against' – was then obtained for the major parties, other than the party positively favoured.

We combined the positive and negative aspects of partisanship to provide indices for the three major party groupings, i.e. Conservative, Labour and Liberal/SDP Alliance. The indices ranged from + 3 to − 3. Very strong identifiers were coded + 3, fairly strong identifiers + 2 and not very strong identifiers + 1. Similarly, those very strongly against a party were coded – 3, those somewhat against – 2, and those not really against – 1. The code '0' was reserved for the small number of refusals to answer, and these have been excluded from the analysis.

The Conservative and Labour indices were straightforward to operationalize by following the procedure described above. Both of these indices were validated when cross-checked against vote in the 1983 general election. For instance, the percentage voting Conservative ranged from 1 per cent of very strongly against (– 3), through 26 per cent of not really against (– 1) to 90 per cent of very strong identifiers (+ 3). The Alliance index, however, created problems in that the negative measure was obtained for both Liberal and Social Democratic parties separately. The solution was to take the average of the Liberal and SDP answers.

7 *The Progress of and Potential for Privatization*

Knowledge of privatization

A potential danger in attitudinal research on policy issues is to assume that respondents know what the question is about. The unwillingness of certain individuals to admit ignorance and the resultant tendency to give opinions even when they have no idea at all about the issue are well documented (e.g. Payne 1951; Schuman and Presser 1981). It is advisable therefore to precede attitudinal questions with knowledge questions, although much research fails to do this. Consequently, before examining attitudes to privatization, we needed to ascertain whether or not respondents knew about privatization.

Towards the beginning of the interview we asked respondents if they had heard of the government's policy of privatization of state industries and services; 86 per cent said they had. We then asked respondents whether they could give us any examples of privatization. Somewhat to our surprise fully 79 per cent of the panel gave at least one example, 59 per cent gave two or more and 34 per cent gave three or more.

The fact that four-fifths of the sample displayed specific knowledge of privatization was impressive evidence of the extent to which the term had entered popular discourse/consciousness. The remaining analytic problem was what to do with the fifth without knowledge. Our solution was to exclude those without knowledge of privatization from subsequent analysis of attitudes, because of patterns in the data. For the first analysis of the level of privatization, those without knowledge were included because the information here was household structural and behavioural data, which are more reliable than attitudinal data.

There is empirical support for our decision to concentrate the attitudinal analysis on those with knowledge. Above we pointed out that all of the five items on the index of attitudes to privatization were significantly associated with each other at the 0.001 significance level. This statement was based only on those with knowledge. Of the ten resultant *tau beta*'s (a measure of association ranging from 0 to 1) only one was less than 0.20. By contrast, when the same exercise was repeated for those without knowledge, only one of the ten associations was significant at even the 0.05 level. Thus those without knowledge were indeed giving random answers to the attitudinal questions. Furthermore, the average level of 'don't know' answers over the five items was more than three times greater for those without knowledge compared with those with knowledge.

In social class terms, *lack* of knowledge of privatization ranged from 30 per cent of workers to 0 per cent of the aptly named 'expert workers' (employing Wright Mark III – see Chapter 2). More importantly, 52 per cent of totally public consumers (-3 on the consumption index) were without knowledge. Therefore those most dependent on state services were the least knowledgeable on privatization. Given that our strategy in the subsequent analysis was to exclude those lacking knowledge, we recognized that the influence of totally public consumers on any overall correlation measures would have to be scaled down accordingly.

The level of privatization

The existence of a panel enabled us to measure the process of service privatization over the three-year period. Table 7.7 summarizes the level of private consumption and the extent of privatization for the four services. Private housing and private transport were more common than in the national population, but the levels of private health and private education were on a par with national figures (in the case of education 2 per cent out of 28 per cent were private, which equals 7 per cent of pupils).

The proportion of the panel households that privatized their consumption over the three-year period was generally low for all four services. The range was from 5.5 per cent in transport to 0.5 per cent in education. The most significant privatization was in

Table 7.7 Levels of private consumption and potential for further privatization in four essential services

	Housing	Transport	Health	Education
% private 1980/1–1983/4	80	68	4	1.5
% privatized 1980/1 – 1983/4	2	5.5	5	0.5
Total % private 1983/4	82	74	9	2
Total % public 1983/4, of whom:	11	26	91	26
% very/quite likely to privatize	1	5	17	2
% not likely/definitely not	10	20	70	24

Source: GMS2 panel.

health, where the level of private insurance more than doubled. This rate of growth was slightly above the national average.

Our figure of 2 per cent privatized in housing was lower than a comparable figure of 5 per cent of households from the *British Social Attitudes* 1985 survey. This is partly owing to the higher level of private housing in our sample to begin with and also to the longer time period involved in the 1985 question.

Transport exhibited the highest level of privatization among our households. However, this must be interpreted with caution as sectoral locations in transport are more volatile than is the case with the other services. Almost as many households deprivatized as privatized their transport – 5 per cent and 5.5 per cent, respectively. Among the old, deprivatization was common. Furthermore, transport consumption was more likely than any of the other services to be mixed. Thus 43 per cent of the households both had access to a private car and used public transport in the week preceding the second interview.

The level of privatization in health was significant, but equally impressive was the overwhelming usage of the NHS. Fully 94 per cent of households had consulted a doctor on the NHS in the three years between the interviews.

Our definition of private health as membership of the big three insurance schemes did not capture the full extent of the private sector in health: 25 per cent of households had used private medicine at some time, which was almost three times the level of big three membership. In fact, only 84 per cent of households with insurance had received private treatment prior to the second interview. Williams *et al.* (1984) pointed out that only 69 per cent of all stays in private hospitals in 1981 were covered by some form of health insurance.

The steady privatization of education was more pervasive than is apparent from Table 7.7. Whilst the proportion of households consuming private education remained constant at around 2 per cent in both interviews, the proportion for state schools fell sharply by 6 per cent. Thus the relative proportion of pupils at private schools increased significantly over the three-year period. Since less than a third of households had children of school age at the second interview, the education sectoral data are somewhat restricted. However, when asked if anyone in the household had ever used private education, the level of private consumption rose to 13 per cent. Other indicators of private education beyond private schools were the 3 per cent of households using private nursery facilities and the 9 per cent who had used private lessons outside school hours for their children.

The potential for further privatization

The data on likelihood of further privatization in the four services are presented in the lower part of Table 7.7. The four categories were compressed into two by merging 'very likely' and 'quite likely', and by combining 'not likely' and 'definitely not'. Nonetheless, for each service the modal answer was 'definitely not', ranging from 67 per cent for housing to 46 per cent for health.

There was clearly very little potential for privatization of housing among our panel. The figure for the likelihood of further privatization of housing (10 per cent) was broadly comparable with previous research. The high level of private housing in our areas had reached saturation point.

Transport offered some potential for further privatization but equally this was likely to be matched by equivalent deprivatization. It may be that private transport was also close to saturation point.

Health offered the most potential for privatization, with 17 per cent of households likely to take up private insurance. On the other hand, a massive 70 per cent were not likely to take up the private option. A third of those households that were likely to privatize health had previously received private treatment, compared with 18 per cent of those not likely to.

Continued steady growth of private education was likely, although the proportion was unlikely to rise drastically. Of those households likely to privatize education, 25 per cent had previously attended a private school, compared with only 7 per cent of those not likely to.

Reasons for privatizing or not

The reasons given for likelihood of privatization in the four services are summarized in Table 7.8. For housing and transport, the 'very/quite likely' categories and the 'not likely/definitely not' categories were combined because of the small numbers involved. In the case of education, only the 'very/quite likely' answers were merged.

The majority of reasons given were pragmatic for all four services and in every 'likelihood' group. Reasons of principle are evident to any degree only for health (23 per cent of 'not likely' and 37 per cent of 'definitely not' responses) and education (21 per cent of 'definitely not').

Cost figured prominently in the reasons for both privatizing and not privatizing housing, while age emerged as an important reason for not privatizing housing. The presence of cost and age corroborated previous research into housing privatization. The 6 per cent of those not likely to privatize their housing for reasons of principle were identical to the figures obtained in the Aberdeen study.

For transport, cost and age were common reasons for those not likely to privatize. It is noteworthy that principled reasons were virtually non-existent (1 per cent of 'not likely' responses) in the case of transport. Private car ownership is clearly an unquestioned norm of modern society.

Cost was a key factor for those households 'not likely' and 'definitely not' going to privatize health. For the 'definitely not's, age was also prominent because of the restricted availability of affordable insurance schemes for the old.

Interestingly, principled reasons in support of the NHS were the most common response for those 'definitely not' taking up private health insurance. The responses on health forced us to provide an extra category of 'cynical' response: 23 per cent of the 'very likely's and 10 per cent of the 'quite likely's supported the NHS in principle but were still intending to privatize (in other words, they were forced to by cuts in the NHS). There was clearly a great deal of principled support for the NHS.

In the case of education, cost was the most important reason for those households 'not likely' to and 'definitely not' going to privatize. Around one-fifth of the 'definitely not's exhibited principled opposition to private schools.

163

Table 7.8 Reasons given for likelihood/unlikelihood of privatization in four essential services

Likelihood of privatization	n	% cost	+ % age	+ % other	= Total % pragmatic	Reasons % principle	% cynical
Housing:							
Very/quite likely	6	50	0	50	100	0	
Not likely/definitely not	70	24	34	36	94	6	
Transport:							
Very/quite likely	32	6	0	94	100	0	
Not likely/definitely not	133	34	31	34	99	1	
Health:							
Very likely	26	0	0	77	77	0	23
Quite likely	88	6	0	83	89	1	10
Not likely	197	34	6	37	77	23	
Definitely not	265	24	21	18	63	37	
Education:							
Very/quite likely	12	0	0	92	92	8	
Not likely	62	52	3	39	94	6	
Definitely not	98	46	3	30	79	21	

Source: GMS2 Panel.

164

Factors influencing private consumption and further privatization

This section examines factors influencing access to private consumption of the four essential services. As in the previous tables, the 'very/quite likely' and 'not likely/definitely not' categories have been combined. In the case of housing, the percentage likely to privatize was excluded because the number involved was too small for meaningful analysis (range 0–2 per cent for all sub-groups). Similarly, the percentage likely to privatize education was too small, so data are presented on the percentage of households that had ever used private schools.

Table 7.9 relates private consumption of services to household social class. There were clear class patterns in the level of private consumption and the likelihood of further privatization for all four services. For housing, the lowest level of currently private consumption and the highest percentage not likely to privatize was found among workers. Significantly, of all the class sub-groups, private housing was most common among employers (100 per cent). The transport data produced similar patterns. Again, the currently least private were workers and the most private were employers (100 per cent). Likelihood of further privatization was associated with the lower class categories, which had not yet reached saturation point.

In the case of health, employers exhibited the highest level of private insurance membership, whilst managers also displayed a high level of private health consumption (14 per cent). Further privatization was most likely among employers and the petty bourgeoisie, with employers being particularly distinctive. The highest previous usage of private schools was found among employers (29 per cent) and the petty bourgeoisie (21 per cent), whereas the lowest category was workers at 9 per cent.

The influence of other factors on the level of private consumption and the likelihood of further privatization is displayed in Table 7.10. The factors were household income, household economic activity, household unemployment and respondent age.

Household income was strongly related to access to private consumption, despite the drawback of having income data only from the first interview. The lowest income group (£50 weekly) was particularly distinctive, with only 51 per cent private housing, 30 per cent private transport and fully 86 per cent not likely to take up private health insurance. The education pattern was less clear-cut, but the indicator used was retrospective (ever used private schools) rather than prospective.

Table 7.9 Access to private consumption by household social class

| Social class | Housing | | Transport | | | Health | | | Education |
	% currently private	% not likely	% currently private	% likely	% not likely	% currently private	% likely	% not likely	% ever private
Employer	100	0	100	0	0	22	32	43	29
Petty bourgeois	94	5	88	0	8	10	20	68	21
Manager	94	5	78	5	14	14	17	63	13
Worker	83	16	65	3	25	8	11	78	9

Source: GMS2 panel.

Table 7.10 Access to private consumption by household income, household economic activity, household unemployment and respondent age

| Variable | n | Housing | | Transport | | | Health | | | Education |
		% currently private	% not likely	% currently private	% likely	% not likely	% currently private	% likely	% not likely	% ever private
Weekly income (£):										
<50	81	51	30	30	1	65	5	4	86	12
51–100	138	70	20	56	9	35	5	9	83	12
101–150	170	87	7	82	7	10	6	20	68	8
151–200	118	92	3	91	4	5	9	20	67	15
200+	116	97	2	92	2	5	17	30	49	18

Economically active:										
0	160	61	23	36	4	58	3	3	91	11
1	198	85	9	80	6	14	10	14	70	13
2	221	90	5	87	5	8	10	25	60	13
3+	106	90	5	90	6	3	11	26	60	14
Current unemployment:										
Yes	100	73	20	77	6	16	8	16	72	8
No	585	83	9	73	5	21	10	17	70	14
Age:										
<21	30	83	13	73	17	7	10	33	47	10
22–29	105	88	8	87	10	4	11	27	52	11
30–39	134	90	4	87	6	6	6	29	58	12
40–49	133	88	4	85	5	11	9	17	70	11
50–59	119	84	13	80	4	15	12	10	74	19
60–69	100	68	17	53	2	43	6	3	90	15
70+	63	59	25	19	0	78	4	0	95	10

Source: GMS2 panel.

Household economic activity, or, more accurately, the lack of it, was related to private consumption of housing, transport and health. Households with no economically active adults were the most distinctive, with only 61 per cent private housing, 36 per cent private transport and fully 91 per cent not likely to take up private health insurance.

Household unemployment proved to be far less of an influence than household economic activity. This suggests that other categories of economic inactivity, especially retirement, were more important. Household unemployment did produce sizeable differences on housing and education, but in the case of health the differences were slight.

Respondent age was a relevant factor for housing, transport and health. The old were least likely to privatize in all three services, thus confirming the importance of the retired category. The young were most likely to privatize health and transport.

In final summary of this section, health privatization clearly had the most potential. It was particularly likely among the well off, the economically active and the young.

8 Attitudes to Privatization

The level of support for the various privatization policies is summarized in Table 7.11. On four out of the five items there were majorities against privatization, although in each case the minority support was substantial (30–43 per cent). The only pro-privatization majority was for council house sales (a bare 50 per cent). On this question, a third of the sample opted for qualified support only in areas with no housing shortage. Overall, there was no mandate in the GMS for the government's accelerating programme of privatization.

Interestingly, on four out of the five items there was greater support for privatization in Torytown than in Labourville as follows: council house sales, 2 per cent; encouraging voluntary social services and selling off nationalized industries, 5 per cent; and, most notably, contracting out local services, 10 per cent.

Although our data were from a local case study, two of our indicators were identical to those used in national-level surveys in 1983. First, the question on council house sales was used in the BSA 1983 survey. Nationally, the percentage pro-privatization was 54 as against the GMS figure of 50 per cent. Second, the private medicine question was identical to that used in the BES

Table 7.11 Support for the various privatization policies

Item	Relevant category	% pro-privatization	% anti-privatization
WSP			
Encourage private medicine	predominantly public	30	64
Encourage voluntary social services	predominantly public	31	64
Council house sales	predominantly private	50	17
NWSP			
Sell off nationalized industries	privatization of provision	33	59
Contract out local authority services	privatization of production	43	52

Source: GMS2 panel.

1983 survey. The national figure of 36 per cent pro-privatization was only marginally higher than the GMS figure of 30 per cent. These examples confirm that our local findings were tolerably close to national results at around the same time.

In the sphere of WSP our expectation was that support for privatization would be greater in predominantly private services than in predominantly public services, and Table 7.11 corroborates this view. Among the WSP items, privatization of the predominantly private service (housing) was more favourably viewed than privatization of the predominantly public services (health and social services). Where state provision was the norm, privatization was rejected by the majority. Where private provision was the norm, privatization was more acceptable. On this basis, we would expect transport privatization to have obtained majority support.

A second expectation was that in the sphere of NWSP support for privatization of production would be greater than for privatization of provision. The frequencies displayed in Table 7.11 are consistent with this. Among NWSP items, privatization of production (contracting out) was more popular than complete privatization of provision (selling off). This suggests that improving the efficiency of/value for money from the state sector was more important than rolling back the frontiers of the state. Admittedly, the limited nature of the test, with only two items, makes it far from conclusive, but the results do conform with the expected pattern.

A third more general expectation was that NWSP would be more favoured than WSP. Evidence for this is less straightforward. Only if we exclude the predominantly private service (housing) does NWSP emerge as more popular than WSP. Certainly, the hypothesis requires reformulation to accommodate the predominantly private/predominantly public distinction. Although the level of support will vary also according to the wording of specific items, a reformulated version might be appropriate as a general rule.

Index of attitudes to privatization
When the five items were combined into a single index, the negative preponderance of attitudes was magnified (see Table 7.12). Over half the sample (57 per cent) scored negatively on the index and only a third (34 per cent) scored positively. At the extremes, 32 per cent were strongly anti (− 3 or less) whereas 19 per cent were strongly pro (+ 3 or more). In the subsequent sections we turn to the more interesting question of what influenced location on the index.

Attitudes to privatization and social class
The first of our bivariate tables concerns the influence of social class on attitudes to privatization. Table 7.13 summarizes class differ-

Table 7.12 Distribution of responses on the index of attitudes to privatization

Score	%		
+ 5 (totally pro)	4		
+ 4	3	19%	
+ 3	12		34%
+ 2	5		
+ 1	10		
0	10		
− 1	15		
− 2	10		57%
− 3	11		
− 4	12	32%	
− 5 (totally anti)	9		

$n = 538$:
Source: GMS2 panel.

170

Table 7.13   Support for privatization by household social class

| Social class | Variable[a] | | | | | |
	PRIVMED % pro	VOLSOC % pro	HOSALES % pro	PRIVNAT % pro	PRIVLA % pro	INDEX mean
Employer	48	39	65	48	65	+ 0.70
Petty bourgeois	38	38	50	48	60	+ 0.29
Controller	30	29	49	36	44	− 0.66
Worker	25	31	50	23	36	− 1.12
All	30	31	50	33	43	− 0.69

Note:
[a] PRIVMED = encourage private medicine
VOLSOC = encourage voluntary social services
HOSALES = council house sales
PRIVNAT = sell off nationalized industries
PRIVLA = contract out local authority services
INDEX = index of attitudes to privatization

Source: GMS2 panel.

ences in attitudes to privatization in terms of both the five specific policies and also the overall index. As indicated earlier, those respondents who lacked knowledge of privatization were excluded from the analysis.

The presence of class-related differences in attitudes to privatization is readily apparent. Employers were the most pro-privatization on all of the five items. The petty bourgeoisie displayed above-average support for privatization on four out of five policies. Thus support for privatization was concentrated among those class categories most implicated in the market system and most inculcated in market values.

Although the most distinctive class, employers, were small in size in our local data, their distinctiveness was confirmed when using larger national samples. For example, when the private medicine question was analysed by class using BES 1987 data, employers remained most in favour of privatization at 52 per cent and workers were the least pro-privatization at 33 per cent.

The influence of social class was strongly corroborated by the scores on the index of attitudes to privatization. The 'highest' class categories all had positive scores, whereas the 'lower' class categories possessed negative scores.

Attitudes to privatization and sectoral location

Variations in attitudes to privatization according to sectoral location are summarized in Table 7.14. This table comprises a breakdown of attitudes by household production sector and household consumption sector. As in Table 7.13, both the five specific items and the overall index of attitudes to privatization are presented.

Turning to the influence of household consumption sectoral location, there were some inconsistencies on individual specific items, but the broad pattern was supportive of our expectation that private sector consumers would be more favourable to privatization than public sector consumers. Totally private households (+ 3) were the most favourable to privatization on four out of the five policies and exhibited above-average support on all five.

At the other extreme of consumption, totally public households (− 3) were the least in favour on four out of the five policies and exhibited below-average support on all five. The largest difference is evident over contracting out local authority services, on which

Table 7.14 Support for privatization by household consumption sector and household production sector

| | Variable[a] | | | | | |
| | PRIVMED | VOLSOC | HOSALES | PRIVNAT | PRIVLA | INDEX |
Sectoral location	% pro	% pro	% pro	% pro	% pro	mean
Consumption sector:						
Totally private	39	46	53	39	56	+ 0.24
Predominantly private	27	27	54	38	49	− 0.52
Predominantly public	24	32	41	26	33	− 1.24
Totally public	21	14	29	29	21	− 2.00
Production sector:						
Controller private	35	33	51	43	56	− 0.08
Controller public	25	26	46	30	33	− 1.20
Worker private	23	28	50	24	36	− 1.28
Worker public	30	35	51	22	36	− 0.88
All	30	31	50	33	43	− 0.69

Note:
[a] The privatization variables are as in Table 7.13.

Source: GMS2 panel.

support ranged from 56 per cent among totally private households to only 21 per cent among totally public households.

The strongest corroboration was provided by the mean scores on the index of attitudes to privatization according to consumption sectoral location. There was a clear gradational relationship, ranging from + 0.24 among totally private households to − 2.00 among totally public households. The latter were notably unfavourable to privatization.

The results for household production sectoral location were only partially consistent with our expectation that private sector producers would be more favourable to privatization than public sector producers. Although private sector controllers were more favourable to privatization on all five items than were public sector controllers, public sector workers did not display the expected pattern. Interestingly, the largest difference among controllers was on contracting out local authority services, with 56 per cent of private sector controllers pro-privatization compared with only 33 per cent of public sector controllers. Contracting out is a component of privatization that directly affects public sector employees.

The index of attitudes to privatization confirmed the patterning among the individual items. Public controller households were more anti-privatization than were private controller households. On the other hand, public worker households were more favourable to privatization than private worker households. Public sector middle-class radicals were in evidence again.

Attitudes to privatization and partisanship

The final hypotheses to be tested addressed the influence of partisanship on attitudes to privatization. Table 7.15 shows attitudes to both the five specific items and the overall index by Conservative and Labour partisanship. Results for the Alliance index of partisanship were not included as there were no significant consistent patterns. Considered together with the evidence in Table 7.15, this suggests that attitudes to privatization were firmly located along the ideological dimension of Conservative–Labour conflict.

Partisanship, especially the Conservative index, shows by far the strongest effect on attitudes to privatization of any of the variables employed in the analysis. Very strong Conservative identifiers (+ 3) were most favourable to privatization on all five policies. Fairly strong Conservative identifiers (+ 2) were the second most favourable on all five policies. At the other extreme, those very

Table 7.15 Support for privatization by Conservative and Labour partisanship

				Variable[a]			
Partisanship	n	PRIVMED % pro	VOLSOC % pro	HOSALES % pro	PRIVNAT % pro	PRIVLA % pro	INDEX mean
Conservative							
+ 3	31	68	48	74	84	81	+ 2.42
+ 2	76	50	47	71	61	76	+ 1.66
+ 1	73	36	37	66	40	60	+ 0.32
− 1	78	36	40	58	37	46	− 0.05
− 2	84	16	21	41	21	36	− 1.62
− 3	177	15	21	30	13	20	− 2.49
Labour							
+ 3	48	10	25	25	11	17	− 2.79
+ 2	72	22	21	28	14	13	− 2.57
+ 1	63	14	25	46	21	24	− 1.78
− 1	121	30	28	54	36	51	− 0.42
− 2	121	36	32	56	34	54	− 0.15
− 3	97	44	51	68	62	74	+ 1.43

Note:
[a] The privatization variables are as in Table 7.13.

Source: GMS2 panel.

strongly against the Conservatives (− 3) were the least favourable on all five items.

The index of attitudes to privatization exhibits a strong gradational relationship with Conservative partisanship. The attitudinal scores ranged from + 2.42 for very strong Conservative identifiers to − 2.49 for those very strongly against the Conservatives. Conservative partisanship was clearly positively associated with support for privatization.

As expected, the index of Labour partisanship produced a pattern that was completely opposite to that of Conservative partisanship. For instance, those very strongly against Labour (− 3) were the most favourable to privatization on all five items. Furthermore, the index of attitudes to privatization ranged widely from + 1.43 among the latter group to − 2.79 among very strong Labour identifiers. Thus, support for privatization was inversely related to Labour partisanship.

Although substantial, the differences produced by Labour

partisanship were less pronounced than those produced by Conservative partisanship. Thus attitudes to privatization were more closely associated with orientation towards the Conservatives, the governing party responsible for introducing the policy. It may well be that the attitudes to nationalization during the period of the last Labour government were more closely associated with orientation towards the Labour Party.

Two further general points are worthy of comment. First, the largest differences in attitudes for both Conservative and Labour indices were on the two NWSP items. This indicates a greater consensus on WSP (mostly unfavourable) than on NWSP. Second, both major parties displayed high levels of negative partisanship. This factor contributes to an explanation of the rise of the Alliance during the period of the panel study. Negative partisanship was especially pronounced for the Conservatives, with a third of the sample very strongly against them. The party in office will tend to attract a higher level of negative partisanship; nonetheless, substantial disaffection with government policies was also indicated.

Attitudes to privatization by social class, sectoral location and partisanship

The final stage in the analysis was to look at the combined effect of social class, sectoral location and partisanship on attitudes to privatization. This could be best achieved by performing a multiple regression on the index of attitudes to privatization on class, sector and partisanship variables. This was performed using the SPSSX regression procedure with blocks of variables entered sequentially.

Partisanship was clearly the strongest influence of the three factors on attitudes to privatization, but was itself influenced by social class and sectoral location. Partisanship should therefore be entered last into the regression model after class and sector. Social class was logically prior to consumption sector in that consumption patterns were partly determined by class location. Furthermore, production sector and social class overlapped in the equivalence of the self-employed sector with the combined employer and petty bourgeois class categories. The public/private sectoral cleavage was therefore applicable only within controller and worker classes. For these two reasons, class was entered first into the regression model, followed by sector and finally partisanship.

As indicated earlier, social class was represented by a set of dummy variables; for example, respondent is/is not an employer. As there were four class categories, only three dummy variables

175

were needed and the worker category was excluded. The procedure was identical to that adopted by Wright (1985, Table 7.7). Class categories that were significantly different from the worker category would emerge in the regression solution.

Similarly, production sector was also measured via a set of dummy variables with the self-employed category excluded. The household self-employed category was excluded also because it was identical to the household employer plus household petty bourgeois categories, and class was to be entered first. Consumption sector was represented by the single index of consumption sectoral location, which stressed the cumulative nature of sectoral consumption of services. Partisanship took the form of the three indices for Conservative, Labour and Alliance. Lastly, respondents for whom no answer was recorded on two or more of the five items were excluded from the analysis.

Table 7.16 summarizes the main features of the multiple regression. The significant variables in each block (class, sector and partisanship) are listed. In addition, the multiple correlation (R) and the proportion of variance explained (R^2) are provided at the end of each stage.

When social class was entered into the model first, a correlation of 0.27 was achieved, which means that class explained 7 per cent of the variation in attitudes to privatization. The significant class categories were respondent employer/petty bourgeois and other adult in the household petty bourgeois. In other words, these categories were significantly different from the excluded worker category.

A further 4 per cent of the variation was explained when the sec-

Table 7.16 Multiple regression of index of attitudes to privatization on social class, sectoral location and partisanship

Block	Significant variables	Correlation
1 Social class	Household petty bourgeois	$R = 0.27$
	Respondent employer	$(R^2 = 0.07)$
	Respondent petty bourgeois	
3 Sectoral location	Household consumption sector	$R = 0.32$
	Household public sector producer	$(R^2 = 0.11)$
3 Partisanship	Conservative index	$R = 0.62$
	Labour index	$(R^2 = 0.38)$

Source: GMS2 panel.

toral variables were added at the second stage, raising the multiple correlation to 0.32. (Sector variables alone produced an R of 0.28 but this included household self-employed, which was entered here under class.) Both consumption sector and production sector emerged as significant, the latter in the form of other adult in the household a public sector producer. The importance of taking account of others in the household was highlighted by the significance of household public sector here and household petty bourgeois in the class block.

The entry of partisanship at the third stage predictably had a powerful effect. The proportion of variance explained rose by 27 per cent to produce a multiple correlation of 0.62. Overall, therefore, the three factors – class, sector and partisanship – together accounted for 38 per cent of the variation in attitudes to privatization.

9 Conclusions

This chapter has attempted to clarify the conceptual confusion surrounding the increasingly important political and economic issue of privatization and has tested several hypotheses derived from the limited previous research into privatization. The GMS data were more comprehensive in coverage and the analysis brought together systematically the different aspects of privatization as well as the various influences on privatization. Although the study was confined to two districts in Greater Manchester, the findings were similar to those obtained in disparate national studies.

Conceptually, we find Kolderie's distinction between privatization of production and privatization of provision most useful, particularly in view of its ready applicability to sectoral cleavage theory. Public sector producers are liable to oppose privatization of both production and provision. On the other hand, public sector consumers may not be opposed to privatization of production if this improves the efficiency of their service or their perceived value for money (see Edgell and Duke 1985).

We propose a further component of privatization to Heald's four, that of encouragement of private consumption of services. This is in fact a dual process of encouraging the private sector whilst at the same time running down the public sector. If anything, this strand of privatization is increasing in importance and is liable to continue to do so. Of the four essential services studied, health exhibited both the most significant privatization during the study period and the most potential for further privatization. This finding must be tempered, however, by the fact that the NHS also received the most principled support of all the services. The dual process described in the previous paragraph fits neatly with the evidence of potential privatization on the one hand and principled support for state provision on the other. In contrast to health, housing and transport appeared to be near saturation point in privatization.

Social class was an important factor in access to private consumption of services. Predominantly private services fragmented the working class, whereas predominantly public services fragmented the middle classes. Household income, household economic activity and age emerged as other important influences on privatization. The first is itself clearly class related. There are clear limits to further privatization of services. Cost factors weighed heavily in decisions to privatize or not, and the Conservative government's economic policies since 1979 have resulted in increased inequality. Thus privatization is part of the growing economic divide in Thatcher's Britain between the haves and have nots.

Several negative trends are evident in the aftermath of privatization, for example, the increase in private housing repossessions and mortgage arrears, and the high proportion of privatization shareholders selling for a quick profit (Buckland 1987). Deprivatization, particularly of industries, is unlikely given the high costs involved. In this one off sense, the term 'special sales of assets' is more appropriate than 'central privatization proceeds'. The Labour Party is striving towards a new policy of social ownership which in part recognizes the status quo after privatization.

Support for privatization varied according to the nature of the service and the form of privatization. Welfare state services that currently were predominantly private constituted more fertile soil for support than predominantly public services, while limited privatization of production found more favour than complete privatization of provision. We found no evidence of a mandate for further privatization except in the case of housing.

There was a clear empirical link between attitudes to privatization and partisanship, in terms of both the strength and the direction of the link. Whereas Conservative partisanship was positively related to support for privatization, Labour partisanship was negatively related. This ideological element in attitudes to privatization was highlighted by the existence of a single underlying dimension on which all the five privatization items were located. Attitudes to welfare state privatization were related to attitudes to non-welfare privatization.

We have noted above that it is the presence or absence of privatization which most distinguishes Conservative and Labour austerity policies since 1974. This divergence in party policy concerning individualism versus collectivism has contributed to a polarization of attitudes to privatization in relation to partisanship. The evidence from the five privatization items in this chapter suggests that privatization may well represent a fundamental ideological cleavage.

The relevance of class and sectoral locations to attitudes to privatization was demonstrated both directly and indirectly via their influence on partisanship. The key factor was the degree of embeddedness of the household in the market system and market values. When sectoral location and class were combined, the crucial role of economic interests in attitude formation was emphasized.

The analysis has also thrown light on several important methodological issues. First, whereas most previous research on privatization has uncritically adopted conventional occupational class categories, in this chapter the appropriateness and usefulness of social class categories is readily apparent. The employers and petty bourgeoisie were distinctive in their support for privatization. Second, the importance of taking into account *both* the class and sectoral location of *all* adults in the household is corroborated. In other words, the findings represent a strong case for systematically investigating class and sector together and for doing so with reference to the whole household. Third, the data suggest the advisability of applying a knowledge filter to the analysis of attitudinal responses. Fourth, panel data are crucial for the study of process and change.

In the case of privatization of industries, government practice on the whole matches government rhetoric. The ideological commitment to privatization has been translated into a steady flow of successive applications to industries. Most of these industries were undervalued to politically manage successful privatizations. Even where there has been no action, the terms of the debate have been switched from nationalization to privatization. By contrast, the reality of privatization of consumption has been less radical than its rhetoric.

Privatization is a policy originating from and distinctively associated with the three Thatcher administrations in Britain. Several other West European governments are currently implementing similar policies. In our view, privatization embodies a package of related measures ranging from contracting out to selling off assets. Only by utilizing a broad definition of privatization, and by comprehensively investigating the interrelated influences on attitudes towards it, is it possible to make sense of the various aspects of this key government policy.

It is important to consider both privatization of consumption and privatization of production within the same overall framework. The distinctiveness of the Conservative era since 1979 lies in the presence of both, plus the encouragement of self-employment/the petty bourgeoisie and a concerted attack on the power of the (mostly public sector) trade unions. Thatcherism is actively undermining the institutions upon which the political strength of the Labour movement rests.

CHAPTER 8

Radicalism and Radicalization in a Period of Change

1 Introduction

Britain at the end of the 1970s was in a stagflationary situation characterized by high inflation, increasing unemployment and a lack of economic growth. These economic conditions, combined with the distinctive political policies adopted by the Conservatives following their electoral success in 1979, provided an ideal historical context in which to assess empirically the validity of competing theories of radicalism and radicalization. The major theoretical contenders included class theory and sectoral theory. To recap from earlier chapters (notably Chapters 1 and 2), class theory relates to changes in the balance of power between employers and employees, which has altered in favour of employers since 1979. Sectoral theory, on the other hand, relates to the patterning of private and public sector production and consumption, which has altered in favour of the private sector since 1979.

2 Class Theory, Sectoral Theory and Radical Social Change

Class theory, especially but not exclusively Marxist, suggests that the economic development of industrial capitalism directly affects class structure, consciousness and action (Mann 1973). Notwithstanding the classical theoretical pedigree of this model and the considerable sociological attention it has received, the exact links in the chain of causality remain the subject of concern and controversy (Lockwood 1981).

During the post-1945 period of economic recovery and growth and relative political stability, the Marxian version of this theory, which concerned successive capitalist economic crises followed by the emergence of a revolutionary working class, was widely regarded as obsolete (for example, Dahrendorf 1959), and was superseded by various non-Marxian theories that focused on the decline of working-class radicalism. Foremost among such theories were Bell's end of ideology thesis (1961) and Zweig's affluent working class thesis (1961). Politically conservative theories like these, which claimed that the working classes of advanced capitalism were integrated and acquiescent, were subsequently discredited as much by events as they were by sociological research (see Goldthorpe *et al.* 1969).

During the more economically uneven and politically turbulent 1960s and early 1970s, class conflict between capital and labour, although typically described as industrial conflict between management and unions, reappeared in theories of the class structure and social change. However, the nature and political significance of class consciousness and action were the subject of considerable sociological debate and political wishful thinking. On the one hand there were those, arguably the majority, who were 'pessimistic' regarding the radical potential of the working classes in Britain (for example, Lockwood 1966; Mann 1973; Roberts *et al.* 1977). On the other hand, some sociologists were more 'optimistic' about the revolutionary role that Marx had assigned to the proletariat, in the sense that they were reluctant to rule out this political possibility (for example, Moorhouse and Chamberlain 1974; Westergaard and Resler 1975).

Both 'pessimists' and 'optimists' accept that a degree of class cooperation and class conflict are always present, but they tend to interpret social stability differently, whatever their explanation of it. Thus, proletarian passivity tends to be viewed by 'pessimists' as a permanent feature of industrial capitalism, whether or not it is caused by the heterogeneity and/or the incorporation of the working classes. For example, certain neo-Weberians have suggested that a new type of home-centred instrumental worker has replaced the more traditional worker categories of proletarian and deferential workers as the prototypical worker of advanced capitalism (Lockwood 1966; Goldthorpe *et al.* 1969). In other words, the working class has become more heterogeneous and an increasing proportion has become incorporated via a new commodity consciousness that engenders acquiescence. 'Optimists', on the other hand, tend to regard proletarian passivity as a temporary phenomenon, again whatever the causes. For example, certain neo-Marxists have recognized the structural divisions and attitudinal variations within the British working class that are related to locality, employment sector, skill, income, gender, and so on, yet claim that it would be quite wrong to assume that 'capital is safe and labour tamed for all time' (Westergaard and Resler 1975: 391).

Thus, whilst both sides acknowledge the coexistence of harmony and dissent in contemporary Britain, the optimists seem to be committed to the possibility of radical social change from below, in marked contrast to the pessimists:

> The British lower class may yet prove more of an active force in making its own future than is often allowed.
>
> (Moorhouse and Chamberlain 1974: 401)

> It seems rather unlikely that the proletariat carries within itself the power to be a class for itself.   (Mann 1973: 73)

The lack of satisfactory empirical evidence to support either of these two divergent views regarding the revolutionary role of the British working class as envisaged by Marx could imply an element of overly deterministic political wishful thinking on the part of all protagonists in the debate. The literature on this subject, though extensive, is flawed on many grounds.

First, there have been very few empirical studies of working-class consciousness *and* action, although there are several literature reviews of the topic (for example, Giddens 1973; Mann 1973; Benson 1978; Marshall 1983; Hindess 1987). More specifically, no primary empirical study in Britain over the past quarter of a century has investigated comprehensively class attitudes *and* action in relation to both the industrial *and* political spheres. Sociologists have concentrated on class imagery and/or purely attitudinal data (see Bulmer 1975; Roberts *et al.* 1977; Gallie 1983). Even the classic three-volume Luton study was based predominantly on attitudinal data, though it did examine both industrial and political matters (Goldthorpe *et al.* 1968a,b, 1969). The only behavioural data used in this research were trade union participation, organizational memberships and vote. By contrast, some political scientists have emphasized action in their analyses but solely in relation to the political sphere and in the absence of a satisfactory conceptualization of class consciousness (see Marsh, 1977). Although Jessop (1974) achieved the latter, his data were political attitudinal to the total neglect of action. Lastly, the major British voting behaviour study by Butler and Stokes (1974) contained virtually no action data beyond vote, in addition to a sociologically ill-informed consideration of class and social change (see also Chapter 3).

Second, not only have studies of class and radicalism concentrated on the working classes to the almost complete exclusion of all other classes (see Goldthorpe and Bevan 1977), there has been a marked tendency to focus on a limited spectrum of economically active male blue-collar workers. In other words, such studies tend to conform to the traditional class analytic framework that was discussed in Chapter 2. Consequently, issues such as the nature and extent of shared values among different classes, raised by Mann over 20 years ago (1970) on the bais of an extensive secondary analysis, cannot be answered by such studies.

Third, sociological analyses of class and radicalism have been preoccupied far more with class consciousness than with class action or the important but problematic relationship between the two (see Miles 1975; Phizacklea and Miles 1980). Not surprisingly, there has been a plethora of attempts to theorize class consciousness and a dearth of attempts to theorize class action or the inter-relationship between class attitudes and action (for example, Parkin 1971; Giddens 1973; Mann 1973; Jessop 1974). Moreover, within the working-class consciousness research tradition, the claim that the working class is more likely to support radical values 'if they are presented as relevant to the respondents' everyday life' (Mann 1970: 429) has been challenged on conceptual and empirical grounds (Moorhouse 1976). In more general terms, it has been argued that 'research into working class consciousness has reached a stalemate between theories of working class instrumentalism and working class ambivalence' and that 'neither of these interpretations is in any way enlightening and ... both may be false' because such theories 'are not substantiated by the survey and attitudinal data from which each has been derived' (Marshall 1983: 263).

The fourth limitation of the research on class and radicalism with special reference to Britain concerns the discontinuity between definitions of class at the theoretical and empirical levels (Weinberg and Lyons 1972). Propositions about the relationship, harmonious or otherwise, between owners and workers are unlikely to be tested satisfactorily by studies that operationalize class on an occupational basis. This problem is exacerbated by the tendency to concentrate empirical research on male workers who are employed full time in manufacturing – a male-dominated conception of work and occupational class of declining representativeness. In other words, such a focus is less and less appropriate in the de-industrialized British economy that is characterized by an increasing number of service workers, female workers, underemployed workers and unemployed workers. In a study that is concerned to investigate, among other things, the classic Marxian thesis regarding the development of capitalism and the growth of working-class radicalism, the mismatch between theory and data would be acute if an occupational class scheme were used yet again and applied exclusively to male industrial workers.

Fifth, and possibly most important of all, is the almost total lack of historical sensitivity exhibited by class researchers (Marshall 1983). Radicalization and de-radicalization are historical processes, yet there is a clear tendency to analyse changes in class consciousness and class action in a static and ahistorical manner. This may be a function of the conceptualization of class that is used, in the sense that occupationally based measures are predicated on the notion of a hierarchy that is perceived as relatively unchanging and about which there is certain value consensus. Consequently, empirical research that operationalizes class in such an essentially static and ahistorical way, and deals in the currency of ideal types, is arguably more adept at describing class conditions than explaining class relations as historical forces (Nichols 1979).

Lastly, in class analysis the potential political importance of sectoral cleavages in general, and consumption in particular, has not been fully recognized, compared with the sociological significance that is conventionally and often uncritically attributed to occupational experiences. This is somewhat surprising in view of the fact that, in the 1960s, the social privatization of affluent workers was advanced as a possible explanation of the historical decline of the radical proletarian worker and the emergence of the basically acquiescent, instrumentally oriented, privatized male worker (Goldthorpe et al. 1969). More recently, the Conservative policy in the 1980s to reduce public sector employment and consumption at the expense of the private sector (see Chapter 7) makes it imperative to distinguish such *economic privatization* from *social privatization* and to examine the possible political implications of the former.

The rise of sectoral theory may be seen, in part, as a response to dissatisfaction with the inconclusive nature of the evidence used to assess theories concerning class and radicalism. It may also be regarded as a response to changes in the structure of public and private sectors brought about by Thatcherism during the 1980s (see especially Chapters 1, 2, 3 and 7). Class analysis on its own is, arguably, insufficient for a thorough consideration of the politics of social division in modern Britain. If class is no longer crucial to the politicization of social groups, then sectoral cleavages may be increasingly important.

During the 1980s, the relevance of a sectoral cleavage explanation of political attitudes and behaviour increased owing to the Thatcherist policy of reducing state intervention in the economy. In a period of massive state retrenchment and restructuring, the interests of public sector producers and consumers were threatened by the twin policies of public spending cuts and private sector growth, as the earlier chapters have shown. Consequently, it became increasingly recognized that social conflict and change in Britain in the 1980s could not be fully understood without reference to the formation and politicization of production and consumption sectoral cleavages (see Edgell and Duke 1983; Duke and Edgell 1984). According to this theoretical model, highly politicized public sector workers and consumers potentially fragment the working class and threaten to replace industrial workers as the new vanguard for radical social change.

There are many ways of transcending these limitations associated with past sociological studies on class and radicalism in Britain, and most of these are implicit in our six interconnected criticisms. In order to contribute to the debate about progressive acquiescence versus progressive radicalism, ideally a research strategy was needed that: (a) involved the investigation of consciousness and action over the whole class structure; (b) utilized a conceptual scheme which was congruent with the class and sector theories that were being addressed; and (c) took into account the historical context in more than just a token manner. Needless to say, this was easier said than done. Our preferred solution, explicated throughout this book, was to undertake a large-scale panel survey of both attitudes and action among representative samples in Greater Manchester (for details, see Appendix 1).

3 Dependent Variables: Radicalism and Radicalization

A wide range of conceptual tools is available for examining the degree of class consciousness evident among different sub-groups in the population. In British empirical research, two basic traditions on class consciousness are discernible: (1) the analysis of subjective class identity and subjective class images; and (2) the application of a framework of dominant and radical values to essentially attitudinal data.

The long tradition of empirical research on class imagery in Britain dates from the 1950s and the operational procedures utilized have varied from standard middle- and working-

(occupational) class dichotomy to complex types of class imagery (see Runciman 1966; Bulmer 1975).

The link between this kind of substantive empirical research and levels of class consciousness was provided by the 'pessimistic' theoretical contributions of Giddens (1973) and Mann (1973). Giddens distinguished three levels of class consciousness:

(1) the lowest level, which simply involves a conception of class identity;
(2) conflict consciousness, which requires the recognition of the opposition of interests with another class or classes;
(3) the highest level, revolutionary class consciousness, which embraces the possibility of an overall reorganization of the power structure through class action.

Mann's comparable model comprised four levels of class consciousness:

(1) class identity of oneself as working class;
(2) class opposition to capitalists and capitalism;
(3) class totality in the sense of recognizing one's own situation and one's society in class terms; and
(4) the conception of an alternative society.

According to Giddens, conflict consciousness is 'inherent in the outlook of the worker in a capitalist society; "revolutionary consciousness" is not' (1973: 202). In a similar vein, Mann concluded that 'revolutionary consciousness is the combination of all four, and an obviously rare occurrence' (1973: 13). More to the point at this stage is the observation that Mann's first two levels of class consciousness are broadly similar to Giddens' first two. Class totality involves the combination of the first two levels, prior to achieving the highest, revolutionary level of class consciousness.

The lower levels of class consciousness noted by Giddens and Mann, namely class identity and class opposition/conflict, are both more common and easier to operationalize than the higher levels. Anyway, it is doubtful whether the ability socially to construct a vision of an alternative socialist society is, or has ever been (even among intellectuals), a precondition for radical class action (Moorhouse and Chamberlain 1974) – although it has been argued that 'revolutionary class consciousness' invariably involves, however tentatively or implicitly, the notion of an alternative society (Wolpe 1970). Unsurprisingly, research on subjective class has tended to concentrate on the first two levels of class consciousness.

The theoretical foundation for the dominant and radical values approach was constructed by Parkin (1967, 1971). He distinguished between three competing meaning-systems; each one 'derives from a different social source, and each promotes a different moral interpretation of class inequality' (Parkin 1971: 81). First, the *dominant value system* derives from the 'major institutional order', endorses the unequal reward structure and encourages the subordinate class to be deferential or aspirational. Second, the *subordinate value system* originates in working-class communities. It neither supports nor opposes the existing order, but involves the negotiation of a compromise and accommodative responses. Third, the *radical value system* derives from the mass political party of the working class and favours an oppositional interpretation of class inequality. Parkin emphasized that these three meaning-systems are the major ones and do not exhaust the normative possibilities. He suggested that: 'all three meaning-systems tend to influence the social and political perceptions of the subordinate class', and that differences 'in the structure of attitudes of groups or individuals within this class are thus to some extent dependent upon differences in access to these meaning-systems' (Parkin 1971: 82).

An instructive example of primary empirical work in this tradition is Jessop's (1974) study of male electors in five constituencies. Drawing upon the work of Lenin (1970), among others, he developed a three-fold model of belief systems that is reminiscent of Parkin's typology: hegemonic, trade union and radical value systems or degrees of class consciousness. Jessop's comment that Parkin 'treats the dominant value system as essentially unchanging' (1974: 39) is particularly pertinent to studies of ideological change and political support during the Thatcher era. He concluded that political research 'should be as concerned with the social bases of meaning systems as with the influence of these systems on political behaviour' (Jessop 1974: 254). Interestingly, his survey also confirmed Mann's (1970) secondary analysis regarding the lack of value consensus, especially among the working class, and his suggestion that dissensus is conducive to social cohesion. Moreover, Mann's review of British and American attitudinal data on the nature and extent of value commitment also employed Parkin's conceptual framework. In other words, like Parkin, he coded supporting values as dominant and oppositional values as deviant or radical (Mann 1970).

In view of the difficulty of utilizing both the subjective class images approach and the dominant/radical values approach in our panel research design, our preference was to adopt the latter framework for the following negative and positive reasons. On the minus side we were aware of: the problems involved in operationalizing the higher levels of class consciousness and the resultant lack of previous empirical research to act as an exemplar; and the restrictive coverage of class imagery data in terms of its concentration on social attitudes. On the plus side, we took into account: that the dominant/radical values framework may be applied to industrial, political and social spheres; and the fact that Mann, in his perceptive confrontation with empirical data, resorted to Parkin's dominant/deviant dichotomy.

Our application of the dominant/radical framework involved constructing three attitudinal scales:

- industrial radicalism,
- political radicalism, and
- public spending radicalism.

Each attitudinal scale was made up of five items, the details of which are provided in Table 8.1. Each item was deemed to have a radical response and a dominant response along the lines developed by Mann (1970). The baseline score on each scale was 5, to which radical responses were added and from which dominant responses were subtracted. Thus, a respondent giving radical replies to all five items would score 5 + 5 = 10; a respondent giving dominant replies on all five items would score 5 − 5 = 0; and a respondent replying with five 'don't knows' or mixed answers (i.e. neither radical nor dominant) would remain on a score of 5. Respondents who did not answer an item through interviewer error or refusal were excluded from the analysis of that particular scale. (The *n* so excluded ranged from 10 to 25.) The justification for scoring the scales from 0 to 10, rather than from − 5 to + 5, is purely presentational. As subsequent tables comprise both mean scores and changes in scores on the scales (for example, Tables 8.4, 8.5 and 8.6), clarity is enhanced by reserving + and − signs solely for measures of change.

The use of five items on each scale afforded greater reliability than the use of single items to classify respondents as dominant, subordinate or radical in their consciousness. Our interpretation of the resultant scale scores was that scores of 7−10 were radical, scores of 0−3 were dominant, and those in between were subordinate. A problem with Mann's (1970) single-item approach to

Table 8.1 Construction of the three attitudinal scales (base = 5)

Radical response (+)	GMS1	% GMS2	Dominant response (−)	GMS1	% GMS2
1 Industrial radicalism scale (0–10)					
Approve of workers occupying factories	32	34	Disapprove	51	55
Agree still necessary for people to strike	72	73	Disagree	23	22
Sympathies generally for strikers	15	18	Against	26	30
Should give workers more say	55	55	Should not	34	39
Union's concern = profits and control	29	29	Pay and conditions	62	62
2 Political radicalism scale (0–10)					
Unions not too much power	30	38	Too much	65	54
Big business too much power	57	60	Not to much	32	30
More nationalization	11	12	Less	46	42
Should redistribute income and wealth	56	56	Should not	34	37
Unions should have close ties with Labour	22	23	Should not	73	70
3 Spending radicalism scale (0–10)					
Should abolish prescription charges on NHS	39	46	Should not	57	50
Should subsidize public transport systems	55	64	Should not	37	32
Should spend more to get rid of poverty	77	82	Should not	17	14
Disapprove of spending cuts	51	63	Approve	37	27
Spending cuts not inevitable	37	48	Inevitable	52	48

Sources: GMS1 and GMS2 panel.

classification is that it frequently excludes the possibility of a subordinate location.

Our purpose in utilizing three attitudinal scales was to compare the pattern of radical/dominant values in different spheres. In his study of American and French workers, Lash (1984) emphasized the importance of the empirical distinction between industrial and political radicalism. The introduction of a separate public spending radicalism scale related to the main *raison d'être* of our panel study (see Chapter 1). This attitudinal scale also addressed the issue of the historical fluidity of dominant values noted earlier with reference to the work by Jessop (1974) and Parkin (1967, 1971). In particular, the construction and use of this scale was indicative of the reassertion of market values at the expense of collective values that is arguably at the heart of Thatcherism. This historically significant shift in the content of the dominant ideology may further be interpreted as an attempt to increase the coherence of the dominant ideology to the extent that public spending is thought to be inconsistent with both the accumulation of capital and the achievement of a meritocratic society (see Abercrombie *et al.* 1980). In addition, it should be noted that, in view of Thatcherism's declared policies towards the state (that is, selectively to reduce its role in the economy) and towards trade unions (that is, to reduce their industrial power and political influence), three out of the five items on the political radicalism scale similarly related to the aims and historical context of our project.

Lastly, the individual items were selected partly on the basis of comparability with previous research and partly in the interests of obtaining a balance of items with dominant and radical majorities. Eight of the 15 items may be located in previous rounds of the British Election Study ranging from 1964 to 1979 (Butler and Stokes 1974; Sarlvik and Crewe 1983). The industrial and political radicalism scales were especially well balanced in that each contained two dominant majority items, two radical majority items and one neither dominant nor radical majority item. Interestingly, in his empirical comparison of the USA and Sweden, Wright's (1985) class consciousness scale was composed of items similar to those in our industrial and political radicalism scales. Wright commented that he limited his analysis to items 'which have the clearest class content' (1985: 146).

All three attitudinal scales possessed both internal and external validity. Each item was significantly intercorrelated with other items on its scale. Of the 30 intercorrelations, 12 were above 0.3 and only 6 were below 0.2. External validity is powerfully

Table 8.2 Attitude to government regulation of trade unions by political radicalism scale

Political radicalism scale score	n	Dominant response (should introduce stricter laws) %	Radical response (should not introduce stricter laws) %
0	65	91	9
1	39	85	10
2	74	74	19
3	68	59	34
4	97	63	29
5	78	45	47
6	75	39	51
7	67	24	64
8	39	10	77
9	43	7	91
10	29	7	93

Source: GMS2 panel.

demonstrated for the political radicalism scale in Table 8.2. Those classified as radical on the scale were overwhelmingly radical on government regulation of trade unions, those classified as dominant on the scale were overwhelmingly dominant on government regulation of trade unions, and those on the mid-point of the scale (5) exhibited neither a radical nor a dominant majority on government regulation of trade unions. The other scales were all similarly validated.

Throughout our study we have stressed the importance of analysing class action as well as class attitudes (see especially section 2 above). Thus, in addition to the three attitudinal scales, we utilized a radical action scale. This related directly to our project's primary concern with the restructuring of public spending. The action scale consisted of a number of acts undertaken by respondents against the spending cuts. Action was defined here in a broad manner in order to encompass both 'orthodox' and 'unorthodox' action, although no attempt is made below to distinguish between the two (see Marsh 1977). It is to be regretted that political participation was almost invariably measured in earlier surveys solely by voting behaviour, which has been discussed already (see Chapter 3), and is of course excluded from the analysis below partly for this reason, but also because the focus of this chapter is radicalism and radicalization.

The action scale represented a simple numerical count of the following types of individual and collective actions taken against the spending cuts: signing a petition, attending a meeting, contacting a Member of Parliament (MP), marching in a demonstration, participating in a sit-in, and refusing to pay a public sector charge for services (for example, rent strike). The first three types of action may be regarded as more 'orthodox' than the last three. The levels of political activity at each stage of the panel survey were remarkably similar at 11.2 per cent ($n = 106$) and 12.3 per cent ($n = 84$), respectively. At the first stage, (1980–1) the most popular form of political protest was attending a meeting, which accounted for over one-third of all protests (4.3 per cent). Signing a petition (2.2 per cent) and marching in a demonstration (1.8 per cent) were the next most common actions. At the second stage (1983–4), petitioning increased markedly to account for nearly half of all reported action (5.5 per cent), demonstrating increased by approximately half (2.8 per cent), and attending protest meetings declined steeply (1.2 per cent). Taking the two surveys together, signing a petition was the most widely reported type of radical political action and accounted for nearly one-third of all protests.

These levels and forms of political action were comparable with the results of surveys in Britain and other representative domocracies in the West (Marsh 1977; Barnes *et al.* 1979). An exception concerned participating in a demonstration. At both stages of our panel survey, the incidence of this type of direct action was higher than that found in other studies, rising to over 20 per cent of all protests at the second stage. In view of the risks associated with this more 'unorthodox' form of political action – including the physical risk of personal injury, the legal risk of arrest, the economic risk of loss of work and the social risk of loss of status – this finding may be significant politically in several respects. For example, it could be interpreted as indicating the relative ineffectiveness of other forms of more 'orthodox' protest under Thatcherism. The urban riots in Britain during 1981–2 and the miners' strike of 1984–5 may also be seen in this light. Alternatively, it could be interpreted in terms of the debate about the increased preparedness of citizens to participate in direct political action in 'mature' democracies (Sanders and Tanenbaum 1983).

The main focus of action at the first interview was education and this was most marked in Torytown (see Chapters 5 and 6). At the second it was still education but now followed closely by health.

Table 8.3 The measurement of radicalization and polarization

	Radicalization/de-radicalization	Polarization
Overall process	Increase in either radical or dominant category for whole sample	Increase in radical and dominant categories for whole sample
Differential process	Increase in either radical or dominant category for specific sub-group	Increase in radical category for one sub-group and dominant category for opposed sub-group

The main organizational vehicle for protest action at both stages was trade unions and this was most noticeable in Labourville (Edgell and Duke 1982).

Our operational scales of radicalism/adherence to the dominant value system (dominantism is too inelegant a term) represented static cross-sectional measures at one point in time. They enabled systemic questions to be addressed, such as the influences on radicalism (what we refer to as the *structure of radicalism*).

Panel data, however, facilitated the measurement of changes over time and therefore opened up the possibility of gauging the *process of radicalization* and the *process of polarization*. Since all the items in the three attitudinal scales and the action questions were asked at both interview stages, evidence of these processes could be sought by analysing changes in the scales over time.

Our approach to measuring radicalization and polarization is summarized in Table 8.3. Both processes may occur either in the overall sample or in specific sub-groups. A proportional movement in the direction of the radical value system was regarded as radicalization; an increase in adherence to the dominant value system was termed de-radicalization, and growth at both extremes of a scale represented polarization.

4   Independent and Intervening Variables

The ways in which we conceptualized and operationalized the key structural independent variables in this study – class and sector –

have been fully discussed in Chapter 2. We used four basic social class locations based on the social relations of production: employer, petty bourgeois, controller of labour and worker.

The procedural decisions applied to both social class (plus occupational class where appropriate) and production sectoral location were the same. First, both respondent and household measures were entered into the full model. Second, the economically inactive were classified according to their previous class/sectoral location.

The first procedure was justified by our finding that attitudinal and behavioural reactions to the spending cuts were based not only on direct personal experience, but also on events in the life of significant others in the household (see Chapter 6). Our preliminary analysis of radicalism was performed using household class and sector. However, the subsequent fuller analyses entered the class and sectoral locations of both respondent and household into the regression model. This solution allowed the influence of either or both to be displayed in the model, thereby addressing in a comprehensive manner the choice of unit of analysis.

The second procedure, which related to the degree of coverage choice, reflected our view that it is not just the economically active who are implicated in the class (and sectoral) structure. We included the economically inactive, such as the unemployed, the retired and housewives, by classifying them according to their previous class/sectoral location. It was in the analysis of the economically inactive that the decision to include both respondent and household measures of class and sector proved particularly useful. Whereas respondent-based measures were typically the most significant for the economically active, in the case of the inactive it was often the household measure that was the most useful.

As noted in Chapter 2, *consumption sectoral location* is more straightforward to operationalize than class and *production sector* to the extent that measurement is inherently at the household level. We operationalized household consumption location on the basis of three services – housing, transport and health. We demonstrated that classifying people by their overall involvement in private or public consumption (a cumulative rather than a non-cumulative measure) revealed important political effects. Each household was classified according to the degree of private or public provision of the three services.

To recap, the basic model to be tested was the influence of class and sector on radicalism, which relates to the theories outlined above. A further stage in the analysis involved the introduction of

Class
RSC = respondent social class
HSC = household social class
ROC = respondent occupational class
HOC = household occupational class

Sector
RPS = respondent production sector
HPS = household production sector
HCS = household consumption sector

Other
SEX
AGE
RUM = respondent union membership
RHE = respondent higher educated

Events
HU = household unemployment
THR = threat of household redundancy
HIS = household impact of spending cuts
AREA = district (Labourville/Torytown)

Party
LAB = Labour partisanship
CON = Conservative partisanship
LSD = Liberal/Social Democratic partisanship

Radical scales
Industrial
Political
Spending
Action

STRUCTURAL ⟶ INTERVENING ⟶ DEPENDENT

Figure 8.1 Influences on the structure of radicalism: variables included in the full model

additional independent and intervening variables into the model which might influence the structure of radicalism. These variables are listed in Figure 8.1 along with their abbreviated names in the regression model.

Other *structural variables* included were: *trade union membership*, which is known to be linked to radicalism (Gallie 1983); *higher education*, the importance of which has been stressed by Inglehart (1977); and *age and sex*, given the greater preponderance of activism among young males as opposed to old females (Marsh 1977). However, it is important to note that, 'when we controlled for economic activity and associated variables such as employment sector and unionization, the differences between men and women in terms of radical attitudes and action in the context of the public spending cuts were insignificant compared to the contrast between the economically active and inactive' (Edgell and Duke 1983: 375).

Two types of *intervening variable* were proposed in the model. First, *events* relating to the specific historical context of high unemployment and public spending cuts; and second, *party* variables relating to the partisanship of the respondent. The events comprised household unemployment since the first interview, the threat of household redundancy, household impact of the spending cuts and whether the household was located in Labourville or Torytown. The latter was included because of the higher levels of actual spending cuts and action against them in Torytown (see Chapter 5). The party variables comprised Labour, Conservative and Liberal/Social Democratic Alliance partisanship. Previous empirical research had consistently established a close link between partisanship and radicalism (for example, Jessop 1974; Gallie 1983).

Whereas the cross-sectional variables outlined above were adequate to examine the static structure of radicalism, the analysis of processes of change required additional *dynamic process variables*. The variables that provide the framework of radicalism may not be the same as the variables that trigger off the process of radicalization. *Changes* in class consciousness may be linked to *changes* in structural position, events, or partisanship. The additional variables included in the full model for changes in attitudes/action are documented in Figure 8.2.

Class locations were relatively stable over the three-year period of the panel study, although there was a marked increase in the size of the petty bourgeoisie (from 4.1 per cent to 6.6 per cent). This is a feature of recessions and has been encouraged by government policies, notably the Enterprise Allowance Scheme (Johnson 1981;

Class
RBS   = respondent become self-employed

Sector
HPH   = household privatized health
HDH   = household deprivatized health
HPE   = household privatized education
HPT   = household privatized transport
HDT   = household deprivatized transport

Other
RBUM = respondent become union member
RDUM = respondent deunionized

Events
HBIS   = household become impacted by spending cuts
HBIC   = household become impacted as consumer
HBIP   = household become impacted as producer
HBU   = household become unemployed
RBU   = respondent become unemployed
SBU   = spouse become unemployed

Party
VCON = vote become Conservative
VLAB = vote become Labour
VLSD = vote become Liberal/Social Democratic
PCON = party become Conservative
PLAB = party become Labour
PLSD = party become Liberal/Social Democratic

Figure 8.2 Influences on the process of radicalization: additional process variables included

Creigh *et al.* 1986). For sectoral changes, a series of indicators were devised to capture household economic privatization/deprivatization of particular services over the panel period (for housing the *n*s proved too low). Only unionization/deunionization were included among the other structural variables, as age, sex and education are less subject to change.

The dynamic events variables related to change between the two interviews in terms of unemployment and impact of the spending cuts. The British party system exhibited a degree of volatility with the rise of the Liberal/Social Democratic Alliance. We employed two sets of dynamic measures: movement to the parties in terms of vote between the 1979 and 1983 elections; and movement to the parties in terms of a change in party identification between the two interviews.

5   Radicalization, De-radicalization or Polarization?

Table 8.4 summarizes the changes in the mean score on the four scales for the panel as a whole. Two of the four scales altered significantly in the direction of radicalization, namely political and spending. Industrial radicalism and action, however, remained at roughly the same level. The changes may also be expressed in terms of the percentage who were radical on each scale at the first and second interviews. For political radicalism, the radical proportion increased by 6 per cent and for spending by 12 per cent, whereas industrial radicalism decreased by 2 per cent and action remained identical at 12 per cent.

Although the level of action remained stable, the main focus of

Table 8.4   Mean scores and changes in scores on the four scales

Scale	*n*	GMS1 Mean	GMS2 Mean	Change
Industrial radicalism	660	5.07	5.02	− 0.05
Political radicalism	675	4.26	4.57	+ 0.31
Spending radicalism	674	5.59	6.32	+ 0.73*
Action against the cuts	685	0.15	0.15	+ 0.02

Note:
* Significant at the 0.01 level.

Sources: GMS1 and GMS2 panel.

199

action switched from consumer groups concerned with education cuts (especially in Torytown), to trade unions concerned with various issues (including education, health and jobs). Behavioural radicalization was displayed by 8 per cent of the panel in the sense that they took action against the cuts prior to the second interview but not the first. For many people, action is occasional rather than continuous, a condition Dowse and Hughes (1977) have termed 'sporadic intervention'.

There is some limited evidence of overall *polarization* among the whole sample. First the standard deviation for all three attitudinal scales was larger at the second interview than at the first, indicating centrifugal tendencies. Second, changes over time in the three attitudinal scales were significantly intercorrelated at the 0.01 level. Third, although the industrial radicalism scale did not display overall polarization, two of the items (occupying factories and sympathy for strikers) evidenced increases in both radical and dominant responses (see the data included in Table 8.1).

Interestingly, the two scales that showed most a tendency to radicalization was present were those most clearly related to the historical context of the panel study. Contextual relevance is further demonstrated by the marked radicalization of attitudes explicitly related to the public spending cuts (see Table 8.1). The proportion of the panel adopting a total oppositional stance to the cuts (i.e. disapproved of the spending cuts in general and viewed them as not inevitable) increased by 11 per cent between the two interviews. From another point of view, these attitudinal changes reflect a degree of political sensitivity to the reassertion of certain dominant values associated with Thatcherism during the 1980s.

Some interesting variations in the pattern occurred when the sample was broken down into respondents who were economically active throughout, respondents who were economically inactive throughout and those who were intermittently economically active (that is, either at the first interview or the second). Table 8.5 provides a breakdown by respondent's level of economic activity.

Examination of the static cross-sectional data at GMS2 revealed the following. First, the expected pattern of the economically active being the most radical and the inactive the least radical emerged distinctly from three of the scales – industrial, political and action. With regard to action, we have demonstrated elsewhere that housewives typically do not have the time to take action owing to the prevailing gender-based division of labour (Edgell and Duke 1983). Second, the reverse pattern was the case for spending radicalism. This is interpretable in terms of the reliance of

Table 8.5 Mean scores and changes in scores on the four scales by respondent's level of economic activity

Respondent level of economic activity	Industrial			Political			Spending			Action		
	GMS2 mean	Change	n	GMS2 mean	Change	n	GMS2 mean	Change	n	GMS2 mean	Change	n
Economically active throughout	5.27	− 0.22	370	4.79	+ 0.36	375	6.18	+ 0.53	378	0.22	+ 0.03	379
Intermittently economically active	4.96	− 0.01	103	4.41	+ 0.03	105	6.32	+ 0.84	105	0.14	− 0.05	108
Economically inactive throughout	4.57	− 0.28	187	4.23	+ 0.36	195	6.61	+ 1.04	191	0.10	+ 0.04	198

Source: GMS2.

the inactive particularly, and the intermittently active occasionally, on state subsidies. The political implications of the expansion of the state-dependent population in Britain are an emerging issue (Dunleavy 1989).

The most radicalized sub-group on all four scales were the economically inactive. Somewhat surprisingly, the radicalization of the inactive was occurring among the retired rather than among housewives or the unemployed. Whereas pensioners might be expected to undergo radicalization on spending, the general character of the effect suggests an awakening of grey consciousness and the possibility of emergent grey power as their numbers increase in the electorate.

A critical sub-group in terms of radicalization and de-radicalization were those respondents who became unemployed between the two interviews. Although only a small group ($n = 24$), there was little evidence of radicalization. They displayed above-average de-radicalization on industrial (-0.38) and below-average radicalization on political ($+0.21$), and were average on spending radicalization ($+0.74$). These findings are very much in line with research undertaken in the USA on political responses to unemployment (Scholzman and Verba 1980) and suggest that it is difficult to generalize in this area since unemployment is a mixed experience in terms of class, age and gender (Allen *et al.* 1986).

6 The Influence of Class and Sector on Radicalism and Radicalization

Table 8.6 summarizes the patterns of radicalism and radicalization for household-based class and sector categories. Observations were made first of all on the static cross-sectional data, that is, the influence of class and sector on the *structure of radicalism*; and secondly on the relationship between class/sector and the *process of radicalization*.

The expected strong relationship between social class and radicalism was present for the industrial, political and spending attitudinal scales. Each of these featured a consistent gradational relationship, with employers the least radical and the workers the most radical. In the case of action, it was the petty bourgeoisie and the controllers who were most active. The distinctiveness of the employer and petty bourgeois classes (especially the former) was apparent for all three attitudinal scales. In other words, the

202

Table 8.6 Mean scores and changes in scores on the four scales by household social class and household production sector

Class/sector	Industrial		Political		Spending		Action	
	GMS2 mean	Change	GMS2 mean	Change	GMS2 mean	Change	GMS2 mean	Change
Household social class:								
Employer	3.64	0.00	2.86	− 0.39	4.71	+ 0.75	0.14	− 0.04
Petty bourgeois	4.07	− 0.29	3.97	+ 0.41	5.36	+ 0.80	0.19	+ 0.05
Controller	5.07	+ 0.04	4.44	+ 0.15	6.33	+ 0.89	0.18	+ 0.05
Worker	5.37	− 0.02	4.98	+ 0.49	6.67	+ 0.55	0.17	+ 0.01
Household production sector:								
Controller private	4.79	+ 0.02	4.04	− 0.14	6.01	+ 0.73	0.12	+ 0.06
Controller public	5.36	+ 0.06	4.86	+ 0.47	6.67	+ 1.06	0.24	+ 0.03
Worker private	5.41	+ 0.11	5.01	+ 0.56	6.82	+ 0.66	0.13	+ 0.01
Worker public	5.32	− 0.24	4.93	+ 0.36	6.42	+ 0.37	0.23	0.00

Source: GMS2

dominant value system was widely held and resilient among the capitalist classes.

The relationship between radicalism and production sector was less straightforward, in the sense that the influence of sector was different in the controller and worker classes. Interestingly, it was not the public sector workers but the public sector controllers who emerged as the more radical on three of the four scales. Similarly, public sector workers were not more radical than private sector workers other than in terms of action. The link between action and public sectoral location is particularly impressive, especially for the controllers.

Consumption sectoral location was excluded from Table 8.6, partly in order to simplify the table, but also because consumption sector was predictably unrelated to industrial and political radicalism. However, there was a marked cleavage between totally private and totally public categories on the spending scale, as might have been expected. The relevant mean scores on spending were: totally private consumers 5.75, mostly private consumers 6.06, mostly public consumers 6.95, and totally public consumers 7.76.

Turning to the dynamic change data, the only social class not to radicalize on three of the four scales were the employers. There is some evidence here of polarization between the bourgeoisie and the rest. Furthermore, it was the controllers rather than the workers who were the most radicalized on three of the four scales. Most telling, however, were the public sector controllers, who radicalized more on the three attitude scales compared with both the private sector controllers and the public sector workers.

To recap thus far: social class was an unequivocal influence on the structure of radicalism. Moreover, the distinctive de-radicalization of employers suggests that one of Thatcherism's most important effects has been to reinforce capitalist values among capitalists. The attitudinal de-radicalization may represent a response to the new right's ideological assault in terms of sweeping away the last vestiges of the post-1945 social democratic consensus in Britain. Also, production sector emerged as a strong influence on the structure of radicalism *and* the process of radicalization in this specific historical context. Of major importance is the finding that it was public sector controllers rather than public sector workers who were in the vanguard of both radicalism and radicalization. This suggests that Parkin's 'middle class radicals' were alive and well in the Thatcherist Britain of the 1980s (Parkin 1968).

The second part of our analysis concerned the relative importance of class and sector on the structure of radicalism. This was achieved by entering both the class and sector variables into a regression model on each of the four scales. As outlined above in the discussion of operationalization, both respondent and household measures of class and sector were entered into the model. A summary of the results is presented in Table 8.7.

The multiple correlations between class/sector and the three attitudinal scales were broadly similar, ranging from 0.211 for industrial radicalism to 0.304 for spending radicalism. Table 8.7 may be further analysed in several ways: first, the relative importance of class and sector variables, which is the main objective; second, the relative importance of social class and occupational class; and, third, the relative influence of respondent and household measures. Each will be considered in turn.

The relative importance of different variables or groups of variables may be gauged by comparing their relative contributions to the increments in variance (change in R^2). Class emerged as substantially more important an influence than sector on industrial and political radicalism. On spending radicalism and action, however, it was sector that proved the most influential. Indeed in the case of action, only sector variables were significant. Interestingly, the influence of consumption sector on action was a reflection not of mostly public consumer activism but of the 'middle class' mostly private consumers taking action over education cuts (especially in Torytown). Production sector was the only category to emerge as a significant influence on all four scales. Consumption sector was predictably not a significant factor in industrial and political radicalism.

On each of the attitudinal scales it was social class which proved the most significant predictor. On two of the three attitudinal scales, a social class variable (RSC or HSC) was the strongest single predictor. Indicatively, the only variable in the class/sector set not appearing as significant in any of the models was household occupational class. This suggests that the fact that others in the household were manual or non-manual was not important. By contrast, the presence of employer or petty bourgeois others in the household clearly was important and reflected in the considerable predictive power of household social class. A by-product of this research exercise was therefore to confirm the greater salience of social class categories.

On all three attitudinal scales, household measures of class/sector were more influential than respondent measures. However, in the case of political radicalism, the difference was slight with relative contributions to R^2 of 0.036 and 0.035. For action, respondent

Table 8.7 The influence of class and sector on the structure of radicalism: multiple correlations between class and sector variables and the four scales

Industrial			Political			Spending			Action		
Variable[a]	R	Change in R^2	Variable[a]	R	Change in R^2	Variable[a]	R	Change in R^2	Variable[a]	R	Change in R^2
1 HSC	0.185	0.034	1 HSC	0.171	0.029	1 HCS	0.190	0.036	1 RPS	0.099	0.010
2 RPS	0.211	0.011	2 ROC	0.222	0.021	2 RSC	0.244	0.023	2 HCS	0.125	0.006
			3 RPS	0.253	0.014	3 HPS	0.278	0.018			
			4 HPS	0.266	0.007	4 ROC	0.296	0.010			
						5 RPS	0.304	0.006			
$R = 0.211$			$R = 0.266$			$R = 0.304$			$R = 0.125$		
$R^2 = 0.045$			$R^2 = 0.071$			$R^2 = 0.093$			$R^2 = 0.016$		
$n = 651$			$n = 666$			$n = 665$			$n = 676$		

Note:

a RSC = respondent social class
HSC = household social class
ROC = respondent occupational class
HOC = household occupational class
RPS = respondent production sector
HPS = household production sector
HCS = household consumption sector

Source: GMS2

production sector was the best predictor. The benefit of including both respondent and household measures was confirmed by the joint emergence of equivalent respondent and household measures for two of the four scales.

7   *Influences on the Structure of Radicalism*

Having tested the basic model of class and sector influences on the structure of radicalism, the next stage was to introduce the additional static variables outlined earlier. The procedure was to enter blocks of variables into the model sequentially, beginning with class and sector, followed by other structural variables, then events, and lastly party variables. At each stage those variables that added significantly to the explanation of radicalism were included in the model. The significant variables and their incremental contribution to the variance explained are provided in Table 8.8.

The multiple correlations outlined for industrial, political and spending radicalism were all above 0.5, with the variance explained at over 30 per cent, and, in the case of political, 45 per cent. Action exhibited a lower multiple correlation of 0.34. It would appear more difficult to explain action than to explain attitudes.

If we examine the relative contribution of the blocks of variables to the variance explained, it was partisanship which was clearly the biggest influence on all three attitudinal scales, despite being entered last into the model (the reason for this was that partisanship itself may be thought of as being determined partly by the other blocks in the model). Indeed, the reason for the lower multiple correlation for action was the absence of partisanship's 'usual' contribution, as in the other scales.

In the case of action, events were the best predictor, especially the variable household impact of the spending cuts. Once again, the relevance of the historical context was amply confirmed, in this instance in relation to action.

Class and sector proved to be the second most powerful influence on the political and spending attitudinal scales. On the industrial attitudinal scale and on action, age emerged as the next best predictor, with the young being the more radical in both cases.

The influential party variables on attitudinal radicalism refer in fact to identifying with Labour and *not* identifying with the Conservatives (a negative coefficient). The moderate middle-of-the-road nature of the new Alliance during this period (the early

Table 8.8 Influences on the structure of radicalism: multiple correlations between groups of variables entered sequentially and the four scales

		Industrial	Political	Spending	Action
	RSC			⋆ (0.023)	
	HSC	⋆ (0.034)	⋆ (0.029)		
CLASS	ROC		⋆ (0.021)	⋆ (0.010)	
AND	HOC				
SECTOR	RPS	⋆ (0.011)	⋆ (0.014)	⋆ (0.006)	⋆ (0.010)
	HPS		⋆ (0.007)	⋆ (0.018)	
	HCS			⋆ (0.036)	⋆ (0.006)
R = (change in R^2)		0.211(0.045)	0.266(0.071)	0.304(0.093)	0.125(0.016)
	SEX			⋆ (0.007)	⋆ (0.006)
OTHER	AGE	⋆ (0.046)	⋆ (0.012)	⋆ (0.008)	⋆ (0.015)
STRUCTURAL	RUM	⋆ (0.029)	⋆ (0.015)	⋆ (0.008)	
	RHE		⋆ (0.008)		⋆ (0.007)
R = (change in R^2)		0.346(0.075)	0.326(0.035)	0.341(0.023)	0.210(0.028)
	HU				
EVENTS	THR	⋆ (0.017)	⋆ (0.011)		
	HIS	⋆ (0.025)	⋆ (0.026)	⋆ (0.031)	⋆ (0.050)
	AREA		⋆ (0.015)		⋆ (0.010)
R = (change in R^2)		0.403(0.042)	0.397(0.052)	0.384(0.031)	0.322(0.060)
	LAB	⋆ (0.127)	⋆ (0.222)	⋆ (0.032)	⋆ (0.014)
PARTY	CON	⋆ (0.031)	⋆ (0.071)	⋆ (0.134)	
	LSD			⋆ (0.006)	
R = (change in R^2)		0.566(0.158)	0.672(0.293)	0.565(0.172)	0.344(0.014)
Final R (R^2)		0.566(0.320)	0.672(0.451)	0.565(0.319)	0.344(0.118)

Note:
⋆ Indicates that the variable emerged as significant at the appropriate stage of entry. Increments to the variance explained (change in R^2) are provided in brackets for significant variables.

Source: GMS2.

1980s) was corroborated by the failure of Liberal/Social Democratic partisanship to emerge in three of the models. The clear link between Labour partisanship and attitudinal radicalism provided strong support for the claim that the Labour Party is the key institutional factor in the persistence of a radical value system in Britain (Parkin 1971).

Household impact of the spending cuts emerged as significant (along with respondent production sector, age and Labour partisanship) on all four scales. This is despite being entered after all the structural variables. Trade union membership was predictably a significant influence on industrial and political radicalism, especially the former. Similarly, it was not unexpected that higher education would prove significant on 'ideological' attitudes (political radicalism) and action.

8 Influences on the Process of Radicalization

The final stage in the analysis was to examine the influences on changes in attitudes and action, that is, on the process of radicalization/de-radicalization. All the static variables included in the last section (and listed in Figure 8.1) and the additional dynamic variables (outlined in Figure 8.2) were entered into the model. The procedure of entry was as described above and the results are summarized in Table 8.9.

In every case the multiple correlation attained for changes in the scale is lower than that for the static analysis. Clearly it is easier to explain the structure of radicalism than the process of radicalization. Dunleavy and Husbands (1985) similarly found it easier to explain support for Conservative and Labour at one point in time than to explain changes in support over time. The highest multiple correlation in our analysis was obtained for changes in action at around 0.07. Interestingly, the action figure was the only one to get near the static figures in Table 8.8.

Partisanship was not the most powerful influence on the process of radicalization, as it was on the structure of radicalism. Only in the cases of political and spending radicalism was partisanship the strongest influence. Instructively, it was events which played the largest part in predicting change on the other two scales (industrial and action). The overall variance explained by changes on the spending scale was lower than that for the other attitudinal scales. This indicates that the radicalization trend here was a general one

Table 8.9 Influences on the process of radicalization: multiple correlations between groups of variables entered sequentially and changes in the four scales

		Industrial	Political	Spending	Action
CLASS	RBS			* (0.008)	
AND	RPS				* (0.016)
SECTOR	HPE				* (0.019)
R = (change in R^2)		0 (0)	0 (0)	0.090(0.008)	0.187(0.035)
OTHER	AGE	* (0.006)			
STRUCTURAL	SEX			* (0.008)	
R = (change in R^2)		0.077(0.006)	0 (0)	0.128(0.008)	0.187(0)
	HBIS	* (0.017)			
	THR	* (0.009)			
EVENTS	AREA		* (0.013)		* (0.013)
	HIS				* (0.023)
R = (change in R^2)		0.179(0.026)	0.116(0.013)	0.128(0)	0.267(0.036)
	VLAB	* (0.015)	* (0.027)		
	VCON	* (0.007)	* (0.015)		
PARTY	WCON		* (0.009)		
	PLSD			* (0.016)	
	PCON			* (0.008)	
R = (change in R^2)		0.233(0.022)	0.254(0.051)	0.200(0.024)	0.267(0)
Final R (R^2)		0.233(0.054)	0.254(0.064)	0.200(0.040)	0.267(0.071)

Note:
* See note to Table 8.8.

Source: GMS2.

which was common to most sub-groups in the population. Both this point and the previous point on the importance of events confirm yet again the salience of the historical context of the public spending cuts.

Most of the change models contain only a few significant variables, so it is informative to consider briefly each of the models. Change in industrial radicalism was simply a combination of events (becoming affected by the spending cuts and the threat of redundancy), plus movement towards the Labour Party and away from the Conservative Party in terms of vote. The latter is probably the result of the very same events.

The process of political radicalization was overwhelmingly linked to changes in partisanship, which were away from the Conservatives and towards Labour. In the case of Labour, this suggested a return to the fold in terms both of party support and of approving the central tenets of the labour movement. The only other variable to emerge as significant on changes in political radicalism confirmed this interpretation. The variable was area and the radicalizing district was Labourville. For spending radicalism, the change effects were small but interesting. Radicalization here was a function of *not* becoming self-employed, being female, and moving towards the Liberal/Social Democratic Alliance and away from the Conservatives.

The most interesting and parsimonious model of change, however, was that of action. The variance explained was split almost equally between events and class/sector. The former influences on action were household impact of the spending cuts and area (with Torytown most active); the class/sector variables were respondent production sector and household becoming privatized in education. Interestingly, the latter involved households (mainly in Torytown) that had been forced into private nursery services because of a lack of public provision. What all of these four variables have in common is their link to the specific historical context of the spending cuts.

The generally lower level of explanation of change is partly a reflection on social science's previous preoccupation with static cross-sectional analysis (and resultant dearth of adequately designed panel studies to replicate), and partly a celebration of the uniqueness of individual human behaviour and social change.

9   Conclusions

The pattern of class and sectoral change revealed in the data is complex and contradictory. There is some evidence for radicalization, de-radicalization and polarization. Most importantly, the basic model concerning the fundamental influence of class and sector on the structure of radicalism was confirmed clearly and consistently. Thus, employees were found to be more radical than employers, and public sector producers and consumers were generally more radical than private sector producers and consumers. Interestingly, the most distinctive feature of the class data was the support for dominant values expressed by capitalists, and the most notable feature of the sectoral data was that production sector emerged as strongly related to action. The public sector controllers appeared as the new vanguard of radicalism and radicalization. These findings are unsurprising given Thatcherism's pro-capital and anti-trade union, pro-private sector and anti-public sector position. In other words, the politico-economic changes wrought by Thatcherism in Britain during the 1980s, had, above all, reinforced the dominant values adhered to by the capitalist class and promoted the public sector controllers to the forefront of class struggle.

These findings confirm the value of panel data and dynamic process variables in the analysis of social change, and, correspondingly, the need to distinguish between the structure of radicalism and the process of radicalization. Moreover, the importance of investigating attitudes and action has been demonstrated, along with the superiority of social class categories over occupational class. This analysis has also demonstrated the applicability of a dominant/radical values framework to the assessment of social consciousness, plus the benefit of using both respondent- and household-based measures of class and sector. However, it is not simply a matter of the inherent superiority of one class scheme compared with another, but more a matter of selecting the most appropriate measures in the light of one's theoretical aims. In this instance, social class categories, in combination with sectoral categories, proved very instructive for the analysis of radicalism and radicalization during the Thatcherist 1980s.

However, it proved easier to explain the structure of radicalism and adherence to dominant values than the process of radicalization/de-radicalization. Moreover, the variables which explained the structure of radicalism were not necessarily the same as those which explained the process of radicalization. At the same time, the historical context of the public spending cuts was affirmed at several points as an important influence on the data.

With regard to the debate over the radical potential of the propertyless classes, both optimistic and pessimistic accounts of class and social change have been shown to be flawed on four main grounds: (a) in their concern with structure rather than process; (b) in their emphasis on attitudes to the relative exclusion of action; (c) in their neglect of the sectoral dimension of political changes;

and (d) in their concentration on the economically active in general, and male manual workers in particular. However, as far as this important historical question is concerned, on balance the evidence would seem to favour the pessimists, although we would empha- size that economic conditions are inherently unstable, and hence political stability is arguably more apparent than real. For example, the relatively acquiescent character of the propertyless classes during the 1980s was not unrelated to mass unemployment, changes in trade union law and the decline of the public sector. Yet, the continued importance of trade unionism, especially in the public sector, and partisanship to radical attitudes and action was amply confirmed. In conclusion, therefore, the persistence of a radical values system in Britain during the 1980s was still associated with the industrial and political wings of the labour movement, despite their relative weakness.

Over the period covered by our study – the 1980s – sociological research on class consciousness and action seemed to have gone out of fashion. As was the case in the 1950s in Britain and elsewhere, and unlike the 1960s and 1970s, the balance of class forces favoured capital. It is as if the relative demise of working-class radicalism was matched by the decline of research into it. In other words, the popularity of class as a research issue seems to be inversely related to the ascendancy of capital.

Apart from our panel study reported here, a second exception to this rule was the Essex cross-sectional research on the importance of class in modern Britain (Marshall *et al.* 1988). Although the aims and methods of this other study were different from our own, as we have seen already in Chapters 2 and 3 their findings related to some of the issues raised by the GMS. On the one hand, we broadly concur with the three main class conclusions reached by the Essex team, namely that class structures social attitudes and political behaviour, and that consequently class analysis is still crucial to an understanding of Britain in the 1980s. On the other hand, our data suggest that the structure of radicalism is influenced by sector as well as class and that the process of radicalization is influenced by historical events. Hence, the argument that, as far as class consciousness is concerned, it is 'a question of how classes are organized in pursuit of class interests' (Marshall *et al.* 1988: 188) needs to be qualified with reference to the fragmenting influence of sectors (see Dunleavy 1989) and the positive or negative influence of the socio-political context (see Scott 1990). If we had to choose one phrase with which to sum up our findings on class con- sciousness and action, it would be 'structured fragmentation'.

Proletarian, controller and capitalist attitudes and behaviour are certainly fragmented in Thatcher's Britain, but they are fragmented in a socially structured way (Piven 1976). Class location, and to a lesser extent sectoral location, have been shown to be important in the fragmented social structuring of both acquiescence and protest. Moreover, the historical situation encountered by all social classes in Britain during the 1980s was found to be relevant to understanding the pattern of socially structured fragmentation.

CHAPTER 9

Thatcherism in Britain during the 1980s: The Reckoning

1 Thatcherism and the Transformation of Contemporary Britain

The Conservative Party led by Thatcher held power in Britain throughout the 1980s. The purpose of this concluding chapter is to consider in which ways and to what extent this period of political domination known as Thatcherism has changed British society.

From the outset, we have argued that the policies pursued since 1979 represent a distinct break with the past: first, in the negative sense that Thatcherism is opposed to the economic theory of Keynesian demand management and its related political ideology of state intervention; second, in the positive sense that Thatcherism favours individualism and an enhanced role for the market in economic life. However, this is not to argue that Thatcherism is a set of unchanging ideas and policies. Thatcherism may have been inspired in the 1970s by certain economic interests and ambitions, both capitalist and nationalist, but it evolved during the 1980s in response to specific political and economic exigencies.

In the first chapter we emphasized the essential coherence of Thatcherism in terms of the interrelatedness of its underlying pro-capital, anti-labour, pro-private, anti-state politico-economic orientation. The fight against inflation and the control of public spending were given top priority from the beginning, and this has not changed. Nor has the Thatcherist dislike of organized labour or the Thatcherist support for capital. However, as circumstances changed, so did the emphasis. Three overlapping phases of Thatcherism may be discerned and summed up by the terms recession, recovery and regression.

During the first stagflationary phase from the late 1970s to the mid 1980s, cutting public expenditure and defeating trade unionism were the central issues. During the second economic recovery phase from the mid to late 1980s, public spending continued to be a key issue and unemployment increased in importance. The third, less buoyant phase, dating from the late 1980s, was characterized by declining North Sea oil revenues and rising interest rates, which threatened the continuation of economic growth in terms of both profits and employment. Public spending remains a prominent issue and the balance of payments problem, last heard of in the 1970s, seemed to have reasserted itself. Throughout the whole era, privatization grew in importance, pre-election booms were engineered, and opposition parties and groups were split within and between themselves.

This, briefly, is the historical context in which we have sought to analyse the sociology of Thatcherism. Our core characterization of Thatcherism as pro-capital and the market, and anti-labour and the state, led us to consider that the most appropriate theoretical categories with which to analyse Thatcherism were social class, plus production and consumption sectoral locations.

The case for a social class, rather than an occupational class, scheme was advanced with reference to the limitations of the traditional analytic class framework, the three choices involved in operationalizing the concept class in a comprehensive manner and the historical context of the research. More specifically, we argued that the traditional analytic class framework based on the occupations of the economically active was deficient in three important respects: (a) it failed to reflect the organizing principle and related power structure of capitalism; (b) it tended to exclude women and the unemployed, amongst others, from class analysis; and (c) it was less compatible with sectoral analysis. Consideration of alternative conceptual class schemes, the unit of analysis and the degree of coverage choices led us to propose a new analytic class framework. This was based on the greater appropriateness of social class to an analysis of Thatcher's Britain, especially in combination with sectoral categories. It also involved a preference for household class in all situations, except when production attitudes and behaviour were the object of the research, and for everyone being included in class analysis. Lastly, we suggested, and have confirmed throughout this study, that, in a period characterized by a concerted attempt to alter the ideological and structural balance of social class and sectoral forces in favour of capital and the private sector, this new analytic class/sectoral framework was particularly apposite.

2 Measuring the Social and Political Effects of Thatcherism

The data presented in Chapters 3–8 reveal a clear pattern of support for and opposition to Thatcherism during the 1980s in Britain that related to social class and sectoral divisions.

In Chapter 3, the social bases of Thatcherism were shown to be narrowly capitalist class based and narrowing in terms of the vote at the 1979, 1983 and 1987 general elections. Opposition to Thatcherism over the same period was similarly social class based to the extent that, as one moved down the class structure, the greater the incidence of anti-Thatcher voting. Although support for and opposition to Thatcherism were primarily and systematically related to social class throughout the whole of the 1980s, household production sector effects within the employee classes had become quite marked by 1987: by this time, public sector controllers and workers were more likely to vote for anti-Thatcher parties than were private sector controllers and workers.

A particularly clear and consistent gradational pattern of support for and opposition to Thatcherism was revealed by the household consumption sector data. These indicated that, the greater the involvement of a household in private consumption, the more likely it was to vote for Thatcherism, and vice versa.

Within the pattern of structured support for and opposition to Thatcherism revealed by the social class and the production and consumption sector data between 1979 and 1987, the highest level of support was to be found among the employers, whereas the highest level of opposition was to be found among totally public consumption households. Support for Thatcherism among the petty bourgeoisie in 1979 and 1983, and among totally private consumers over the whole period, was marked but not as high as among the employers. Similarly, opposition to Thatcherism among workers was consistently high over the whole period but not as high as among the totally public consumers.

Summarized in this way, the voting data showed not only that class dealignment is a myth in Thatcher's Britain, but that the social class and sectoral pattern of support for and opposition to Thatcherism is exceedingly distinctive. The two self-employed classes in our neo-Marxist social class scheme were noticeably pro-Thatcher and the workers were consistently, though less markedly, anti-Thatcher. Moreover, a clear majority of totally private consumption sector households were pro-Thatcher, in contrast to those who were totally dependent upon the public sector, the vast majority of whom were anti-Thatcher.

These findings emphatically validated the adoption of a social class model of the class structure in which the ownership of property dimension is fundamental. This key element of electoral support for and opposition to Thatcherism would have been at best obscured and at worst entirely hidden by an essentially occupational class analysis of voting. The very distinctive household consumption sector voting patterns similarly validated the adoption of a sectoral approach to the study of voting in Thatcher's Britain. In fact, the highest measure of anti-Thatcher voting (75 per cent) in all the data presented was among the totally public consumption households for the 1979 election.

These voting patterns were in line with the pro-capital, anti-labour, pro-private sector, anti-public sector ideology and policy that have been espoused and implemented since 1979. The Conservative attack on trade unionism and the public sector, especially during the first phase of Thatcherism, led to a considerable measure of support among the capitalist classes. Conservative electoral support during the 1980s was reinforced by policies designed to favour capital in general, and to expand the role of the private sector in particular. In other words, consumption sector political effects remained high throughout the period and production sector political effects grew in strength. Over the three elections analysed, support for Thatcherism declined but remained relatively united compared with the anti-Thatcher vote. Thus, the electoral success of Thatcherism has been due in part to a fragmented opposition in party, social class and sectoral terms, and in part to a narrowly based but relatively united Conservative vote. Last but not least, Thatcherism's mandate has been essentially a parliamentary one, predicated upon Britain's system of non-proportional representational voting.

A second measure of Thatcherism concerns the nature and extent of support for core Thatcherist policies. In terms of general attitudes to cutting public spending and specific attitudes to spending on welfare state services (Chapter 4), we found that throughout the 1980s the majority of people disapproved of Conservative government policy, especially cuts in the health services, and that the overall direction of attitudinal change was of increased opposition. The capitalist classes, totally private sector consumers and Conservative identifiers were the most prominent in their support for cuts in public spending in general and cuts in welfare state spending in particular. However, strong approval of the cuts did not extend to defence and police spending. Attitudes to other aspects of Conservative policy during the 1980s, notably inflation, unemployment and local government autonomy, exhibited a similar pattern. In other words, apart from significant numbers of employers, totally private consumers and Conservative partisans, most people were opposed to government policies on these issues.

Apart from certain aspects of privatization (see below), the only exception to this lack of support for Thatcherist policies concerned trade union reform. In this instance, although trade unions and strikes were regarded as necessary, a majority (albeit a declining one) were in favour of the Conservative policy of restricting the power of trade unions. Yet again, there was a predictable social class, sectoral and party patterning of attitudes to trade unionism.

In sum, the distinct, narrow and highly ideological social class and sectoral basis of Thatcherist support was clarified and amply confirmed. The Conservative faithful were in a minority on most policy issues and were concentrated among the capitalist classes and the totally private sector consumers. Supporters of Thatcherism were also distinctive in the sense that, although they tended to approve of cuts in public spending in general, they were in favour of increased defence and law and order spending.

Our third measure of Thatcherism focused on the attempt by Conservative central governments throughout the 1980s to control local government with the aim of reducing this element of public spending (Chapter 5). On the basis of a case study of two politically contrasting local authorities in Greater Manchester, we found that, once the total expenditure data had been disaggregated into individual services, the party effect was crucial in relation to the local impact of Thatcherist central government policies. In the early 1980s, Conservative-controlled Torytown implemented Thatcherism at the local level in a more thoroughgoing and enthusiastic way than Labour-controlled Labourville. A marked degree of partisanship was also evident in the political positions adopted by the local press in the two case study areas.

In other words, political obedience characterized the relationship between Conservative central government and Conservative local authorities, whereas reluctant political obedience, and even political disobedience, characterized the relationship between Conservative central government and Labour local authorities. Conservative attempts to control local government in general and their spending policies in particular have been politically unpopular and therefore not entirely successful. The driving force behind the attempt to emasculate local political democracy during the 1980s was the Thatcherist ambition to reduce public expenditure. Although local government may have been transformed in certain respects (for example, in terms of its subordination to central government), the economic impact of Thatcherism has been uneven owing to the mediating role of the controlling local party. Lastly, political obedience also characterized the relationship between the local press and the dominant local party.

A fourth measure of Thatcherism related to the social impact of Conservative policies on different groups over time (Chapter 6). The data on perceived impact of the public spending cuts showed that, in the early phase, consumer impact (especially education in Torytown) was most apparent, as was the impact on households with children. During the panel study period (1980–4), producer impact (especially unemployment in Labourville) increased, along with the impact on households with retired persons. Our panel findings on the perceived impact of the cuts also revealed a clear social class pattern that became more marked over time, to the relative disadvantage of employees compared with employer and petty bourgeois households. Thus, the social impact of cuts in welfare state spending was divisive and this measure of Thatcherism validated, yet again, our social class and sectoral approach.

A fifth measure of Thatcherism pertained to privatization, broadly defined to reflect the diversity of this increasingly important policy (Chapter 7). On this issue, we found that support for privatization varied according to the nature of the service and the form of privatization. Predominantly private services (e.g. housing) constituted more fertile ground for support than predominantly public services (e.g. health), while limited privatization of production was more popular than complete privatization of provision. This suggests that the vast majority of people in Britain recognized that health services can be provided effectively and fairly only by the state on the basis of need, and not by capital on the basis of price. As with the first two measures of Thatcherism (electoral support and policy attitudes), we found little evidence of a mandate for further privatization. In fact, the only pro-privatization majority out of five privatization policies was for council house sales.

Detailed consideration of the pattern of support for and opposition to privatization revealed a clear link with partisanship in relation to both the strength and direction of the link. Unsurprisingly in the light of the other findings, Conservative partisanship was related in a positive way to support for privatization and Labour partisanship was related negatively. In addition to this element of ideological polarization, class and sector were once again prominent in the analysis. When social class and sectoral location were combined, the crucial role of economic interests in attitude formation was highlighted: for example, employers and the petty bourgeoisie were both distinctive in their support for privatization. On a more methodological note, the data on attitudes to privatization yet again affirmed the appropriateness and usefulness of our social class categories both on their own and in combination with sectoral categories, and both with reference to the whole household.

Our sixth and last measure of Thatcherism, namely the nature and extent of radicalism, radicalization and polarization in Britain during the 1980s, produced the most ambiguous findings (Chapter 8). On the one hand, there was some evidence of radicalization over time, namely in the political and spending radicalism scales, reflecting the relevance of the historical context of the research. On the other hand, there was a slight decline in industrial radicalism, and the level of action against the cuts remained stable. Regarding the latter measure, there was a change in the focus of action from consumer groups to producer groups. Anti-Thatcher radical action was not continuous but sporadic; in other words, it was fragmented. The data also revealed some limited evidence of overall polarization, especially with reference to attitudes to public spending.

Social class and sectoral location both influenced the structure of radicalism and the process of radicalization. First, there was a consistent relationship in the expected direction between class and radicalism, with employers being the least radical and workers the most radical. Second, it was public sector controllers, rather than public sector workers, who emerged as part of the vanguard of both radicalism and radicalization in Thatcher's Britain.

On balance, this complex and contradictory measure of Thatcherism provided marginally more support for 'pessimistic' accounts of class-based radical social change than it did for 'optimistic' accounts. Thatcherism has not radicalized the whole of the working class, only parts, and these at different times (not to mention the 'middle-class' radicals evident in the public sector). Although there was some evidence of overall polarization, there was also some evidence of de-radicalization. The fragmented working classes contrast with the more unified capitalist classes, whose support for dominant values seems to have been reinforced by the experience of Thatcherism.

221

3 The Sum of the Measures of Thatcherism

What do all these measures of Thatcherism add up to? Throughout this sociological analysis of Thatcher's Britain in the 1980s, the same variables have cropped up time and time again, notably social class, production and consumption sectoral locations and partisanship. For example, political attitudes and behaviour towards Thatcherism were found to be related clearly and consistently to social class and sectoral location. Thus, the pattern of results generated by our social class and sectoral location categories and the analyses based upon them amply demonstrates the usefulness of our approach.

On the one hand, this was illustrated by the tendency for the highest and strongest electoral and attitudinal support for Thatcherism to be expressed by a relatively narrow and unified range of social groups, namely the employer and petty bourgeois classes, together with the totally private consumption sector location households and Conservative partisans. At the same time, these were also the social groups who were affected the least in negative terms, and the most in positive terms, by Thatcherist policies.

In contrast, the opposition tended to be based more widely but was somewhat fragmented. This social fragmentation took many forms – including attitudinal, behavioural, organizational and temporal. Workers, especially those employed in the public sector, public sector controllers, totally public sector consumers, trade unionists, the elderly and the unemployed were all prominent in their opposition to Thatcherism from time to time on a variety of issues, but during the 1980s this broadly based opposition tended to be more divided than united and never coalesced into a mass radical movement. This was a matter of design *and* default in the sense that labour was arguably as much weakened by the recession as by the political attack by Thatcherism.

The fragmented character of the opposition to Thatcherism did not extend to Parliament, where, on the basis of minority electoral support, the Conservative Party led by Thatcher was able to dominate the House of Commons. However, the Thatcherist political programme to change British society was far less popular outside Parliament. Public support was limited to the Conservative policy to reform trade unions plus certain forms of privatization, notably council house sales at discount prices. Among the many unpopular Thatcherist policies during the 1980s, the most unpopular was the 'reform' of the National Health Service, the archetypal socialized service available on the basis of need rather than price. In the most recent phase of Thatcherism, the introduction of the community charge and the steep rise in the mortgage interest rate threatens the continued support of even the most pro-Thatcher social groups. However, opposition to the regressive and therefore unfair poll tax may not be translated into electoral defeat, since it discourages people to register to vote.

Overall, therefore, attitudinal and behavioural opposition to and, to a lesser extent, support for Thatcherism in Britain during the 1980s were characterized by structured fragmentation. That the support for Thatcherism, especially in Parliament, was less fragmented than the opposition is of great political significance. However, whatever the changing degree of fragmentation, both support and opposition are socially structured, notably, according to our data, by social class and sectoral cleavages. Moreover, historical circumstances, including the content and perceived credibility of government and opposition party policies, influence the social patterning of the political process, often in contradictory ways. For example, Conservative policies such as the privatization of local authority housing erode the social bases of Labour support, while other aspects of the same general policy, such as the attempt to extend the role of the market into all spheres of everyday life, including education and the massively popular socialized health service, swell the opposition to Thatcherism. Throughout the 1980s, the problem for the non-Thatcherist opposition was an inability to translate popular support into parliamentary support.

4 Thatcherism, Dominant Values and Political Practice

The content of the dominant ideology of late capitalism can be listed under five main headings: capitalism, statism, managerialism, consumerism and nationalism. Abercrombie *et al.* discussed the first three elements with special reference to Britain, albeit in a rather static way, but declined to examine consumerism on the grounds of 'flimsy' evidence and failed to discuss nationalism at all (1980: 189). However, they did consider inconsistencies between and within the elements that they regarded as the key ones in the dominant ideology of late capitalism – for example, the possible conflict between welfare statism and capital accumulation, and between different fractions of capital.

In the post-1945 period to the late 1970s, there existed a broad political consensus in Britain to the extent that both Conservative and Labour administrations attempted to implement a Keynesian version of this dominant ideology. This involved operating with a welfare state capitalist model characterized by state intervention in a mixed economy, the growth of the welfare state and the maintenance of full employment. Confronted by the economic failure of policies predicated on this model, the Labour government of the late 1970s started to depart from Keynesian policies on pragmatic grounds. Economic failure was followed by political downfall.

In 1979 the victorious Conservative Party led by Thatcher engaged in a more principled and complete rejection of Keynesian politico-economic policy. In the process of adopting a monetarist view of the role of individual choice in a free market, Thatcherism moved ideologically to the right by virtue of its advocacy of laissez-faire capitalism. This recrudescence of market values involved a redefinition of the two key elements of the dominant ideology in Britain during the 1980s: capitalism and statism. State intervention in the economy was to be reduced and the public–private mix was to be altered in favour of the private sector, the growth of the welfare state was to be reversed, and government responsibility for full employment was to be abandoned. Thus, the revised dominant ideology gave a greater priority to capital at the expense of the state, and, by implication, correspondingly demoted the interests of labour and the public sector. In ideological terms, it can be argued that Thatcherism in government broke with the 'one nation' Conservative tradition of Churchill, Macmillan and Heath. Henceforth, One Nation Conservatives were known as 'wets' and became an endangered species in successive Conservative cabinets during the 1980s.

In sum, One Nation Conservatism and Two Nation Thatcherist Conservatism represent contrasting variants of the dominant ideology of advanced industrial capitalism. The basic difference between them is that the former favours *welfare state capitalism* whereas the latter advocates *laissez-faire capitalism*. In this respect, Thatcherism's dominance in the Conservative Party is ideologically distinctive. However, from the perspective of the dominant ideology, Thatcherism is far less distinctive; it has merely reasserted its adherence to certain core values. Thus, it is important to specify the standard being used to measure Thatcherism.

Furthermore, from the standpoint of political practice, Thatcherism also appears less distinctive. In order to achieve its stated objectives of cutting public expenditure in general and welfare state spending in particular, and of introducing market forces into all areas of economic life, Thatcherism has been obliged to expand the role of central government in various ways. First, local government has been emasculated while the power of central government has been enhanced. Second, defence and law and order spending have been increased (popular with Conservative identifiers as well as with Thatcher governments), partly at the expense of welfare state spending and partly in response to the effects of cuts in the welfare state. Third, the state has intervened in innumerable ways to ensure that market values operate in all spheres of social life. Thus it is now a state requirement that virtually everything from rural transport services and the supply of tap water, to the performance of general practitioners and the provision of university courses, has to be measured in terms of pecuniary values. In Veblenian terminology (1970), Thatcherism has aspired to spread pecuniary culture more deeply and widely than any other post-1945 government in Britain. Interestingly, and unsurprisingly, in the process of trying to effect this change it has been calculated that: 'the Thatcher era has produced more legislation than any other government in British history' (Benyon 1989: 177).

In sum, Thatcherism represents an attempt to transform British society from above: it has attempted, on the basis of its majority support in Parliament but with only minority popular support, to propagate capitalist values and practices. However, it has been far more successful in spreading capitalist values than capitalist practices in all spheres of life. Moreover, in attempting to create a more free-market type of society, the state has become more authoritarian. According to Gamble, this gap between the theory and practice of Thatcherism constitutes its 'great contradiction' (Gamble 1988: 205). In other words: 'Despite the anti-state rhetoric the Thatcher Governments have proved remarkably interventionist and dirigiste. The state has had to be considerably strengthened in order that the Thatcher Governments can press ahead with freeing the economy' (1988: 205–6).

5 Capitalism, the Welfare State and Thatcherism

In the attempt to reassert the role of market forces in British society during the 1980s, Thatcherism has increased the internal coherence of the dominant ideology to the extent that it has been successful in reducing the welfare role of the capitalist state. Moreover, the contradiction between the capitalist economic system and welfare state institutions in Thatcher's Britain has been further reduced by introducing the logic of the market into the production and distribution of welfare state services. Even the finance of the welfare state depends less and less on redistributive collectivist principles, and more and more on charging the consumers of the welfare state. In other words, a large measure of capitalism, in both quantitative and qualitative terms, was introduced into the welfare state by Thatcherism during the 1980s.

The welfare state not only contradicts the market price value that lies at the heart of capitalism, but it is also inherently contradictory. As far as capital accumulation is concerned, the welfare state is both 'functional' and 'dysfunctional'. It is functional in the sense that it contributes to the creation of a healthy, educated and passive labour force, thereby achieving social harmony and legitimation. It is dysfunctional in the sense that it involves considerable economic and political costs by virtue of the fact that it has to be financed out of the private sector and potentially threatens the theory and practice of individualism. From this perspective, Thatcherist policies have tended to enhance the functional dimension of the welfare state while at the same time attempting to reduce the dysfunctional dimension. For example, cuts in welfare state spending are intended to achieve the latter, whereas it is hoped that the privatization of the welfare state will achieve the former. This is yet another illustration of the attempt by Thatcherism to move the ideological goalposts in favour of capital.

Consequently, the coherence of the dominant ideology in Thatcher's Britain during the 1980s was doubly improved – first, by expanding capitalism at the expense of welfare statism, and, second, by expanding the functional elements of the welfare state at the expense of its dysfunctional elements. Thatcherism has been able to implement these social changes from above by winning the political argument, and with it three successive general elections. It has been helped in this endeavour by an opposition weakened by a recession and internal divisions that have been encouraged and exploited by Thatcherism.

However, the Thatcherist policy of concentrating on the state of the economy at the expense of the economy of the welfare state potentially exacerbates the inherent contradictions of both, but especially the latter. Thus, the social casualties of an increasingly deregulated industrial capitalist Britain not only represent a moral indictment of the economic system, but raise the possibility of a 'legitimacy crisis' if the political demands by those dependent to a greater or lesser extent upon the state remain unmet. To recognize such political demands is also problematic because containment (that is, social control) is costly in terms of law and order spending as well as welfare spending.

The sociological significance of Thatcherism is that it has questioned and altered the conventional wisdom regarding the mixed economy and in the process reversed the historical association between advanced capitalism and the growth of the welfare state. One of Thatcherism's main achievements has been the degree to which market values are used in contemporary Britain to measure a person's welfare needs. The recrudescence of capitalist values (including the attack on public spending) is not unique to Thatcher's Britain. Privatization programmes have been undertaken by governments of all political persuasions, not just Conservative ones, throughout Western Europe during the 1980s, for example, coalition governments in Italy and West Germany, and governments led by socialists in Spain and Sweden (Vickers and Wright 1988). One consequence of this ideological and practical assault on the public sector has been to give credence to the 'public = bad, private = good' equations. Only the passage of time will reveal whether or not this political policy is a permanent feature of British and other Western European societies. If this key aspect of Thatcherism is not reversed, an acute social division between 'private opulence and public squalor' (Galbraith 1962: 211), which is increasingly evident in employment, housing, health, transport and education, is likely to be the most significant and lasting social and political legacy of Thatcherism.

6   Postscript: Thatcher's Resignation – the End of an Era?

At the time of going to press (November 1990), Mrs Thatcher resigned her premiership. The demise of the longest-serving British prime minister this century, and only woman ever to hold this office, was the culmination of increasingly visible internal divisions within her own party. In the main, these divisions concerned her autocratic style of government and certain key policy areas, notably European integration and the poll tax. In a period of economic difficulty and poor by-election results, many Conservative MPs were understandably anxious about their electoral prospects. When Michael Heseltine challenged Mrs Thatcher in a leadership contest, the internal divisions became publicly acute. At this critical juncture, the so called 'iron lady' resigned within twenty-four hours of declaring 'I fight on. I fight to win'. It is entirely appropriate that the 'elected dictator' should be toppled by a palace (of Westminster) coup and not be defeated at a general election.

The key question in any social audit of Mrs Thatcher's reign is the degree to which Thatcherism will outlive Thatcher. Her resignation can be interpreted as an attempt to ensure that if she could not carry on, then someone else who is arguably more sympathetic to Thatcherism than Michael Heseltine, should be enabled to do so, namely one of her more recent and loyal cabinet colleagues like Douglas Hurd or John Major. Mrs Thatcher's resignation is also indicative of the limits of Thatcherism; a sufficient number of Conservative MPs were of the view that the same leader, with the same strident and undemocratic style, pursuing the same policies, had become more of an electoral liability than an electoral asset.

The success of John Major, Thatcher's personal preference, means that there will be a semblance of continuity, and therefore Thatcherism will survive the end of Thatcher, at least in the short term. However, the change of leadership is likely to involve the dilution of Thatcherism as a politically distinctive era with respect to both its economic and ideological dimensions. In other words, the restructuring of Britain's economy in favour of the private sector and the ideological realignment of the political culture that accompanied it, is likely to be less forcibly advocated and less thoroughly implemented in the post-Thatcher era. For example, during the two week campaign for the leadership of the Conservative Party and therefore the government, the process of revising the post-Thatcher political agenda was initiated in earnest. Discussion focused on a review of the poll tax and on a higher priority being given to education and training, both of which imply more rather than less public spending. In a pre-general election context, it is therefore possible that Majorism will herald a more state interventionist form of Thatcherism. In the longer term, judgement about the nature and extent of the persistence of Thatcherism will have to be suspended until all the evidence is available, and then, as always, much will depend upon the measures used.

The Greater Manchester
Study

1   Origins

The change of government in May 1979 heralded a new era in the history of post Second World War Britain. We contend that it is an era characterized by a distinctive set of 'new right' policies designed not merely to halt but to reverse Britain's long-term economic decline.

The central target of Conservative policy in 1979 was to cut public expenditure in general and welfare state spending in particular. Late in 1979 we realized that the historical significance and ramifications of this change in the direction of British society from increasing collectivism to increasing individualism warranted sociological investigation. In March 1980 we submitted a research grant application to the Social Science Research Council (SSRC) with the general aim of studying the 'new right' central government policies, their social effects and political reactions to them. More specifically we were concerned to survey the following theoretically important and policy-relevant issues: (a) how people see and react to major changes in social policy; (b) the role of these reactions in relation to competing theories of politicization; and (c), arising out of (a) and (b), the social and political policy implications of these social changes. We were subsequently awarded a grant and the first stage of the project began in September 1980.

In November 1981 we sent a report to the SSRC (Edgell and Duke 1981) in which we argued that our findings strongly supported the basic premise of the research project, namely that the public expenditure cuts were highly salient to the research sample in terms of knowledge and perceived impact, and involved a potential polarization situation. We further argued that, to investigate socio-political changes fully, a more dynamic research design was necessary. We considered that a follow-up study using our ready-made panel would enable us to assess changes in the impact of the 'cuts' over time, to test theories of social stability more effectively and to establish more confidently the longer-term policy implications. The renamed SSRC, the Economic and Social Research Council (ESRC) awarded a second research grant and the fieldwork stage of what was now a longitudinal project was begun in September 1983. A report was sent to the ESRC in February 1985 (Edgell and Duke 1985). Both surveys commenced approximately six months after a Conservative general election victory, which enabled us to ask detailed questions regarding political party attitudes and voting behaviour, and to relate these to the data collected on the perceived effects of government policies.

In the interval between the two parts of our SSRC/ESRC panel study we were awarded an internal grant by the Campaign to Promote the University of Salford (CAMPUS) to look in more detail at the changing local economic and political situation.

In addition to those jointly awarded research grants, further funding to us as individuals was forthcoming from the Nuffield Foundation in 1985. These grants took the form of a research fellowship, to enable one of us to concentrate upon analysing and writing up some of the accumulating mass of data, and an award under their Social Science Small Grants Scheme, which enabled the other to employ a research assistant to recode the class data on a household basis.

2   Research Design

One of the main factors influencing the research design of the GMS was the observation during the autumn of 1979 that local authorities did not all react in the same way to the Conservative central government policy of cutting public expenditure. Basically, local authorities controlled by the Conservative party seemed at that time to respond more positively and with more urgency to the 'cuts' policy than local authorities controlled by the Labour Party. Moreover, the keen response of certain Conservative-dominated local authorities in the Greater Manchester District had sparked off a spate of anti-cuts campaigns. Some of these groups, notably those concerned with fighting cuts in the education service in a Conservative-controlled local authority, involved public sector producers and consumers and thus comprised both 'middle-class' and 'working-class' protesters. Consequently, after consideration of the relevant sociological and political science literatures, we decided from the outset of our study to build these two observations into our research design. In practice this meant controlling for the possibility of local authority mediation in the implementation of public spending cuts required by policies emanating from the central government. It also meant sampling a sufficient number of people in the two selected local authorities to achieve representativeness, especially in terms of the various possible sub-groups when the data were disaggregated for analysis.

Hence, we chose one district controlled locally by the Conservative Party and represented by a Conservative MP (Torytown) and another district controlled locally by the Labour Party and represented by a Labour MP (Labourville). Within these districts the 1971 Census enabled us to select two urban wards, one from each district, which were comparable in several significant social respects, with the key exception of local political control. The two wards selected were comparable in population size (just under 11,000 and just over 12,000 private residents, respectively) and, as can be seen from Table A1.1, equivalent in terms of social composition.

Table A1.1 shows that both wards were mixed in terms of occupational class, though predominantly manual working class. The high degree of owner-occupation was also central to the research design because several press commentators at that time attributed Conservative success in the 1979 election to the defection to the Conservatives of manual house-owners. Significantly, in the May 1980 local government elections both wards were captured by Labour, although they are both traditional Conservative strongholds – in the case of Labourville, a Conservative outlier in a Labour sea. Both wards exhibited a negligible proportion of immigrants/residents from the New Commonwealth, thus avoiding the possibility of racial cleavage and/or the existence of an ethnic subordinate class (i.e. the contamination of the class data

Table A1.1 Comparison of ward characteristics: 1971 Census

Characteristic	Torytown	Labourville
% owner-occupied	63	67
% council housing	11	12
% professional/managerial	16	16
% skilled/semi-skilled/unskilled	49	55
% New Commonwealth	0.7	0.8

by race). In sum, Labourville and Torytown were not located at the extremes of the class structure; they were neither privileged nor deprived ghettos.

Having decided to survey the social and political effects of the public spending cuts in two politically contrasting yet socially similar local authority wards, we considered it imperative to extend our local knowledge of the two districts systematically by: (a) collecting official statistics on changes in public expenditure at the local level from Labourville and Torytown district councils (LDC and TDC) and from publications of the Chartered Institute of Public Finance and Accountancy (CIPFA); and (b) monitoring local press reports on the 'cuts' in the two local authority districts (*Labourville Bugle* and the *Torytown Echo*). Although the project was designed with the large-scale social survey as the core of the project, the incorporation of two other data sources from the beginning opened up the opportunity of undertaking a triangulation of official data, press data and survey data. (See Figure A1.1, which summarizes the basic structure of the GMS research design.) Furthermore, in an effort to enhance our local knowledge of the highly variegated policy to 'cut' public spending, we collected official statistics at the regional level with respect to the Greater Manchester Council (GMC). We also monitored the regional

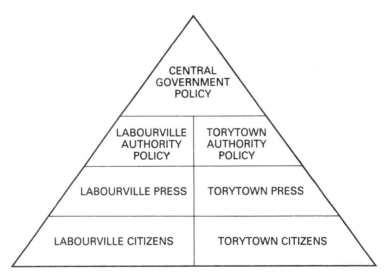

Figure A1.1 The Greater Manchester Study research design

press, namely the *Manchester Evening News* (MEN), for its coverage of public spending issues throughout Greater Manchester, including our two districts.

Although it was anticipated from the outset that the project should ideally be designed as a longitudinal one, the intensification of the economic crisis during the early 1980s convinced us of the need to build upon our original survey and other data sources by converting the project to a panel study. We considered that the most appropriate way to investigate sociologically historical processes such as polarization and radicalization was to adopt a dynamic research design. The collection of survey data from the same people at two points in time facilitates two types of data analysis – cross-sectional and panel. The former is more commonly undertaken and involves the comparison of the full samples at the first and second interviews and allows one to compare the relationship between variables at one point in time. Panel data draw upon only those interviewed twice, which facilitates the measurement of individual changes over time. More generally, in a highly fluid political economic situation, it is preferable to extend the time period of the investigation in order to be able to judge accurately and fully the social consequences of changes in government policy. In other words, a research design based on a panel of respondents is recognized as the best survey research method for studying trends in attitudes and behaviour because it makes it possible not only to measure degrees of change, but also to identify and analyse those who change.

3 Aims

The initial project had three main aims, all of which were associated primarily with the survey data:

1 To collect data on the comprehension, perception and impact of changes in public spending plus people's attitudinal and behavioural reactions to them. These were to be analysed with reference to individuals, family/household groups, electoral wards and various social groups (social/occupational class and public/private production and consumption sector).

2 To evaluate the conceptual and empirical validity of the variety of general theories regarding the social cohesion of British society. With this particular aim in mind, it was considered imperative to collect data on both attitudes and action plus

233

sufficient information to be able to operationalize the key concept class in a variety of ways.

3 To consider the policy implications of the changes in public spending and their political impact in the broadest sense. Our policy analysis tended to focus on specific categories of public spending such as health, education, transport and social services, as well as general policy implications such as local authority employment.

In addition to these three main aims, the first stage of the project was concerned with three subsidiary objectives:

4 To investigate the extent to which local political control is a mediating factor in the nature and severity of the central government policy to cut public spending.
5 To consider the role of the press in the local political process with special reference to the two local papers located in our research districts of contrasting political complexion.
6 To examine the pattern of political party loyalty in relation to attitudinal and behavioural reactions to the 'cuts' in the context of the emergence of the Social Democratic Party and its electoral alliance with the Liberal Party.

At the second stage of the project, the original three main aims and their constituent elements remained. At the same time, two issues were upgraded into additional aims of the project:

7 To investigate the sectoral dimension of the impact of, and reactions to, the restructuring of public spending.
8 To assess the privatization dimension of 'new right' economic and political policies.

Both these strands had been present since the beginning of the project, but by the second stage they had become far more significant politically and so it was important to incorporate them into the main aims of the project. The sectoral dimension directly relates to the social cohesion issue (see main aim (2) above) in the sense that sectoral theory had emerged as the major alternative to the theory that class represented the principle line of cleavage in Britain in the 1980s. The privatization dimension not only underpins the growing importance of sectoral divisions in contemporary Britain and as such has considerable policy implications (see main aim (3) above), but is exceedingly important in relation to party politics at both the local and national levels of government.

Although the aims of the research were conceived in very broad terms, and we were able to modify them in response to changes in central government policy, they were interrelated in various ways, as has been indicated throughout.

4 Sampling and Fieldwork

Prior to conducting the first survey, we undertook a pilot survey in another part of Greater Manchester in the summer of 1980. In the light of the pilot study, a full-scale interview survey was conducted by a team of social science graduate interviewers between September 1980 and March 1981. The target was a 10 per cent systematic sample selected from the electoral registers in each ward. We wrote to every potential respondent prior to an interviewer calling on them. The final response rates were remarkably similar for each ward and are presented in Table A1.2.

Although the main interview survey took approximately six months to complete, over 90 per cent of the interviews were conducted in the first three months of the fieldwork period. The interviewers were instructed to make a minimum of three calls at different times, although they often made more. Considerable efforts were made to trace and interview respondents who had moved within the area, whereas respondents who had moved out of the district were excluded. In Torytown, for example, over a dozen respondents who had moved within the district were traced and interviewed. Table A1.2 shows that, as a result of these efforts, a total of 948 people were eventually interviewed, which represents 63 per cent of the initial sample of 1,499 people and 76 per cent of those known to be eligible. Table A1.2 also shows that the response rates in the two wards were more or less identical and that virtually every potential respondent was traced in both Torytown and Labourville.

The interview combined both open (minority) and closed (majority) questions and all interviewers were instructed to note respondents' comments when they answered pre-coded questions. The questions ranged from those that were specifically developed for this project, to the standard political survey questions culled from other studies, particularly the British Election Study (BES) and *British Social Attitudes* (BSA) series, to facilitate comparability (see Appendix 2). On average, the first 'wave' interview took

Table A1.2 First interview survey response rate

	Number		Proportion of all names drawn (%)		Proportion of all those known to be eligible (%)	
	Torytown	Labourville	Torytown	Labourville	Torytown	Labourville
Moved	87	78	11.3	10.7	—	—
Deceased	6	12	0.8	1.6	—	—
Too old/ill/senile	24	35	3.1	4.8	—	—
Interviewed	487	461	63.3	63.2	74.7	76.2
Refused	161	130	20.9	17.8	24.7	21.4
Always out/untraced	4	14	0.5	1.9	0.6	2.3
Totals	769	730	100% (769)	100% (730)	100% (652)	100% (605)

35 minutes, although many of course took much longer, especially in the case of respondents who regarded themselves as very knowledgeable on public spending cuts.

In order to find out as much as possible about those who had refused to be interviewed or had not been traced, we sent out a postal questionnaire to the 'refusals/non-availables' in June 1981. Questionnaires were sent to 290 people, of which 91 (31 per cent) were completed and returned. The final overall response rate was thus nearly 70 per cent (1,039) of the original number of potential respondents and over 83 per cent of those known to be eligible. The postal questionnaire produced additional information on key issues from a further 7.3 per cent of respondents, thus improving the representativeness of the first sample. This is because it contained proportionally more older females who are traditionally reluctant to admit interviewers (31 per cent older females compared with 15 per cent in the main survey). Most importantly, the additional data collected via the postal questionnaire differed little from the main survey. Thus the postal questionnaire data tended to validate the main survey findings and conclusions.

At the end of the main interview schedule we asked respondents if they would be prepared to be re-interviewed about government policy at a later date, and over 90 per cent said yes. The follow-up survey, or second 'wave', was conducted between September 1983 and March 1984 and, as with the first wave, the vast majority of interviews were completed in the first three months of this fieldwork period. Of the original respondents, 685 were re-interviewed, which constituted 72 per cent of the first sample and approximately 86 per cent of those known to be eligible for re-interview. Once again the response rates in the two wards were almost identical and over half of the original fieldwork research team were employed, alongside some additional social science graduates.

Before re-entering the field, we checked again on the representativeness of the samples with the 1981 Census Small Area Statistics. As can be seen from Table A1.3, at the time of the 1981 Census, Torytown and Labourville wards were socially comparable in terms of age, sex, employment status and housing tenure. Table A1.3 also shows that, at the first and second stages, the youngest and oldest age groups were slightly under-represented; the former owing mainly to the inclusion of 16–18 year olds in the Census but not in our surveys, and the latter owing to the lower response rate among older respondents. The over-representation of controllers of labour at both stages in both wards was due to the

Table A1.3 Labourville and Torytown: 1981 Census, first interview cross-section (1980–1) and second interview cross-section (1983–4)

Indicator	Census %	Labourville GMS1 % (n = 461)	GMS2 % (n = 334)	Census %	Torytown GMS1 % (n = 487)	GMS2 % (n = 351)
Age:						
16–19 (Census)	27			29		
18–29 (GMS)		21	17		23	23
30–39	16	20	22	17	18	18
40–49	16	18	22	13	16	17
50–59	15	15	16	14	17	19
60–69	14	17	18	13	11	12
70–79	10	9	7	10	13	10
80 +	3	1	0.5	4	3	1
Sex:						
Male	47	49	48	48	49	53
Female	53	51	52	52	51	47
Employment status (social class):						
Self-employed + employees (i.e. employer)	2	3	2	3	4	3
Self-employed – employees (i.e. petty bourgeois)	4	5	8	5	4	10
Supervisor of others (i.e. controller)	22	29	30	24	32	30
Employee (i.e. worker)	71	64	59	68	60	57
Housing tenure:						
Owner-occupied	73	79	82	69	77	81
Council rented	13	14	12	11	11	9

more restrictive operational definition of this social class adopted in the Census compared with the one used in this study (see Chapter 2). The noticeable increase in petty bourgeois respondents at the second stage reflects the tendency for some redundant workers to become self-employed (Gerry 1985). The increase in owner-occupiers at the second stage was partly the result of the economic privatization of local authority and housing association tenants. Notwithstanding these caveats, Table A1.3 clearly shows that, when our two samples were compared with the 1981 Census data, those interviewed at each wave were broadly representative of the total population of the two wards.

5   Questionnaires

In the interests of space we have not included the full questionnaires here. For those attitudinal questions employed in the tables in this book, detailed question wording is provided with the tables. The full questionnaires for GMS1 and GMS2 have been published previously (Edgell and Duke 1981, 1985).

APPENDIX 2

Other Data Sources: British Election Study and British Social Attitudes

The Greater Manchester Study panel survey (GMS1 and GMS2) provided a wealth of social and political data on our households in Greater Manchester. We also employed two national surveys in order to check our findings on national samples and to update the material to 1987. The two surveys are the 1987 British Election Study and *British Social Attitudes* survey for 1987. Both of these were obtained from the ESRC Data Archive at the University of Essex.

The 1987 British Election Study cross–section survey was a nationally representative probability sample interviewed following the 1987 general election. The study was directed by Anthony Heath, Roger Jowell and John Curtice as a collaborative venture between Social and Community Planning Research and Nuffield College, Oxford.

British Social Attitudes: The 1988 Report was the fifth in an annual series of surveys started by Social and Community Planning Research in 1983 under the direction of Roger Jowell. The survey was designed to yield a representative sample of adults aged 18 or over living in private households in Great Britain.

APPENDIX 3

Key Sample Sizes: GMS1 1980–1 and GMS2 1983–4, BES 1987 and BSA 1987

In order to avoid cluttering the often complex class and sector cross-tabulations in the book, we have omitted the sample size of sub-groups from the tables. The base *n*'s are provided in Table A3.1 for the main social classes, sectoral locations, partisanship and

Table A3.1 Sample sizes

Category	GMS1	GMS2	BES	BSA
Social class:				
Employer	45	28	279	186
Petty bourgeois	76	72	249	237
Controller	380	286	894	620
Worker	436	299	2,278	1,706
Consumption sector:				
Totally private	61	60	514	340
Predominantly private	519	400	1,797	1,369
Predominantly public	210	133	704	527
Totally public	65	41	441	361
Production sector:				
Controller private	198	145	483	320
Controller public	174	140	405	300
Worker private	246	184	1,299	974
Worker public	173	110	951	728
Partisanship:				
Conservative	299	222	1,461	1,081
Labour	357	246	1,225	824
Liberal/SDP Alliance	57	122	682	533

class/sector combined categories. This information covers all our data-sets – the Greater Manchester Study (GMS1 and GMS2), the British Election Study (BES) and *British Social Attitudes* (BSA). Many of these sub-groups figure repeatedly in several of the chapters. The actual *n* in a given table may be marginally lower than the figure quoted here, if there were missing data on the dependent variable in the table.

REFERENCES

Abbott, P. 1987. Women's social class identification: Does husband's occupation make a difference? *Sociology* 21: 91–103.

Abbott, P. and Sapsford, R. 1987. *Women and Social Class* (London: Tavistock).

Abercrombie, N., Hill, S. and Turner, B. 1980. *The Dominant Ideology Thesis* (London: Allen & Unwin).

Abrams, M. *et al.* 1960. *Must Labour Lose?* (London: Penguin).

Acker, J. 1973. Women and social stratification, *American Journal of Sociology* 78: 936–45.

Acts of Parliament: Education Act 1980, Employment Act 1980, Housing Act 1980, Local Government Planning and Land Act 1980, Employment Act 1982, Local Government Finance Act 1982, Transport Act 1982, Rates Act 1984, Trade Union Act 1984, Local Government Act 1985, Housing Planning Act 1986, Social Security Act 1986, Education Reform Act 1988, Local Government Finance Act 1988.

Alber, J. 1988. Is there a crisis of the welfare state? Cross-national evidence from Europe, North America and Japan. *European Sociological Review* 4: 181–207.

Allen, J. and Massey, D. (eds) 1988. *Restructuring Britain: the Economy in Question* (London: Sage–Open University).

Allen, S. *et al.* 1986. *The Experience of Unemployment* (London: Macmillan).

Alt, J. 1971. Some social and political correlates of county borough expenditures. *British Journal of Political Science* 1: 49–62.

Ascher, K. 1987. *The Politics of Privatisation* (London: Macmillan).

Ashford, D. 1974. The effects of central finance on the British local government system. *British Journal of Political Science* 4: 305–22.

Ball, M. 1983. *Housing Policy and Economic Power* (London: Methuen).

Barnes, S. *et al.* 1979. *Political Action: Mass Participation in Five Western Democracies* (London: Sage).

Bassett, K. 1982. Which way for Labour councils? *Local Government Studies* 8: 8–13.

Beaumont, P. 1987. *The Decline of Trade Union Organisation* (London: Croom Helm).

Bechhofer, F. 1969. Occupations. In M. Stacey (ed.), *Comparability in Social Research* (London: Heinemann).

Bell, D. 1961. *The End of Ideology* (New York: Collier).

Benson, L. 1978. *Proletarians and Parties* (London: Tavistock).

Benyon, J. 1989. Ten years of Thatcherism. *Social Studies Review* 4: 170–8.

Bevan, G. *et al.* 1981. Cash limits and public sector pay. *Public Administration* 59: 379–98.

A Measure of Thatcherism

Beynon, H. 1975. *Working for Ford* (London: Allen Lane and Penguin Education).

Biggs, S. 1987. Quality of care and the growth of private welfare for old people. *Critical Social Policy* 20: 74–82.

Birch, S. 1986. Increasing patient charges in the National Health Service: a method of privatising primary care. *Journal of Social Policy* 15: 163–84.

Boaden, N. 1971. *Urban Policy Making* (Cambridge: Cambridge University Press).

Boddy, M. and Fudge, C. (eds) 1984. *Local Socialism* (London: Macmillan).

Boleat, M. 1983. The prospect for council house sales. *Housing Review*, September–October: 147–8.

Bosanquet, N. 1986. Interim report: public spending and the welfare state. In R. Jowell *et al.*, *British Social Attitudes: the 1986 Report* (Aldershot: Gower).

Bottomore, T. and Brym, R. 1989. *The Capitalist Class: an International Study* (London: Harvester Wheatsheaf).

Bramley, G. *et al.* 1989. How far is the poll tax a community charge? The implications of service usage evidence. *Policy and Politics* 17: 187–205.

Brewer, R. 1986. A note on the changing status of the Registrar General's classification of occupations. *British Journal of Sociology* 37: 131–40.

Brindley, T. and Stoker, G. 1988. Housing renewal policy in the 1980s: the scope and limits of privatisation. *Local Government Studies* 14(5): 45–67.

Bristow, S. 1982. Rates and votes: the 1980 district council elections. *Policy and Politics* 10: 163–80.

Britten, N. and Heath, A. 1983. Women, men and social class. In E. Gamarnikow *et al.* (eds), *Gender, Class and Work* (London: Heinemann).

Broadbent, T. 1977. *Planning and Profit in the Urban Economy* (London: Methuen).

Brown, P. and Sparks, R. (eds) 1989. *Beyond Thatcherism: Social Policy, Politics and Society* (Milton Keynes, Open University Press).

Buckland, R. 1987. The costs and returns of the privatisation of nationalised industries. *Public Administration* 65: 241–57.

Bulmer, M. (ed.) 1975. *Working Class Images of Society* (London: Routledge & Kegan Paul).

Butcher, H. *et al.* 1990. *Local Government and Thatcherism* (London: Blackwell).

Butler, D. and Kavanagh, D. 1980. *The British General Election of 1979* (London: Macmillan).

Butler, D. and Kavanagh, D. 1984. *The British General Election of 1983* (London: Macmillan).

Butler, D. and Kavanagh, D. 1988. *The British General Election of 1987* (London: Macmillan).

Butler, D. and Stokes, D. 1974. *Political Change in Britain* (London: Macmillan.

References

Camley, M. 1987. Employment in the public and private sectors 1981 to 1987, *Economic Trends* (London: HMSO) no. 410: 98–103.

Carter, R. 1985. *Capitalism, Class Conflict and the New Middle Class* (London: Routledge & Kegan Paul).

Casey, B. and Laczko, F. 1989. Early retired or long term unemployed? *Work, Employment and Society* 3: 509–26.

Cashmore, E. 1989. *United Kingdom? Class, Race and Gender Since the War* (London: Unwin Hyman).

Castells, M. 1977. *The Urban Question* (London: Edward Arnold).

Cawson, A. and Saunders, P. 1983. Corporatism, competitive politics and class struggle. In R. King (ed.), *Capital and Politics* (London: Routledge & Kegan Paul).

Clegg, T. 1982. Social consumption, social investment and the dual state: the case of transport policy in the Paris region. Paper presented at the Political Studies Association conference, University of Kent, April.

Cockburn, C. 1977. *The Local State* (London: Pluto).

Conservative Party, 1979, 1983. Election Manifestos. (London: Conservative Central Office.

Cooper, N. and Stewart, J. 1982. Local government budget closer to targets. *Public Finance and Accountancy*, June.

Cox, H. and Morgan, D. 1973. *City Politics and the Press* (Cambridge: Cambridge University Press).

Creigh, S. *et al.* 1986. Self-employment in Britain: results from the labour force survey 1981–1984. *Department of Employment Gazette* 94: 183–94.

Crewe, I. 1973. The politics of "affluent" and "traditional" workers in Britain. *British Journal of Political Science* 3: 29–52.

Crewe, I. 1981. Why the Conservatives won. In H. Penniman (ed.), *Britain at the Polls 1979* (Washington DC: American Enterprise Institute).

Crewe, I. 1984. The electorate: partisan dealignment ten years on. In H. Berrington (ed.), *Change in British Politics* (London: Frank Cass).

Crewe, I. 1985. How to win a landslide without really trying. In A. Ranney (ed.), *Britain at the Polls 1983* (Washington DC: American Enterprise Institute).

Crewe, I. 1986. On the death and resurrection of class voting: some comments on how Britain votes. *Political Studies* 34: 620–38.

Crewe, I. 1987. Tories prosper from a paradox. *Guardian*, 15 June.

Crewe, I. and Searing, D. 1988. Ideological change in the British Conservative Party. *American Political Science Review* 82: 361–84.

Crewe, I. *et al.* 1977. Partisan dealignment in Britain 1964–1974. *British Journal of Political Science* 7: 129–90.

Crompton, R. 1989. Class, theory and gender. *British Journal of Sociology* 40: 565–87.

Crompton, R. and Mann, M. 1986. *Gender and Stratification* (Cambridge: Polity).

245

Dahrendorf, R. 1959. *Class and Class Conflict in Industrial Society* (London: Routledge & Kegan Paul).

Dale, A. *et al.* 1985. Integrating women into class theory. *Sociology* 19: 384–409.

Davies, B. *et al.* 1972. *Variations in Children's Services among British Urban Authorities* (London: Bell).

Davies, C. 1980. Making sense of the census in Britain and the USA: the changing occupational classification and the position of nurses. *Sociological Review* 28: 581–609.

Day, P. 1988. The public regulation of private welfare: the case of residential and nursing homes for the elderly. *Political Quarterly* 59: 44–55.

Dearlove, J. 1979. *The Reorganisation of British Local Government* (Cambridge: Cambridge University Press).

Delphy, C. 1981. Women in stratification studies. In H. Roberts (ed.), *Doing Feminist Research* (London: Routledge & Kegan Paul).

Denver, D. 1986. Review of how Britain votes. *Political Studies* 34: 485.

Department of Employment 1987. *New Earnings Survey* (London: HMSO).

Dex, S. 1985. *The Sexual Division of Work* (Brighton: Wheatsheaf).

Dowse, R. and Hughes, J. 1977. Sporadic interventionists. *Political Studies* 25: 84–92.

Duke, V. and Edgell, S. 1984. Public expenditure cuts in Britain and consumption sectoral cleavages. *International Journal of Urban and Regional Research* 8: 177–201.

Duke, V. and Edgell, S. 1987. Attitudes to privatisation: the influence of class, sector and partisanship. *Quarterly Journal of Social Affairs* 3: 253–84.

Duncan, S. and Goodwin, M. 1982. The local state and restructuring social relations. *International Journal of Urban and Regional Research* 6: 157–85.

Duncan, S. and Goodwin, M. 1988. *The Local State and Uneven Development* (Cambridge: Polity Press).

Dunleavy, P. 1979. The urban basis of political alignment: social class, domestic property ownership, and state intervention in consumption processes. *British Journal of Political Science* 9: 409–43.

Dunleavy, P. 1980a. *Urban Political Analysis* (London: Macmillan).

Dunleavy, P. 1980b. The political implications of sectoral cleavages and the growth of state employment: Part 1. *Political Studies* 28: 364–83.

Dunleavy, P. 1980c. The political implications of sectoral cleavages and the growth of state employment: Part 2. *Political Studies* 28: 527–49.

Dunleavy, P. 1986. Explaining the privatisation boom: public choice versus radical approaches. *Public Administration* 64: 13–34.

Dunleavy, P. 1987. Class dealignment in Britain revisited. *West European Politics* 10: 400–19.

Dunleavy, P. 1989. The end of class politics? In A. Cochrane and J. Anderson (eds), *Politics in Transition* (London: Sage–Open University).

Dunleavy, P. and Husbands, C. 1985. *British Democracy at the Crossroads* (London: Allen & Unwin).

Economic Progress Reports: no. 100, 1978; no. 110, 1979; no. 145, 1982; no. 168, 1984; no. 183, 1986; no. 195, 1988; no. 196, 1988 (London: Treasury).

Economic Trends, 1984. Annual Supplement (London: HMSO).

Edgell, S. and Duke, V. 1980. Social and political effects of the public expenditure cuts. Funding application to the Social Science Research Council.

Edgell, S. and Duke, V. 1981. The social and political effects of the public expenditure cuts. *Social Science Research Council Report* HR 7315.

Edgell, S. and Duke, V. 1982, Reactions to the public expenditure cuts: occupational class and party realignment. *Sociology* 16: 431–9.

Edgell, S. and Duke, V. 1983. Gender and social policy: the impact of the public expenditure cuts and reactions to them. *Journal of Social Policy* 12: 357–78.

Edgell, S. and Duke, V. 1985. Changes in the social and political effects of the public expenditure cuts. *Economic and Social Research Council Report* GOO23107.

Elcock, H. 1982. *Local Government* (London: Methuen).

Elcock, H. 1986. Learning from local authority budgeting. *Public Policy and Administration* 1(2): 1–22.

Elliott, R. 1986. The growing problem of public sector pay. *Public Policy and Administration* 1(2): 33–48.

Else, P. and Marshall, G. 1981. The unplanning of public expenditure: recent problems in expenditure planning and the consequences of cash limits. *Public Administration* 59: 253–78.

Employment Gazette, 1979–90 (London: Department of Employment).

Erikson, R. 1984. Social class of men, women and families. *Sociology* 18: 500–14.

Erikson, R. and Goldthorpe, J. 1988. Women at class crossroads: a critical note. *Sociology* 22: 545–53.

Evans, C. 1985. Privatisation of local services. *Local Government Studies* 11(6): 97–110.

Ferlie, E. and Judge, K. 1981. Retrenchment and rationality in the personal social services. *Policy and Politics* 9: 311–30.

Field, F. (ed.) 1983. *The Wealth Report 2* (London: Routledge & Kegan Paul).

Finance and General Statistics (London: CIPFA).

Fleming, A. 1988. Employment in the public and private sectors 1982 to 1988. *Economic Trends* no. 422: 119–29.

Fleming, A. 1989. Employment in the public and private sectors. *Economic Trends* no. 434: 91–9.

Flynn, R. 1983. Co-optation and strategic planning in the local state. In R. King (ed.), *Capital and Politics* (London: Routledge).

Flynn, R. 1988. Political acquiescence, privatisation and residualisation in British housing policy. *Journal of Social Policy* 17: 289–312.

Forrest, R. and Murie, A. 1986. Marginalisation and subsidised individualism: the sale of council houses in the restructuring of the British welfare state. *International Journal of Urban and Regional Research*, 10: 46–65.

Franklin, M. 1985. *The Decline of Class Voting* (Oxford: Oxford University Press).

Fried, R. 1976. Comparative urban policy and performance. In F. Greenstein and N. Polsby (eds), *The Handbook of Political Science*, vol. 6 (Reading, Mass.: Addison-Wesley).

Friedman, M. 1977. *Inflation and Unemployment: The New Dimension of Politics*. Occasional Paper No. 51 (London: Institute of Economic Affairs).

Galbraith, J. 1962. *The Affluent Society* (London: Penguin).

Gallie, D. 1983. *Social Inequality and Class Radicalism in France and Britain* (Cambridge: Cambridge University Press).

Gallie, D. (ed.) 1988. *Employment in Britain* (Oxford: Blackwell).

Gamble, A. 1988. *The Free Economy and the Strong State* (London: Macmillan).

General Household Survey (London: HMSO).

George, V. and Wilding, P. 1984. *The Impact of Social Policy* (London: Routledge).

Gerry, C. 1985. Small enterprises, the recession and the disappearing working class. In G. Rees *et al.* (eds), *Political Action and Social Identity* (London: Macmillan).

Gibson, J. 1987. The reform of British local government finance: the limits of local accountability. *Policy and Politics*, 15: 167–74.

Giddens, A. 1973. *The Class Structure of the Advanced Societies* (London: Hutchinson).

Giddens, A. 1985. Review of E. Wright, *Classes*. *New Society*, 29 November, 383–4.

Glennerster, H. 1985. *Paying for Welfare* (Oxford: Basil Blackwell).

Golding, P. and Middleton, S. 1982. *Images of Welfare* (Oxford: Martin Robertson).

Goldthorpe, J. 1983. Women and class analysis: in defence of the conventional wisdom. *Sociology* 17: 465–88.

Goldthorpe, J. 1984. Women and class analysis: a reply to the replies. *Sociology* 17: 491–9.

Goldthorpe, J. 1987. *Social Mobility and Class Structure in Modern Britain* (Oxford: Clarendon Press).

Goldthorpe, J. and Bevan, P. 1977. The study of social stratification in Great Britain: 1946–1976. *Social Science Information* 16: 279–334.

Goldthorpe, J. and Hope, K. 1974. *The Social Grading of Occupations: A New Approach and Scale* (Oxford: Clarendon Press).

Goldthorpe, J. and Payne, C. 1986. On the class mobility of women: results from the different approaches to the analysis of recent British data. *Sociology* 20: 531–55.

Goldthorpe, J. *et al.* 1968a. *The Affluent Worker: Industrial Attitudes and Behaviour* (Cambridge: Cambridge University Press).

Goldthorpe, J. *et al.* 1968b. *The Affluent Worker: Political Attitudes and Behaviour* (Cambridge: Cambridge University Press).

Goldthorpe, J. *et al.* 1969. *The Affluent Worker in the Class Structure* (Cambridge: Cambridge University Press).

Goodwin, M. 1989. The politics of locality. In A. Cochrane and J. Anderson (eds), *Politics in Transition* (London: Sage).

Gough, I. 1979. *The Political Economy of the Welfare State* (London: Macmillan).

Gough, I. 1982. The crisis of the British welfare state. In N. Fainstein and S. Fainstein (eds), *Urban Policy under Capitalism* (London: Sage).

Gough, I. 1983. Thatcherism and the welfare state. In S. Hall and M. Jacques (eds), *The Politics of Thatcherism* (London: Lawrence & Wishart).

Gould, F. and Roweth, B. 1980. Public spending and social policy: the United Kingdom 1950–77. *Journal of Social Policy* 9: 337–57.

Greenwoood, R. 1981. Fiscal pressure and local government in England and Wales. In C. Hood and M. Wright (eds), *Big Government in Hard Times* (Oxford: Martin Robertson).

Habermas, J. 1976. *Legitimation Crisis* (London: Heinemann).

Hakim, C. 1980. Census reports as documentary evidence: the census commentaries 1801–1951. *Sociological Review* 28: 551–80.

Halford, R. 1985. The literature on local government contracting out. *Local Government Studies* 11(2): 77–83.

Hall, D. 1983. *The Cuts Machine: The Politics of Public Expenditure* (London: Pluto Press).

Hall, J. and Jones, D. 1950. The social grading of occupations, *British Journal of Sociology* 1: 31–55.

Hall, S. 1980. Popular democratic versus authoritarian populism. In A. Hunt (ed.), *Marxism and Democracy* (London: Lawrence & Wishart).

Hall, S. 1983. The Great Moving Right Show. In S. Hall and M. Jacques (eds), *The Politics of Thatcherism* (London: Lawrence & Wishart).

Hall, S. 1985. Authoritarian populism: a reply to Jessop *et al. New Left Review* 151: 115–24.

Hall, S. 1988. *The Hard Road to Renewal: Thatcherism and the Crisis of the Left* (London: Verso).

Hall, S. and Jacques, M. (eds) 1983. *The Politics of Thatcherism* (London: Lawrence & Wishart).

Hamnett, C. 1989. Consumption and class in contemporary Britain. In C. Hamnett *et al.* (eds), *The Changing Social Structure* (London: Sage–Open University).

Harris, C. 1987. *Redundancy and Recession in South Wales* (Oxford: Blackwell).

Harris, R. and Seldon, A. 1979. *Over-ruled on Welfare* (London: Institute of Economic Affairs).

A Measure of Thatcherism

Harrop, M. 1988. Voting and the electorate. In H. Drucker *et al.* (eds), *Developments in British Politics 2* (London: Macmillan).

Hastings, S. and Levie, H. (eds) 1983. *Privatisation?* (Nottingham: Spokesman).

Haug, M. 1973. Social class measurement and women's occupational roles. *Social Forces* 52: 86–98.

Hawthorne, M. and Jackson, J. 1987. The individual political economy of federal tax policy. *American Political Science Review* 81: 757–74.

Heald, D. 1983. *Public Expenditure: its Defence and Reform* (Oxford: Martin Robertson).

Heald, D. 1985. Will the privatisation of public enterprises solve the problem of control? *Public Administration* 63: 7–22.

Heald, D. and Thomas, D. 1986. Privatisation as Theology. *Public Policy and Administration* 1: 49–66.

Heath, A. and Britten, N. 1984. Women's jobs do make a difference. *Sociology* 18: 475–90.

Heath, A. *et al.* 1985. *How Britain Votes* (Oxford: Pergamon Press).

Heath, A. *et al.* 1987. Trendless fluctuation: a reply to Crewe. *Political Studies* 35: 256–77.

Henry, S. 1982. The working unemployed: perspectives on the informal economy and unemployment. *Sociological Review* 30: 460–77.

Hill, S. 1976. *The Dockers* (London: Heinemann).

Hill, S. 1981. *Competition and Control of Work* (London: Heinemann).

Himmelweit, H. *et al.* 1985. *How Voters Decide* (Milton Keynes: Open University Press).

Hindess, B. 1987. *Politics and Class Analysis* (Oxford: Blackwell).

HMSO, 1979a. *The Government's Expenditure Plans 1979–80 to 1982–83*, Cmnd 7439 (London).

HMSO, 1979b. *The Government's Expenditure Plans 1980–81*, Cmnd 7746 (London).

HMSO, 1979c. *Fifth Report on the Standing Reference – Royal Commission on the Distribution of Income and Wealth, John Diamond*, Cmnd 7679 (London).

HMSO, 1980. *The Government's Expenditure Plans 1980–81 to 1983–84*, Cmnd 7841 (London).

HMSO, 1984. *The Government's Expenditure Plans 1984–85 to 1986–87*, Cmnd 9143 (London).

HMSO, 1986a. *Paying for Local Government*, Cmnd 9714 (London).

HMSO, 1986b. *The Government's Expenditure Plans 1986–87 to 1988–89*, Cmnd 9702 – I and II (London).

HMSO, 1987. *The Government's Expenditure Plans 1987–88 to 1989–90*, Cmnd 56 – I and II (London).

HMSO, 1988. *The Government's Expenditure Plans 1988–89 to 1990–91*, Cmnd 288 – I and II (London).

Hoggart, K. 1987. Does politics matter? Redistributive policies in English cities 1949–74. *British Journal of Political Science* 17: 359–71.

Hogwood, B. 1989. The hidden face of public expenditure: trends in tax expenditures in Britain. *Policy and Politics* 17: 111–30.

References

Holmes, M. 1985. *The First Thatcher Government 1979–83* (Brighton: Wheatsheaf).
Hurstfield, J. 1987. *Part-timers under Pressure: Paying the Price of Flexibility.* Pamphlet No. 47 (London: Low Pay Unit).
Husband, C. 1982. *Race in Britain* (London: Hutchinson).
Hyde, M. and Deacon, B. 1986. Working class opinion and welfare strategies: beyond the state and the market. *Critical Social Policy* 18: 15–31.
Hyman, R. 1984. *Strikes*, 3rd edn (Aylesbury: Fontana).

Inglehart, R. 1977. *The Silent Revolution: Changing Values and Political Styles among Western Publics* (New Jersey: Princeton University Press).

Jary, D. 1978. A new significance for the middle-class left. In J. Garrard *et al.* (eds), *The Middle Class in Politics* (Farnborough: Saxon House).
Jessop, B. 1974. *Traditionalism, Conservatism and British Political Culture* (London: Allen & Unwin).
Jessop, B. 1978. Capitalism and democracy: the best possible political shell? In G. Littlejohn *et al.* (eds), *Power and the State* (London: Croom Helm).
Jessop, B. *et al.* 1985. Thatcherism and the politics of hegemony: a reply to Stuart Hall. *New Left Review* 153: 87–101.
Jessop, B. *et al.* 1988. *Thatcherism: A Tale of Two Nations* (Cambridge: Polity).
Johnson, P. 1981. Unemployment and self-employment: a survey. *Industrial Relations Journal* 12: 5–15.
Jowell, R. and Airey, C. 1984. *British Social Attitudes: The 1984 Report* (Aldershot: Gower).
Jowell, R. and Witherspoon, S. 1985. *British Social Attitudes: The 1985 Report* (Aldershot: Gower).
Jowell, R. *et al.* 1986. *British Social Attitudes: The 1986 Report* (Aldershot: Gower).
Jowell, R. *et al.* 1987. *British Social Attitudes: The 1987 Report* (Aldershot: Gower).
Jowell, R. *et al.* 1988. *British Social Attitudes: The Fifth Report* (Aldershot: Gower).
Judge, K. *et al.* 1983. Public opinion and the privatisation of welfare: some theoretical implications. *Journal of Social Policy* 12: 469–90.

Kahan, M. *et al.* 1966. On the analytical division of social class. *British Journal of Sociology* 17: 122–32.
Kaser, G. 1988. Value for money in the public services. *Capital and Class* 36: 31–57.
Kavanagh, D. 1987. *Thatcherism and British Politics* (Oxford: Clarendon Press).
Keegan, V. 1984. *Mrs Thatcher's Economic Experiment* (London: Allen Lane).
Kelley, J. and McAllister, I. 1985. Class and party in Australia: comparison with Britain and the USA. *British Journal of Sociology* 36: 383–420.

Kelly, A. 1989. An end to incrementalism? The impact of expenditure restraint on social services budgets 1979–1986. *Journal of Social Policy* 18: 187–210.

Kelly, J. and Bailey, R. 1989. British trade union membership, density and decline in the 1980s: a research note. *Industrial Relations Journal* 20: 54–61.

King, A. 1983. Margaret Thatcher: the style of a prime minister. In A. King (ed.), *The British Prime Minister* (London: Macmillan).

King, D. 1987. *The New Right, Politics, Markets and Citizenship* (London: Macmillan).

King, R. and Raynor, J. 1981. *The Middle Class* (London: Longman).

Kolderie, T. 1986. The two different concepts of privatisation. *Public Administration Review* 46: 285–91.

Krieger, J. 1986. *Reagan, Thatcher and the Politics of Decline* (Cambridge: Polity).

Labour Research (London: LRD Publications).

Laczko, F. *et al.* 1988. Early retirement in a period of high unemployment. *Journal of Social Policy* 17: 313–33.

Laing, W. 1987. *Laing's Guide to Private Health Care* (London: Laing and Buisson).

Lash, S. 1984. *The Militant Worker* (London: Heinemann).

Leat, D. 1986. Privatisation and voluntarisation, *Quarterly Journal of Social Affairs* 2: 285–320.

Leete, R. and Fox, J. 1977. Registrar General's social classes: origins and uses, *Population Trends* 1–7.

Le Grand, J. 1982. *The Strategy of Equality* (London: Allen and Unwin).

Le Grand, J. and Robinson, R. 1984. *Privatisation and the Welfare State* (London: Allen and Unwin).

Le Grand, J. and Winter, D. 1986. The middle classes and the welfare state under Conservative and Labour governments. *Journal of Public Policy* 6: 399–430.

Leiulfsrud, H. and Woodward, A. 1988. Women at class crossroads: a critical reply to Erikson and Goldthorpe's note. *Sociology* 22: 555–62.

Lenin, V. 1970. *What Is To Be Done?* (London: Panther).

Lewis, A. 1982. *The Psychology of Taxation* (Oxford: Martin Robertson).

Lewis, A. and Jackson, D. 1985. Voting preferences and attitudes to public expenditure. *Political Studies* 33: 457–66.

Likierman, A. 1988, *Public Expenditure: The Public Spending Process* (London: Penguin).

Local Government Studies, January 1988. Special issue on Education Reform Bill.

Local Government Trends (London: CIPFA).

Lockwood, D. 1966. Sources of variation in working class images of society. *Sociological Review* 14: 244–67.

Lockwood, D. 1981. The weakest link in the chain? Some comments on the Marxist theory of action. In S. Simpson and I. Simpson (eds), *Research in the Sociology of Work*, vol. 1 (Greenford, Conn.: JAI Press).

Lomas, E. 1980. Employment in the public and private sectors 1974–1980. *Economic Trends*, no. 325: 101–9.

McAllister, I. and Rose, R. 1984. *The Nationwide Competition for Votes: The 1983 British Election* (London: Frances Pinter).

McAllister, I. and Studlar, D. 1989. Popular versus elite views of privatisation: the case of Britain. *Journal of Public Policy* 9: 157–78.

MacInnes, J. 1987. *Thatcherism at Work* (Milton Keynes: Open University Press).

McKenzie, R. and Silver, A. 1968. *Angels in Marble* (London: Heinemann).

Mann, M. 1970. The social cohesion of liberal democracy. *American Sociological Review* 35: 423–39.

Mann, M. 1973. *Consciousness and Action among the Western Working Class* (London: Macmillan).

Marsh, A. 1977. *Protest and Political Consciousness* (London: Sage).

Marshall, G. 1983. Some remarks on the study of working class consciousness, *Politics and Society* 12: 263–301.

Marshall, G. 1988. Classes in Britain: Marxist and official. *European Sociological Review* 4: 141–54.

Marshall, G. *et al.* 1988. *Social Class in Modern Britain* (London: Hutchinson).

Martlew, C. 1982. Institutional diversity and the reform of local state finance. Paper presented at the Political Studies Association conference, University of Kent, April.

Marx, K. [1894] 1974. *Capital, Vol. 3* (London: Lawrence & Wishart).

Marx, K. and Engels, F. 1848. *Manifesto of the Communist Party* (Moscow: Foreign Languages Publishing House).

Midwinter, A. 1980. The Scottish Office and local authority financial planning: a study of change in central–local relations. *Public Administration Bulletin* 34: 21–43.

Miles, R. 1975. Radical values and radical action. *Sociology* 9: 485–9.

Miliband, R. 1969. *The State and Capitalist Society* (London: Weidenfeld & Nicolson).

Mohan, J. 1986. Private medical care and the British Conservative government: what price independence? *Journal of Social Policy* 15: 337–60.

Mohan, J. 1988. Restructuring, privatisation and the geography of health care provision in England 1983–87. *Transactions of the Institute of British Geographers* 13: 449–65.

Monk, D. 1985. *Social Grading on the National Readership Survey* (London: Joint Industry Committee for National Readership Surveys).

Moorhouse, H. 1976. Attitudes to class and class relationships in Britain. *Sociology* 10: 469–96.

Moorhouse, H. and Chamberlain, C. 1974. Lower class attitudes to property. *Sociology* 8: 387–405.

Morris, L. 1987. Local social polarisation: a case study of Hartlepool. *International Journal of Urban and Regional Research* 11: 331–50.

Mouritzen, P. 1987. The demanding citizen: driven by policy, self-interest or ideology? *European Journal of Political Research* 15: 417–35.

Murphy, D. 1976. *The Silent Watchdog: The Press in Local Politics* (London: Constable).

Murphy, R. 1984. The structure of closure: a critique and development of the theories of Weber, Collins and Parkin. *British Journal of Sociology* 35: 547–67.

National Travel Survey 1978–79 (London: HMSO).

Newby, H. 1977. *The Deferential Worker* (Middlesex: Penguin Books).

Newton, K. and Karran, T. 1985. *The Politics of Local Expenditure* (London: Macmillan).

Newton, K. and Sharpe, L. 1977. Local outputs research: some reflections and proposals. *Policy and Politics* 5: 61–82.

Nichols, T. 1979. Social class: official, sociological and Marxist. In J. Irvine *et al.* (eds), *Demystifying Social Statistics* (London: Pluto Press).

Nicholson, R. and Topham, N. 1972. Investment decisions and the size of local authorities. *Policy and Politics* 1: 23–44.

Niskanen, W. 1973. *Bureaucracy – Servant or Master?* (London: Institute of Economic Affairs).

O'Connor, J. 1973. *The Fiscal Crisis of the State* (New York: St. Martins).

Offe, C. 1975. The theory of the capitalist state and the problems of policy formation. In L. Lindberg *et al.* (eds), *Stress and Contradiction in Modern Society* (London: Lexington).

Oliver, F. and Stanyer, J. 1969. Some aspects of the financial behaviour of county boroughs. *Public Administration* 47: 169–84.

OPCS 1980. *Classification of Occupations* (London: HMSO).

Osborn, A. and Morris, T. 1979. The rationale for a composite index of social class and its evaluation. *British Journal of Sociology* 30: 39–61.

Page, E. 1978. Why should central–local relations in Scotland be different to those in England? *Public Administration Bulletin* 28: 51–72.

Parkin, F. 1967. Working class Conservatives: a theory of political deviance. *British Journal of Sociology* 18: 280–90.

Parkin, F. 1968. *Middle Class Radicalism* (Manchester: Manchester University Press).

Parkin, F. 1971. *Class, Inequality and Political Order* (London: MacGibbon & Kee).

Payne, S. 1951. *The Art of Asking Questions* (Princeton, NJ: Princeton University Press).

Phizacklea, A. and Miles, R. 1980. *Labour and Racism* (London: Routledge & Kegan Paul).

Piven, F. 1976. The social structuring of protest. *Politics and Society* 6: 297–326.

Pliatzky, L. 1984. *Getting and Spending: Public Expenditure, Employment and Inflation* (Oxford: Blackwell).

Pond, C. 1982. Taxation and public expenditure. In A. Walker (ed.), *Public Expenditure and Social Policy* (London: Heinemann).

Poulantzas, N. 1973. *Political Power and Social Classes* (London: New Left Books).

Price, R. and Bain, G. 1983. Union growth in Britain: retrospect and prospect. *British Journal of Industrial Relations* 21: 46–68.

Proctor, I. 1990. The privatisation of working class life: a dissenting view. *British Journal of Sociology* 41: 157–80.

Radical Statistics Health Group 1987. *Facing the Figures: What Really is Happening to the National Health Service?* (London: Radical Statistics).

Rallings, C. 1975. Two types of middle-class Labour voter. *British Journal of Political Science* 5: 102–12.

Ranade, W. and Haywood, S. 1989. Privatising from within – the NHS under Thatcher. *Local Government Studies* 15(4): 19–34.

Rayner, G. 1986. Health care as a business? The emergence of a commercial hospital sector in Britain. *Policy and Politics* 14: 439–59.

Redcliffe-Maud, Lord 1967. Local governors at work: could they do better? *Public Administration* 45: 347–52.

Reid, I. 1989. *Social Class Differences in Britain*, 3rd edn (Glasgow: Fontana).

Rex, J. and Moore, R. 1967. *Race, Community and Conflict* (Oxford: Oxford University Press).

Rex, J. and Tomlinson, S. 1979. *Colonial Immigrants in a British City* (London: Routledge).

Rhodes, R. 1979. Research into central–local relations in Britain: a framework for analysis. In *Central–Local Government Relations* (London: SSRC).

Riddell, P. 1985. *The Thatcher Government* (Oxford: Basil Blackwell).

Riddell, P. 1989. *The Thatcher Decade: How Britain Has Changed during the 1980s* (Oxford: Blackwell).

Roberts, K. *et al.* 1977. *The Fragmentary Class Structure* (London: Heinemann).

Robertson, D. 1984. *Class and the British Electorate* (Oxford: Blackwell).

Rose, D. (ed.) 1988. *Social Stratification and Economic Change* (London: Hutchinson).

Rose, D. and Marshall, G. 1986. Constructing the (W)right classes. *Sociology* 20: 440–5.

Rose, H. 1981. Rereading Titmuss: the sexual division of welfare. *Journal of Social Policy* 10: 477–502.

Rose, R. and McAllister, I. 1986. *Voters Begin to Choose: From Closed-Class to Open Elections in Britain* (London: Sage).

Rose, R. and Page, E. (eds) 1982. *Fiscal Stress in Cities* (Cambridge: Cambridge University Press).

Rowley, K. and Feather, N. 1987. The impact of unemployment in relation to age and length of unemployment. *Journal of Occupational Psychology* 60: 323–32.

Rowntree, B. 1901. *Poverty: A Study of Town Life* (London: Nelson).

Runciman, W. 1966. *Relative Deprivation and Social Justice* (London: Routledge & Kegan Paul).

Sanders, D. and Tanenbaum, E. 1983. Direct action and political culture: the changing political consciousness of the British public. *European Journal of Political Research* 11: 45–61.

Sarlvik, B. and Crewe, I. 1983. *Decade of Dealignment* (Cambridge: Cambridge University Press).

Saunders, P. 1981. *Social Theory and the Urban Question* (London: Hutchinson).

Saunders, P. 1982. Why study central–local relations? *Local Government Studies* 8: 55–66.

Saunders, P. 1984. Rethinking local politics. In M. Boddy and C. Fudge (eds), *Local Socialism* (London: Macmillan).

Saunders, P. 1986. Reflections on the dual politics thesis: the argument, its origins and its critics. In M. Goldsmith and S. Villadsen (eds), *Urban Political Theory and the Management of Fiscal Stress* (Aldershot: Gower).

Saunders, P. 1990. *A Nation of Homeowners* (London: Unwin Hyman).

Savas, E. 1982. *Privatising the Public Sector* (Chatham, NJ: Chatham House).

Scholzman, K. and Verba, S. 1980. *Injury to Insult: Unemployment, Class and Political Response* (Cambridge, Mass.: Harvard University Press).

Schuman, H. and Presser, S. 1981. *Questions and Answers in Attitude Surveys* (New York: Academic Press).

Scott, A. 1990. *Ideology and New Social Movements* (London: Unwin Hyman).

Scott, J. 1985. *Corporations, Classes and Capitalism* (London: Hutchinson).

Semple, M. 1979. Employment in the public and private sectors 1961–78. *Economic Trends*, no. 313: 90–108.

Sharpe, K. and Newton, K. 1984. *Does Politics Matter?* (Oxford: Clarendon).

Skidelsky, R. (ed.) 1988. *Thatcherism* (London: Chatto & Windus).

Smith, D. 1989. *North and South: Britain's Economic, Social and Political Divide* (London: Penguin).

Social Trends (London: HMSO).

Stallworthy, M. 1989. Central government and local government: the uses and abuses of a constitutional hegemony. *Political Quarterly* 60: 22–37.

Stanworth, M. 1984. Women and class analysis: a reply to Goldthorpe. *Sociology* 18: 159–70.

Stark, T. 1987. *Income and Wealth in the 1980s* (London: Fabian Society).

Stevenson, T. 1928. The vital statistics of wealth and poverty. *Journal of the Royal Statistical Society* 91: 207–20.

Stoker, G. 1988, *The Politics of Local Government* (London: Macmillan).

Tapper, T. and Salter, B. 1986. The assisted places scheme. *Journal of Educational Policy* 1: 315–30.

Tawney, R. 1952. *Equality* (London: Allen & Unwin).

Taylor-Gooby, P. 1983. Legitimation deficit, public opinion and the welfare state. *Sociology* 17: 165–84.

Taylor-Gooby, P. 1985. *Public Opinion, Ideology and State Welfare* (London: Routledge).

Taylor-Gooby, P. 1986. Privatisation, public opinion and the welfare state. *Sociology* 20: 228–46.

Taylor-Gooby, P. 1988. The future of the British welfare state: public attitudes, citizenship and social policy under the Conservative governments of the 1980s. *European Sociological Review* 4: 1–19.

Taylor-Gooby, P. and Bochel, H. 1988. Attitudes to welfare policy in the House of Commons. *Political Studies* 36: 334–40.

Thomas, W. 1928. *The Child in America* (New York: Knopf).

Titmuss, R. 1958. *Essays on 'The Welfare State'* (London: Allen & Unwin).

Titmuss, R. 1962. *Income Distribution and Social Change* (London: Allen & Unwin).

Townsend, P. 1979. *Poverty in the United Kindom* (London: Allen Lane).

Treasury and Civil Service Committee, Fifth Report 1981–2. *The Government's Expenditure Plans 1982–3 to 1984–5* (London: HMSO).

Urry, J. 1981. Localities, regions and social class. *International Journal of Urban and Regional Research* 5: 455–73.

Veblen, T. 1970. *The Theory of the Leisure Class* (London: Allen & Unwin).

Vickers, J. and Wright, V. 1988. The politics of privatisation in Western Europe: an overview, *West European Politics* 11(4): 1–30.

Walker, A. 1981. Social policy, social administration and the social construction of welfare. *Sociology* 15: 225–50.

Walker, A. (ed.) 1982. *Public Expenditure and Social Policy* (London: Heinemann).

Walker, A. and Walker, C. (eds) 1987. *The Growing Divide: A Social Audit 1979–1987* (London: Child Poverty Action Group).

Wedderburn, D. 1974. *Poverty, Inequality and Class Structure* (Cambridge: Cambridge University Press).

Weinberg, A. and Lyons, F. 1972. Class theory and practice. *British Journal of Sociology* 23: 51–65.

Westergaard, J. and Resler, H. 1975. *Class in a Capitalist Society* (London: Heinemann).

Westergaard, J. et al. 1989. *After Redundancy: The Experience of Economic Insecurity* (Cambridge: Polity).

Whiteley, P. 1981. Public opinion and the demand for social welfare in Britain. *Journal of Social Policy* 10: 453–76.

Whiteside, N. 1988. Unemployment and health: an historical perspective. *Journal of Social Policy* 17: 177–94.

Whitfield, D. 1983. *Making It Public* (London: Pluto).

Whitty, G. *et al.* 1986. Assisting whom? Benefits and costs of the assisted places scheme. Paper presented to the British Educational Research Association conference, University of Bristol, September.

Wicks, M. 1987. The decades of inequality. *New Society*, 6 February, pp. 10–12.

Williams, B. *et al.* 1984. Analysis of the work of independent acute hospitals in England and Wales 1981. *British Medical Journal* 289: 446–8.

Williams, N. *et al.* 1986. Council house sales and residualisation. *Journal of Social Policy* 15: 273–92.

Wilson, E. 1977. *Women and the Welfare State* (London: Tavistock).

Wolpe, H. 1970. Some problems concerning revolutionary consciousness. In R. Miliband and J. Saville (eds), *The Socialist Register 1970* (London: Merlin Press).

Wright, E. 1976. Class boundaries in advanced capitalist societies. *New Left Review*, no. 98: 3–41.

Wright, E. 1979. *Class, Crisis and the State* (London: Verso).

Wright, E. 1980. Class and occupation. *Theory and Society* 9: 177–214.

Wright, E. 1985. *Classes* (London: Verso).

Wright, E. 1989a. Women in the class structure. *Politics and Society* 17: 35–66.

Wright, E. 1989b. *The Debate on Classes* (London: Verso).

Wright, E. and Perrone, L. 1977. Marxist class categories and income inequality. *American Sociological Review* 42: 32–55.

Yearbook of Labour Statistics, 1987 (Geneva: International Labour Office).

Young, K. 1988. The challenge to professionalism in local government. *Policy Studies* 9(1): 60–72.

Young, S. 1986. *Privatisation and Planning in Declining Areas* (London: Croom Helm).

Zweig, F. 1961. *The Worker in an Affluent Society* (London: Heinemann).

AUTHOR INDEX

259

261

SUBJECT INDEX

References in italics are to figures

Aberdeen study 145–6
accountability, local 88
accumulation 91–2, 191, 223, 226
acquiescence 182, 185–6, 213
action, radical 192–3, 199–209, 211–12, 221,
    233, Tables 8.4, 8.5, 8.7
  class 183–5, 192–3, 213
  radical action scale 192–4
affluent worker study 23, 142, 185
age 157
  and private consumption 163, 168, 178,
    Table 7.10
  and radicalism 197, 207, 209
alignment theory 19, 50–3, 61, 68, 119
Alliance 49, 61, 64–5, 68, 159, 199, 211
  partisanship 78, 84–5, 173, 175, 209
asset sales 14–15, 139, 141, 178, 180
Assisted Places Scheme 148
Associated British Ports 10
attitudes, public 19–20, 70–85, 212, 218–19,
    221–3, 230, 233
  and issue voting 58, 60
  and radicalism 189, 191
  attitudinal scale 189–92, Tables 8.1, 8.2
  class 192
  on local government 80–3
  on privatization 149–57, 168–77, 221,
    Tables 7.4, 7.5, 7.11, 7.12
  on public spending 71–8, Tables 4.1, 4.2
  on trade unions 83
  on unemployment 78–80
authoritarianism 225
autonomy
  local 70, 80–3, 90, 95, 114, 219, Table 4.5
  state, relative 115

balance of payments 216
block grant 87
borrowing, government 4, 6
bourgeoisie 30, 35, 204
British Aerospace 10
British Airways 10
British Census *see* Census
British Election Studies (BES) 17–18,

45, 74, 149, 158, 191, 235,
240, 242
  (1983) 83, 150, 168–9
  (1987) 70, 83, 171, Table 2.5
British Gas 10, 50
British Petroleum Company 4
British Rail 14, 147
British Social Attitudes (BSA) 17–18, 70, 78,
  145, 149, 235, 240, 242
  (1983) 79, 82, 148, 168
  (1984) 150
  (1985) 145, 148, 161
  (1987) 75, 79–80, 82
  (1988) 147, 150
British Sugar Corporation 14
British Telecom 10, 14, 150
Britoil 10
budgets 4, 6–8
Building Societies Association 145
bus deregulation 147

Cable and Wireless 10
Callaghan, James 2, 4
capital 12, 19, 22, 24, 51, 83, 92–3, 131,
  182–3, 213, 215–16, 218, 224, 226
  monopoly 91–2, 115
capitalism 187, 204, 216, 223–5
  industrial 19, 181–2
  laissez-faire 224
  welfare state 224–7
capitalists 23, 30, 35, 57, 204, 212, 217–18
car
  company 89
  ownership 16, 42–4, 62, 146, 151, 163,
    Table 2.4
cash limits 4, 88, 92, 137
Census 23, 25, 31, 38, 231, 237–9
central government
  and local government 80–2, 86–116,
    Table 4.5
  finance 94
  strong 71, 225
  see also state
charges 15–16, 77, 88–90, 98,

Index

Index

Index